Acting

Acting

An Introduction to the Art and Craft of Playing

Paul Kassel

State University of New York at New Paltz

Boston ■ New York ■ San Francisco
Mexico City ■ Montreal ■ Toronto ■ London ■ Madrid ■ Munich ■ Paris
Hong Kong ■ Singapore ■ Tokyo ■ Cape Town ■ Sydney

Series Editor: *Molly Taylor*
Marketing Manager: *Suzan Czajkowski*
Editorial Assistant: *Suzanne Stradley*
Senior Production Administrator: *Donna Simons*
Manufacturing Buyer: *JoAnne Sweeney*
Composition Buyer: *Linda Cox*
Cover Administrator: *Kristina Mose-Libon*
Editorial Production Service: *WestWords, Inc.*
Electronic Composition: *WestWords, Inc.*
Illustrator: *Barry Rockwell*

Between the time website information is gathered and then published, it is not unusual for some sites to have closed. Also, the transcription of URLs can result in typographical errors. The publisher would appreciate notification where these errors occur so that they may be corrected in subsequent editions.

Cataloging-in-Publication data unavailable at press time.

ISBN 0-205-44002-9

Printed in the United States of America

10 9 8 7 6 5 4 3 2 1   10 09 08 07 06

CONTENTS

EXERCISES

PREFACE TO THE TEACHER/COACH

These are the premises on which this book is based: 1) Acting is an art and actors are the primary artists in making theater. 2) Theater is a collaborative art and the actor must be the most flexible, the most giving, and yet the most resilient of all the artists who collaborate to make theater. 3) The actor must serve—the playwright, director, designers, other players, and most important, the audience. It is the actor who embodies a performance and delivers it to the audience. It is the actor who gives life to words, who makes a world out of scenery, who translates a director's ideas into action.

The basic elements of acting have been known for a very long time. Teachers of acting and books on acting all struggle with the same two tasks—how best to articulate the elements of acting and how to facilitate the development of the actor. The grandfather of modern acting is Stanislavski, of course. Every textbook on acting since has covered similar territory. What has changed is our understanding of human beings. Each generation of actor and acting teachers utilize current understanding of being human, and subtly but substantively alter the discussion on acting and training actors.

Besides the teachers I mention in the acknowledgements, I am indebted to several authors for much of the foundation of my thinking. Viola Spolin's *Improvisation for the Theatre* is still a preeminent text on acting and actor training. Not only is it an immense resource of games and exercises, but it also articulates an approach to training that is pertinent to this day—student-centered, nonjudgmental, joyous. Robert Cohen turned a theoretical eye on acting in his important book, *Acting Power.* He combined his considerable knowledge of communication and behavior with his deep understanding of the acting process to forge a book of major significance. He articulates the fundamental aspects of acting and suggests ways an actor might employ this knowledge. Robert Benedetti's *The Actor at Work* is also a powerful and important work. Benedetti's focus is on facilitating the actor's development through a clear and comprehensive program, touching on nearly all aspects of acting. These books remain seminal texts in the ongoing discussion of acting and actor training.

However, these texts, as important as they are, are not the last word on acting. Although most acting texts cover similar ground, they offer different perspectives, different emphases, and sometimes advances in our understanding of the acting process and actor training. This book offers a different perspective and emphasis, and hopefully at least a small advance in our understanding. Like Spolin, I believe in the primacy of the student—that the central task of the teacher is to offer opportunities to learn. Like Cohen, I believe that the essence of acting is in the interplay between actors—that the central task of the actor is to play actions. Like Benedetti, I believe examining the play of energy between human beings will lead to a clear and comprehensive program of training—the central task of training is to expand the range of human expression. What differences I offer here arise out of my experience first as an actor, second as a teacher, and third as a researcher. I believe that these differences, while they may be subtle, are nonetheless significant—for actors and the teachers of actors.

My approach to actor training is synthetic. I use ideas and exercises from a number of sources, including those already mentioned. I have endeavored to write the book that complements the work in the classroom, discussing theory and providing practical examples, both to prepare students for what is to come, and for them to reflect upon what they have done. This book covers all the usual ground that many books cover, but attempts to marry theory and practice, and *de*scribe rather than *pre*scribe, as others have put it. I utilize simple formulas and charts, not to boil acting down to a set of mechanics, but rather to employ as *conceptual conveniences.* The concepts of art and acting are elusive, so I have attempted to make them as clear as possible by means of these conveniences—charts, formulas, pictographs. Acting is simple, but it is not easy. Elusive concepts rendered elusively would make matters less comprehensible. I propose basic terms that more clearly state the nature of the acting process. None of these terms are new, but are sometimes differently employed. For example, the term "task" here is used instead of objective or intention. My goal is to find the most simple and open, yet apt, term to describe an aspect of the acting process. When possible, I cite every resource from which the concepts have clearly arisen; all other concepts and assertions are mine. The exercises presented here are a combination of original and "public domain." When I know the source of an exercise, I credit the individual who either created it or who taught it to me. Yet, inevitably, there will be omissions, and for that I apologize in advance.

All of the exercises and theories in this book have been used in the classroom with beginning students—both majors and nonmajors—for more than a decade. The exercises are intended to focus on the acting process, from which a performance product may emerge. But naturally, the teacher/coach must encourage students to stick to the process and not manufacture results (as they invariably will be tempted to do). The chapters are organized into general areas and function as outlines for workshops in each area. They may be followed sequentially or as the teacher/coach sees fit. Playing actions are conceived as part of the core of the work and are integrated into the basic warm-up (see the sample warm-up at the end of Part Two—**The Tools for Playing**).

Actors and acting teachers are also not usually writers. As of this writing, there is no journal devoted exclusively to acting (although one is in development). Textbooks on acting are the only avenues to continue a discourse on the acting process. I greet each new text as an opportunity to expand my understanding of the process and to enhance my work in the classroom. It is my hope that the teacher/coach will find similar opportunities here.

In a panel at the 2000 Conference of the Association for Theater in Higher Education, the following goals were proposed as a new basis for the training of actors at the university.

1. To expand/enhance the range of expressiveness and creativity via the unique tools of the performer, including vocal, physical, imaginative, and felt expressiveness (work on the self).
2. To develop an understanding of the process of human interaction (work with others).
3. To facilitate choice-making as performing artist, thinker, and producer (application of knowledge toward end results).
4. To explore human interactions through a set of value systems, life experiences and/or life circumstances different from one's own (connecting the work to a diverse world).

These seem an apt basis on which to build a program. The actor who is an artist will find ways to continue to practice, venues in which to perform, and fellow artists with whom to work. This book is an attempt to state as clearly as possible what the actor does and how the actor does it, and to help students begin the lifelong journey of discovery as their talents, skills, and creative imagination unfold.

Acknowledgments

Teacher/coaches and Colleagues

Barbara Swearingen, Barry Witham, Lin Conaway, Manuel Duque, Stuart Vaughan, Joel Friedman, John Basil, Patrick Tucker, Tom Casciero, Craig Turner, Norma Bowles, Ann Klotz, Marc Powers, David Krasner, Pamela Chabora, David Wiles, Brant Pope

Authors

Susanne K. Langer, Viola Spolin, Northrup Frye, Joseph Chaiken, Robert Benedetti, Hollis Huston, Robert Cohen

Professional Actors

Betty Oliver, Karl Redkoff, Charles Ludlam, Bill Irwin, Monica Horan, Tyrone Wilson, Jennifer Prescott, Lewis Stadlen, James Earl Jones, Tony Freeman, and the members of Asylum Theater Company: Deborah Mayo, Valeri Lantz Gefroh, Steven Marsh, Steven Lantz Gefroh, Laura Ross, Jean Giebel

Students

All my students, but especially Alixa Englund, Jon Malamie, Bill Gross, Rosalie Bahmer, Adam Lewis, Dawn Jourdan, Amy Elizabeth Clark, Meredith Richardson, Glen Cullen, Robyn Berg, Liz Bresnak-Arata, Josh Adler, Lisa Casper, Marianna McClellan, Douglas Nyman—truth-tellers all—and Russell Dembin, actor and indexer.

Manuscript Reviewers

Ken Bush, Eastern Oregon University; Evelyn Carol Case, California State University Fullerton; Sandra Forman, Northern Kentucky University; George Maguire, Solano Community College; Marc Powers, University of South Florida; Randy Reinholz, San Diego State University; and James B. Williams, University of North Dakota.

Thank you to the patient and able individuals for shepherding this book through the publication process—Molly Taylor, Donna Simons, and Suzanne Stradley (Allyn & Bacon), and the experts at WestWords.

Finally, I must acknowledge my partner, Kit Kassel, and my children, who inspire me daily.

PREFACE TO STUDENT PLAYERS

Acting cannot be learned from a book—you have to do it to learn it. However, a book does provide an important aspect of training that is often overlooked in the rush of producing and rehearsing a play or in the precious minutes of a class. In addition to just doing it, you must *reflect* on the doing. This book is a companion to your work in class, in rehearsal, and on stage. My hope is that it amplifies, verifies, and supports the learning opportunities your teacher/coach provides. Class time should be devoted to practice. The book is a guide for what is to come and a reference for what has occurred. It is where theory *converges* with practice.

Articulating theory requires clear language, so considerable effort has been made to define the terms clearly. Terms such as action, performance, or role are different from *jargon* such as "upstaging" or "cheating." Terms we use casually make for casual acting, so it is very important to take care and consider carefully the words we use to describe acting. As we will discuss later, art is a language unto itself, and so a beginning acting class can be seen as a vocabulary and grammar class for the actor. A beginning acting class also ought to begin at the beginning—not just *how,* but *why* do actors do what they do? We will take time to thoroughly examine the nature of the acting process and the actor's tools for playing. The better, richer, deeper your understanding of the tools and process of the actor, the more in charge you will be of your development. We attempt to discover the very fundamental aspects of playing and thereby empower you to continue to grow, learn, and become the kind of player you wish to be.

When working on a scene in class or beginning the rehearsal process for a show, the beginning actor typically asks, "how should I say this line?" For Constantin Stanislavski, the great Russian actor, director, and acting teacher of the early twentieth century (see Text Box—**Stanislavski**) the central question for the actor is, "how shall I *do* this?" About fifty years later, another genius of the theater, Jerzy Grotowski (see Text Box—**Grotowski**) posed the question in this way: "What must I *not* do?" (1968: 207) All three questions amount to the same thing—**acting is doing.** What follows is an approach to acting that deals with the central challenge for the actor—performing clear and effective actions.

Theater is a game, similar to baseball or hide-and-go-seek. The best players are students of the game—not only *how* to play, but *what,* exactly, you are playing, and *why.* The best players

A. Are masters of the subtleties and nuances of the game because they understand the essence and nature of the game.
B. Always return to the fundamentals of the game, to enrich both their understanding and their skill in playing.

Stanislavski, Constantin Sergeyevich (1863–1938)

Born of a wealthy family, Stanislavski (a stage name he took in 1885 to avoid embarrassing his family with his artistic endeavors) was a lifelong investigator of the acting process. Determined to find a system whereby a high level of artistry could be maintained from performance to performance, he devised an approach to training that he hoped would lead actors to "living the part." This system had two essential aspects—work on the self and work on the role. Work on the self included investigating one's inner resources of imagination and emotion. Work on the role included exploration of physical and vocal choices. Over the years he amended and altered the system, even retracting or discarding some earlier ideas. His influence on acting in the West cannot be overstated. Former pupils brought his early ideas to the United States where they gained great popularity, but also generated great controversy. Two of the most influential aspects of his system are his work on emotional recall and the so-called method of physical actions. Stanislavski discarded the former, while the latter has been claimed as his true legacy. What is important to remember is that both Stanislavski and Grotowski continued experimenting and searching their entire lives, and no doubt would have continued. Toward the end of his life, Stanislavski published his ideas, but the English translations are now suspect. As of this writing, a new translation is in the offing, but has not yet been completed.

C. Understand that what they do is only a game and is meant for the entertainment of the audience.

Although a game played without an audience can be fun, art is a special kind of game—meant for the perception of others. The wonderful thing about theater is that when it is played well, everyone wins—players and audience.

Part One explores the Preparation for Playing—the basic terms, underlying processes, and tools needed to play well. In Chapter One we examine the basic

Grotowski, Jerzy (1933–1999)

Grotowski was born in Poland and studied the Stanislavski system in his youth. He is the founder of a number of theater groups, the most famous of which is the Polish Lab Theater. Whereas Stanislavski's approach built up a character through the accumulation of details, Grotowski worked "via negativa"—that is, by eliminating all but the most essential behaviors in a performance. He published *Towards a Poor Theater* in 1968, which became a central text of the experimental theater movement of the late sixties and seventies. Later, his experiments led him away from theater and into spiritual explorations, although toward the end of his life he returned to his roots. Thomas Richards published *At Work with Grotowski on Physical Actions,* based on Richards's work with Grotowski in Italy in the nineties.

impulses that lead to symbolic expression; generally define art, acting, performing and theater; and propose some guidelines for training. In Chapter Two we discuss the optimal creative environment for actor training and how to engender it. Chapter Three introduces the central concept of "*ki*," or energy, and the generating, focusing, transforming, and exchanging of *ki* in playing.

Part Two begins the exploration of the Tools for Playing. Chapters Four through Seven examine the actor's tools (the body, voice, imagination, and feelings), propose methods by which the tools may be optimally developed, and suggest a working vocabulary for each tool that you may draw on in service to theatrical material. Chapter Eight examines the form of action, what the fundamental actions for playing are, and how to harness the specific energy necessary to act. Part Two concludes with two "intermissions." The first concerns the nature of the theatrical illusion and the second provides a sample warm-up with which to begin each class.

Part Three examines the game of theater itself: what it is and how to begin to apply your skills to playing effectively. In Chapter Nine we examine the four basic tasks of playing and the play of energy between actors, actors and objects, and actors and audience. Chapter Ten examines the interplay of text and acting; Chapter Eleven examines character—what it is and how to fulfill the demands of a role. Chapter Twelve explores the interplay of design and acting—set, lighting, costume, and sound. Chapter Thirteen examines your relationship to teachers of acting, to directors, and to the theater. The book concludes with the Curtain Call, exploring the spirit of play and the nature of *presence.*

The exercises in this book are drawn from many sources; some have been adapted and changed from their original structure, others have not. This synthetic approach is purposeful—there is no single way or method of actor training that is the be-all and end-all. There are fundamental aspects of training and many means by which these aspects may be explored. Your teacher will have his/her own exercises. This book attempts to provide a context for exercises. You may use them in a class or with a partner, or even by yourself. You can also make up your own exercises, bearing in mind that the exercise is a means, not an end. All the exercises focus on the play of energy—within you, and between you, your partner(s), and the audience. The emphasis is on *how,* on the **process** of acting, rather than the *what,* or the **product** of performance. Trust the process and the results will come. Impatience and shortcuts will undermine your work. The exercises go step by step. Attend to these steps and they will lead you to effective playing.

Two Terms to Consider

The following are two terms you ought to consider carefully. You may have some familiarity with these words, but they are employed here rather specifically and play a central role throughout the book.

Attending

Attending means to be present, to be there—in class, at rehearsal, in performance, and for your partners. Most of us spend our time in the "then and there" rather than the "here and now." We worry about what has happened, what will happen, and fail to attend to what's going on in the moment. Instead of *listening* to what people have to say, we're thinking about what we're going to say. Instead of *noticing* how the other person is behaving, we focus on how we appear to them. Instead of using our sensitivity to discern how someone else may be feeling, we tend to be obsessed with our own feelings. It is as if we do not trust ourselves, as if the words we speak, the body we inhabit and the feelings we have are not actually our own, thus requiring constant monitoring. In the theater we can tell which actors are in the "then and there"—they are not attending, they are thinking about their next line or the fit of the costume or whether or not the audience likes them.

Effective playing requires attention—to the task at hand, to your partner, and to the process. Throughout the book, you will be invited to attend to things you may ordinarily take for granted.

There is no element of playing that demands less than your full attention.

Ki

Acting is doing—the application of energy to a task. This energy may be physical, but isn't always. Physical actions are clearly perceivable, but prior to any behavior there exists the *potential* energy for action. When we speak of "sparks flying" in a confrontation, or the "electricity" of a moment, or the "chemistry" between individuals, we are referring to this energy. It is the *energy of the possible*. It is the possibility of action that makes performance compelling—the question of what will happen next that keeps us connected to the performer. In such interactions we *feel* the current, even if we don't see or hear it. This current of energy provides a common denominator to all forms of performance. There are many terms for this energy, but particularly apt is the Japanese concept of "*ki*."[1]

Ki is the central concept employed throughout the book. It is used to discuss the play of energy in performance and in the exercises. Sometimes following the exercise will be tips—*Ki points*—about how to focus your energy to get the most out of the exercise (see Text Box—*Ki or Chi*).

Some exercises are designed to explore concepts (mostly in Chapter One, but throughout the book as well). Exercises designed to develop you as an actor always do at least one of the four following things.

- **Generate energy**—foster and nurture impulses
- **Focus energy**—shape and form impulses
- **Transform energy**—change the form and shape of an impulse
- **Exchange (assimilate** and **emit) energy**—allow impulses to flow in and out of you

Ki or *Chi*

In essence, the character *ki* 木 means:

- spirit, mind, soul, heart, intention
- bent, interest, mood, feeling, temper, disposition, nature, care, attention, air, atmosphere
- flavor, odor
- energy, essence, indications
- taste, touch, dash, shade, trace
- spark, flash

by J. Aikyama. from www.aikiweb.com/language/ki_phrases.html

(The first initials—**G, F, T, E**—are placed after the name of an exercise and identify the function of the exercise throughout the book.)

In collaboration with your instructor, this book is designed to empower *you,* the actor, to be in charge of your artistic choices and your development as an artist.

Now, let's play.

N O T E S

1. "Ki" (or "Chi" in Chinese) is the Japanese word for life or spirit energy, as in Tai **chi** or Aikido. In 1994 Craig Turner introduced me to the concept of "ki" in his workshop on applying the martial arts to movement training at the Webster Movement Institute in Webster Groves, Missouri. "Dynami-sphere" is a term coined by Rudolf Laban from the Greek *dynethsthia,* "to be able." In a 1992 course manuscript, Tom Casciero defines it as "the space into which our energy is infused, the space in which we are able." "Personal space" is a common term from psychology that David Myers has defined as "the buffer zone we like to maintain around our bodies" (568). Stanislavski used the term "invisible rays" to describe a similar phenomenon (Smeliansky, Anatoly. "Stanislavski Revisited." Panel Presentation. Association for Theatre in Higher Education. San Francisco. 1995).

PART ONE

Preparation for Playing

CHAPTER

1 Acting and Performing

"We ask ourselves, who am I to be brilliant, gorgeous, talented and fabulous? Actually, who are you not to be?"
—Nelson Mandela, from Inaugural Speech (1994)

In this chapter we will examine:

- Who you are and how you function
- What is meant by "acting" and "performing"
- What art is and the particular art form that is acting
- How we can train to become effective actors

Acting is

- Simple, but it isn't easy
- Fun, but it's hard work
- Not real, but its illusion can be most compelling
- Not holy, but it can be spiritual

Great acting is compelling—it commands attention. Great actors create compelling performances through bold, imaginative choices, and the intimate connection they generate between each other and an audience. The goal of actor training—from a beginning acting class to a multi-year conservatory program—is to facilitate developing a technique that will result in a compelling performance every night when the lights go up, or every time a director calls "Action!" Although it is imperative that training is grounded in a clearly articulated philosophy of theater art and artistry, any approach, no matter its foundation, ought to adapt to and nurture your individual talents. You have unique challenges to face, as well as unique talents and abilities. This book is your companion and, in conjunction with your teacher/coach, is designed to guide the process of discovery and give you freedom to explore, make mistakes, and find joy in playing.

Ultimately, actor training must focus on nurturing your individual artistry and expanding your range of expression. The unique individual is what finally "sells" in the marketplace, regardless of whether the market is entertainment, law, public service, or science, and your original artistic vision, supported by a full range of physical, emotional, and intellectual expressiveness, cannot help but enrich your life as well as the lives of those touched by your artistry. Can you be a great actor? Who are you not to be?

Let us begin at the beginning then. Who are you? What is art? What are theater and acting? How do you begin the enormous tasks of understanding the acting process, developing your skills, and playing effectively? Impossible questions. But the impossibility of answering them has never stopped anyone from trying.

Who We Are and How We Function

You are an organic system and process energy following the same physical laws as any organic system. These laws govern all your behaviors, all your actions. *Everything you do in your study of acting, every exercise, improvisation, scene work and performance, follows these laws.* Therefore, it seems a good idea to review them, because from these laws the fundamental laws of art, theater, and acting arise.

1. Energy is neither lost nor destroyed.
   You have some, you use some, it goes somewhere, and you go get more. There are many forms of energy—light, sound, food, feelings—all of which have an impact upon you.
2. Energy tends toward the most stable state.
   This is the second law of thermodynamics, and is related to the Newtonian concept of inertia—things at rest tend to stay at rest, things in motion tend to stay in motion. It is also related to the biological concept of **homeostasis**— "the tendency of an organism to *maintain a uniform and beneficial physiological stability within and between its parts; organic equilibrium*" (Webster's Dictionary).
3. An organism does everything it can all the time.
   From the simplest single cell to the most complex forms of life, any organic system is in a continual relationship with itself and its environment, busily maintaining its life. That is all it can do. As you read this, you are doing all that you can do—not all you *may* do, but all you *can* do. You may choose to do something else, but at the time of doing something, that is all you can do. You can do only one thing at a time. That time may be quite brief, seemingly instantaneous, but nevertheless, it is a time during which you can do only one thing. It may appear that you are doing two things at once—eating and talking, thinking and scratching, *playing a character and managing a performance* (the so-called double consciousness of the actor)—but actually there is just a shift of attention, however brief and minute, from one thing to the other.

4. Human beings can choose how to use their energy.
Your ability to choose enables you to deny or yield to urges, place yourself in or out of danger, and create art.

Acting and Performing

An **act** is a thing you do to create or forestall change. You do things because you *must* to remain alive and balanced.[1] You are acting, therefore, *all the time*. **Acting** is doing—doing to, acting upon (see Text Box—**Acting Is Everything**). The most basic definition for acting is the application of energy to a task. The task may or may not be accomplished, but the energy applied must be sufficient to accomplish the task in order for the action to be effective.

When it comes to acting as an art and in the theater, generating and applying the specific energy for a clear task can be quite challenging. It is the specificity of the action that differentiates the average actor from the consummate one. The consummate actor performs the specific action at the precise moment and in the exact manner to accomplish a task with grace and ease.

Performing occurs when a person assumes a position relative to an Other. The Other could be an inanimate object (like a statue, photograph, the door to the bathroom when you have to go), but usually the other is another perceiving being. The other even could be you. **Performing** is *acting designed for perception*. That is, the task is to *make perceivable* the energy applied. Some actions are functional, such as work. Digging a ditch is a functional action; it's work. But, when the boss comes around to see how you are working, digging becomes a performance. There is a subtle but clear shift of energy from work to performance—a kind of "lift." You shift from doing something to "I am doing something." The assumption of "I" creates a position relative to an Other. Not just digging, but "See, Boss, I'm digging!"

Performance occurs in other perceptive modes besides the visual. Speaking is always a performance for the very act is predicated upon perception (the aural mode). We may *vocalize* (yell "ow" when a hammer hits the thumb), but that is not necessarily a performance—unless we want someone to hear our pain and come and take care of us. Chatting in a chat room online is a performance. The point is that performance is *felt* in the shift of energy from doing to doing something for perception. The rise in energy that occurs in performance is what the audience and actor feels.

Acting Is Everything

We have words to designate different *kinds* of acting: eating, sleeping, work, and play. Learning to be an actor is learning to play the game of theater. You already know how to play. For some, the gift of play, understood intuitively as a child, has been lost, forgotten, or suppressed. For others, playing comes easily, naturally. But in both cases, what is wanted is a way to play effectively and consistently, with intelligence, passion, and joy.

Found Performance

1. Observe life—in residence hall or apartment, cafeteria, class—wherever—and discover performances. When do you see people "acting out?" or "putting on a show" for someone else? Jot down your observations, even to snippets of dialogue you may overhear. Write up a scene using this found material, editing or adding as little as possible. For example, perhaps you see a man and a woman arguing about who was supposed to call whom. Perhaps the man claims it was not a definite promise to call, but more of a "whatever." Perhaps the woman sees it differently. Record the dialogue and behavior as faithfully as possible.
2. Perform this "found performance" for the class (using partners as needed).
3. Discuss what makes it theater for you. What might have occurred before the scene? What might happen afterward? Is this a funny or serious play?
4. Reflect on a recent performance you gave in your daily life—who were you performing for? What did you want them to see ("See, I'm digging")? Was it effective (did they believe you were "digging")?

Who are you? An organic system that follows physical laws. What is acting? Acting is doing and playing is a kind of acting. What are you playing? The game of theater. Although you may have encountered the next impossible questions in other contexts, it is imperative to try to answer them from the point of view of the player/actor. What is art and what is theater?

Art and Theater

The philosopher Susanne Langer defined art as "the creation of forms symbolic of human feeling" (1948: 40). A form is a shape or vessel or means by which a concept is conveyed. A symbol is a mental image of a thing—"this for that." The ability to symbolize is a uniquely human activity, and from this activity arises our ability to imagine, remember, think, and communicate. Langer argues that each art form is a language unto itself, each expressing in its own unique way indescribable human feelings that cannot be adequately conveyed by other means. Art is a language, a mode of communication. Before spoken language arose as the dominant mode, communication probably occurred via all means of expression.[2] Utterances, movement, markings, and enactments, all were methods by which primitive beings sought to gain some control over the environment (space, time, natural forces) and their own impulses (instinctual acts and reactions, as well as volitional acts). Initially, these acts were not means of communication, but were enlisted into such means.[3] Communication requires that both communicator and recipient have the capability of symbolic expression (this for that).

Over time and through a process of natural selection, spoken language became the dominant mode of communication, while other modes—movement, marking, enactments—became utilized in more specialized circumstances when ordinary speech would not do. Complex feelings do not easily boil down to one word or sentence. A picture—or movement, sounding, enactment—is indeed worth a thousand words. These other means of communication arose out of necessity—*there were and are no other means of expressing complex feelings.* In prehistory, it seems likely that what we now call art was part of the daily repertoire of communication, although not elaborated into the art forms that have since been formalized.

Over time, as spoken and written language developed, these other modes of communication developed as well, elaborating and finding more specific forms. So, perhaps, markings became painting, movement elaborated into dance, sound and rhythm into music, and *enactments into theater.* These forms are not fixed, but rather are determined by the feelings the artist is attempting to symbolize. Only when people started thinking and writing about art did the forms become to be seen as more distinct. In order to think about something it is necessary to classify it, define it, and examine its parts. This is in some ways antithetical to art making, which arises out of prerational intuitions about life feelings.

The life feelings that the artist attempts to symbolize deal with the nature of change. As stated previously, all acts are done in order to create or forestall change—internally and externally. Changes are typical; that is, changes occur in discernible patterns and under discernible circumstances. Some changes are sudden, some slow, some occur in clear steps, some all at once. In the human world we see typical changes in the development from childhood to adulthood (coming of age), from adulthood to old age, etc. Erik Erikson proposed eight stages of life that typify the developmental changes that occur in a human lifetime. (Erikson 1950)[4] The nature of change is what art recreates, or **imitates.**[5]

Change is made perceivable[6] through the **energy** exerted to make a change, whether or not change actually occurs. Whether or not change will occur creates the feeling of aliveness of a work of art, and as *suspense/anticipation/apprehension/ expectation.* These are the basic qualities all art has in common.

Each art form reveals change in a way particular to the form, what Langer calls the "commanding form." This form creates a *semblance* of life processes. The seeming liveliness of art is not real, but *virtual,* an *illusion.* For example, a pattern in wallpaper might have an appearance of movement; it might look as if the pattern were moving. But, of course, it is not moving. The appearance of movement is virtual, not actual. Every art form creates a kind of virtual world of its own, based on the commanding form of the art. Art imitates life. It imitates life processes. Life processes are about change. All art is an attempt to symbolize the nature of particular change in a particular way.

Theater reveals change through *action*—things done by someone or something. *Action is theater's commanding form.* Things may be done physically, musically, verbally, and may even be merely implied visually (scenically), but finally it is the *doing* that offers itself for the contemplation and entertainment of the audience. The doings are revealed in relationship with other doings—interaction—and are composed, or put in some order, by the artists (writer, director, and/or actor). Patterns of change in action (plots) are what hold the audience's interest. The play of actions performed by actors before an audience is what makes theater, no matter the genre, style, or milieu. *The illusion theater creates is the appearance of energy between actors.*

Tug-o-War (G, T, E)

1. With a partner, square off about four or five feet apart, holding an imaginary rope in your hands.
2. Pull the rope, focusing on the rope—its width, length, heft, texture. You and your partner must really engage your muscles in the act of pulling. As you pull, go ahead and yell or shout or "talk trash" to your partner. Once you've started talking, speak a memorized text such as a nursery rhyme or lyrics to a song or the words of a poem or monologue you know very well.
3. The audience should call out when they "see" the imaginary rope.

The object of the game is to make the rope "appear" to the audience. When you are fully engaged physically in the game, the audience will "see" a rope that isn't there. That is the illusion of theater. Note your experience:

a. What physical things happened to you when the rope appeared? Were your muscles engaged? Did you get tired?
b. What did you notice happened to your voice? Were you louder or softer? Did you strain? What happened when you spoke a memorized text? Was it different? If so, how?
c. Did your feelings change? Did you experience any particular emotion or any psychological charge? Did your feelings toward your partner change at all?
d. When you observed the tug-o-war, when the rope appeared, what did you observe about the players—their physical and vocal behavior? What change, if any, occurred in your feelings? Did you root for one player over another? Was your attention compelled?

Acting

Every human being applies energy to a task. Everyone **performs** actions. So, what is the difference between what everyone does and what the actor does? The actor performs actions under special, **theatrical conditions.** These conditions are of two types.

1. The *actual* conditions of the performance
   - the environment in which the performance occurs (the space and whatever elements of design are employed).
   - the play of energy between the actors and between the actors and audience.
2. The *virtual* conditions of the performance
   - the imaginary world evoked by the theater artists (the who, what, where and when *asserted* by the artists—actor, playwright, director, designers, etc.) and *accepted* by the audience.

These theatrical conditions **determine** the action; that is, the conditions *influence* and *give form* to the action. Finally, any action is taken to accomplish a task. So, now our operating definition of acting is:

> **Performing an action determined by the theatrical conditions to accomplish a task.**

Found Performance, Part II

1. Go back to the scene you found. What was the task being attempted? For example, in our scenario of the missed phone call, we might say that the young man was trying to "win over" the young woman, or "dismiss her complaints."
2. What conditions affected the scene? Did it happen outside or inside? In a crowded or unpopulated area? What other things may have affected the way the scene played?
3. What was the main action? Was one person *pushing* the other around? Was one person *urging* another to come along? Was one person *calming* the other person down? Try to describe the action as you understood it.
4. What was the nature of the performance? Was it personal—between friends or lovers? Was it social—between a person and a group? Was it political—between opposing powers? What roles were being played? Who was the intended audience?

Impossible questions cannot be answered easily or briefly. Full consideration would take volumes. However, it is sufficient for our purposes to pose the questions and begin the process of answering them. You will spend the rest of your life pondering these questions (and probably have spent a lot of time on them already). Let us now turn to our last impossible question. How do you begin the enormous task of understanding the acting process, developing your skills, and playing effectively?

The Three A's of Acting.   In learning a new game, there is a general process that occurs for nearly everyone. An initiation to the game is often accompanied by the thrill of initial success—you hit the ball, you scored a goal, you made a basket. This thrill is what induces you to go on, to try again and possibly to stick with it. Inevitably, this initial phase is usually followed by a long and frustrating series of failures and successes. What at first seemed like child's play is now an unattainable agony. Most alter their relationship to the game at this point, letting go of professional ambitions but perhaps maintaining an interest—sometimes passionate, sometimes mild—and participating in the game for pleasure. If this difficult phase is passed successfully, which may take years, you will arrive at a place where you have attained a certain level of competence. This is actually the most dangerous phase;

you may be fooled into thinking that you know what you're doing. However, those who wish to attain mastery realize that it is at this point that one must begin all over again. At that point, knowing what you know, you may truly learn the game and see in the first lessons deep implications for the most advanced levels of play. Presumably, you are at the beginning—an exciting phase that will hopefully segue to that wonderful thrill of initial success. Although different teacher/coaches, theorists, and practitioners may express it differently, all training, including acting training—progresses through three levels: *Awareness, Availability,* and *Articulation.*

Awareness: The cognition of, and sensitivity to, your internal and external environment. You must be aware of your own psychophysical status each moment, and aware of other actors, the audience, and the physical environment (lights, costume, set, props). To be fully aware, you must acknowledge the presence of all things affecting performance (in other words, everything).

Availability: The degree to which you are affected by the impact of energy on your system. Energy is generated via the imagination, other actors, the audience, and the physical environment (lights, costume, set, and props). To be fully available is to *get out of the way* of one's natural and organic impulses to act, and *allow* impulses to manifest themselves through actor's tools.

Articulation: To be fully expressive in, and have command over, the actor's tools. Articulation is the ability to make a wide range of choices regarding the use of those tools in performance. An articulate voice is characterized by clear speech, wide range, and is connected to the action. An articulate body is characterized by clear gestures and movement, a wide range of motion, and is connected to the action. The articulate imagination is characterized by specificity of image, a wide range of imaginings, and is connected to the action. An actor fully expressive in feelings has access to specific and a substantial range of feelings that are connected to the action.[7]

The Practice of Practice

Every acting class involves participating in exercises of one kind or another, so it might be worthwhile to examine just what an exercise is and what it is supposed to do. Exercises work in two ways: 1) Work on the actor's tools, and/or 2) work on the acting process. This work is done directly and/or indirectly. Direct exercises identify a specific objective and work toward achieving that objective. A breathing exercise to develop lung capacity is an example of a direct exercise. Indirect exercises identify a process or concept and work analogously or metaphorically to help you achieve a grasp of the process or concept. Most acting games are examples of indirect exercises.

Like all exercises and games, there is a level of risk involved in the practice and playing. If you attempt certain physical or emotional challenges for which you are not prepared you can damage your musculature or psyche. The acting teacher/coach is like a personal trainer—spotting, recommending types of workouts to develop acting tools and skills, and partially responsible for the safety of trainees.

The following is a short list of things to keep in mind when you are doing an exercise.

■ Keep a beginner's mind. Suspend judgments and assumptions. Stay open. Only by suspending judgments and assumptions may you encounter an exercise with the greatest opportunity to learn from it. Release yourself from the need to achieve some goal or produce an effect beyond those identified by you and your teacher/coach.

■ Be "in-the-moment." Acting teacher/coaches love this phrase, but what does it mean? It means the good part is now, not soon or a minute ago—this moment—this place is the best. Love it, honor it, give in to it.

■ Do first; ask questions later. This precludes trying to "figure out" the exercise so as to "do it right."[8] It often occurs that as soon as you engage your mind (a reflexive process), you disengage from your body (a physical process). "Get out of your head!" a teacher/coach may exclaim from time to time. The positive version of this exhortation might be "get into your body!" When your body is fully engaged in an activity, the mind—the repressive judgment of the mind—ceases at least temporarily. Then you may participate fully in the work and learning may occur.

■ Attend to the task at hand. Each exercise and improvisation presents a task to accomplish. If you are not clear as to the task, ask. Once you understand, then you may observe others more critically and identify behavior that is *extraneous* and *unnecessary* to the exercise. In "real life" you may always stand with your hips hitched in one direction or another. While this may be comfortable, it may not be necessary in an exercise, and may even hinder your progress.

■ Trust the process. It is the journey, not the destination that matters most in your work both in the classroom and on stage. Trust that the process will get you to your destination. Do not rush to a result. If the ground is well prepared the plant will grow. You cannot shove a stick in the ground and call it a tree! Neither can you manufacture expressions (mugging) and behaviors (indicating) and call it acting. (This will be discussed in more detail in Chapters Eight and Ten.)

■ Find the fun. Take pleasure and find joy in the work; sometimes exercises can be discomforting, distressing, disconcerting. But, if the learning environment established is safe, open, and collaborative, then you may find pleasure even when it feels like nothing is working.

Improvisation

Many exercises are improvisations; that is, the events and actions that occur are unscripted. Viola Spolin's book, *Improvisation for the Theater,* remains the seminal text on improvisation and is also a source of numerous improv games. These games can be used to create new theater pieces, from comic sketches to entire plays. But in the classroom, their primary function is to explore the acting process and develop the actor's tools. The following are guidelines to assist you in getting the most out of improvisations.

1. *Play by the rules.* Rules are structure and without structure there is no game. Follow the rules with the utmost fidelity and learn them until they are second nature.
2. *Play with the rules.* Those who are students of the game, who have a profound understanding of the game's nature and know how to bend the rules of the game, are the best actors. It is important to remember, however, that the beginner must first play by the rules. Only when a game is mastered may you begin to play with the rules—and only if your teacher/coach allows it.
3. *Play your part.* Every game has roles. In tag, for example, the roles are "it" and "not-it." Fulfill your role with commitment and purpose. There is a tendency among some actors to play all the roles to "help" the game (see Text Box—**The "Save the Show" Syndrome**). But, in fact, that only hinders the game and the development of the actors.
4. *Blend.* All energy you encounter is a gift—accept it, transform it, use it, say "Yes" to it (see Text Box—**Saying "Yes"**). Working with a partner,

The "Save the Show" Syndrome

Sometimes in performance things just don't go well—energy flags, voices aren't projecting, lines are dropped, entrances are missed. You may feel an impulse to do something to save the show (or the exercise), such as speak very loudly, make a big entrance or speak another actor's lines. Although understandable, this is usually not a good idea. Play the action, play your part. For example, in *Tug-o-War* your job is to pull your side of the rope. Pull it! If your partner isn't pulling and you "help" by easing off, neither you nor your partner will have played effectively.

Saying "Yes"

"Saying 'yes'" is a traditional concept in improvisation. Saying "yes" means agreeing to a premise or relationship asserted by your scene partner or the audience. By saying "yes," you allow the improv to move forward. However, "yes" can be coercive. If someone asserts a dominating role upon you (e.g., "Nurse, examine this man."), you must assent to it or you are not saying "yes." *Blending* describes a **mode of action** (a way of doing) rather than prescribes a text, and therefore is more fundamental to playing. Dr. Amy Seham's book, *Whose Improv Is It Anyway?* (University of Mississippi Press, 2001) provides an insightful examination of the practice and ethics of improvisation.

dealing with the environment, and connecting to the audience are all matters of blending. The instinctual act is to defend against your partner's attack, or overcome the environment, or control an audience. But these are acts of fear. It takes courage to not only face your partner, environment, and audience, but to cooperate with each and all. In later chapters we will elaborate on how to apply the concept of blending to specific acting challenges.

5. *Live in the Land of I-Don't-Know.* Not knowing what to do next is often a greatly feared moment in any exercise or game. However, that moment is also a source of great power and opportunity. Knowing what to do means being in control. A controlled performance is more predictable, less spontaneous and therefore less compelling. Spontaneity is highly valued in improvisation because it allows the audience to witness an actual event or decision. Not knowing what to do next invites possibilities. It is not the specific decision made that is important. Once a decision is made the audience need not attend as closely, for decisions have inevitable consequences. Once someone jumps up, we all know they will come down. It is the *deciding* to jump that creates suspense. Trust not knowing. Live in the "Land of I-Don't-Know."

6. *Focus.* Focusing means aligning your energy with your intent. If your intent is to not look silly, your attention is on yourself, and not on the acting task. If your intent is to please the audience, it is also not on the task at hand. Focus on the acting task.

7. *Work from impulse.* Impulses are urges to change. We tend to resist, mistrust, and even fear change. **Allow** the impulse to come forth, **nurture** its development and finally, **cultivate** it in service of the dramatic moment. Working from the impulse means getting out of the way of energy as it emerges, letting it grow, and shaping it.

8. *Trust.* Give up control and trust your intuition to guide you. There is a tendency to try to figure things out, to think through an action before attempting it. But this is a fear response. You have already lived through a lot and know what to do when encountering energy, but over time negative reinforcements have replaced the daring you once had as a child with caution. In Chapter Two we will look at how trust is most effectively created in the classroom (and rehearsal and performance).

9. *Dare to fail gloriously.*[9] Your attitude ought to be "what the hell!" Go for it. Dare to fail and you will likely succeed. Your willingness and commitment to the game determine the amount of energy you will apply to the tasks of the game. A half-hearted attempt at anything will not likely succeed. But if you willingly dive in, if you happily embrace foolishness, then you may succeed.

10. *Success.* It is the **quality** of our interactions, and the value that we attribute to those interactions, that defines success. Improvisation is not a game to win, but to play effectively. When improvs are played with spontaneity, ease, grace, élan, spirit, camaraderie and joy, *everyone*—actors, audience, technicians, and designers—*wins.*

We have considered the impossible and suggested some ways to begin the study of acting. Next, we look at how together we may bring out the best in our fellow players and ourselves. It is imperative that the environment fosters your creativity. You, your fellow players, and your teacher/coach have the responsibility to make the classroom a safe place to play.

NOTES

1. "Every act of a living unit transforms its situation and necessitates action under the impact of that new development as well as any fortuitous changes coinciding with it" (Langer 27). Things happen. You deal with it. It changes things. You deal with it. Sometimes these changes can be lucky for you, sometimes not.

2. We do not know how language arose, although there are many theories. My contention is that we do everything we can all the time and we obey the second law of thermodynamics. An infant experiences the feeling of hunger. Unable to do anything else, it cries. Food arrives and a connection is made between crying and the arrival of food. Through the process of natural selection, we discovered means of satisfying basic needs. Apparently, the most effective means of getting a number of needs satisfied is through spoken language, but that is not the only means.

3. New acts (such as speech) do not typically arise from old acts developmentally, but rather the new act is **adapted** to new needs. For example, vocal utterances were probably not originally designed for communication, but were found to be handy means by which to communicate. See Langer, *Mind: An Essay on Human Feeling,* Volume II, especially chapters 16–18.

4. See http://psychology.about.com/blsub_isterik.htm for information about Erikson and developmental stages.

5. Imitation is a loaded term that has fallen into some disrepute. Imitation seems to imply false or fake, but that is a second meaning. To imitate first means "to do or try to do after the manner of." (Webster 483) There has been considerable argument about this term ever since Aristotle discussed the concept in *Poetics.* I believe the word is apt, if we look at its supposed original meaning rather than the meanings that have accumulated over time.

6. By perception, I mean all the modes available to any individual—all the psychophysical senses.

7. The use of "articulation" is suggested by Anne Dennis in her book, *The Articulate Body: The Physical Training of the Actor* (New York: Drama Publishers, 1995).

8. For a number of reasons—cultural, economic, personal—there is a tendency in learning new things to "get it right." We all do this, either to show off our prowess, please the teacher, or to better our competitors. But this urge to get it right subverts the learning process and puts the focus on end results. We see exercises as ends, rather than means to an end. Viola Spolin saw this clearly and in her introduction to *Improvisation for the Theatre* suggests a number of ways to get around "getting it right."

9. This is the class motto used in my class, borrowed from my mentor as a teacher/coach, Ann V. Klotz.

CHAPTER

2 The Creative Environment

"Creativity comes from trust."

—Rita Mae Brown

In this chapter we will examine:

- Commitment
- Risk
- Breath

Except for love stories, perhaps the oldest stories we tell are about groups of people coming together to overcome impossible odds. From the *Odyssey* to *Henry V* to *The Seven Samurai* to *A League of Their Own* the pattern is familiar. A collection of misfits join (or are forced) together, face terrible obstacles and problems, fall apart, but then finally come together and save the day. (You may recognized this pattern if you have ever rehearsed and performed a play!) We probably like these stories so much because we enact them over and over throughout our lives. Acting classes may follow this pattern, too. Your learning is incredibly dependent upon your fellow players, so it is imperative that you all get along well enough to rise to the challenges you will encounter.

Two true stories. Two professional actors were preparing a scene for a showcase (a collection of scenes presented to agents and casting directors to "showcase" the actors' work). In the scene the actors were to kiss passionately. It was not going well. The director said to them, "Listen. The kiss isn't working. She needs to know that the kiss doesn't mean anything more than it does, and he needs to know that she doesn't think he wants something more from the kiss. Go work that out." The actors did not trust each other and the scene was not effective. Two other professional actors were working on *How I Learned to Drive,* by Paula Vogel. The play revolves around the characters "Lil' Bit" and her "Uncle Peck," who molests her. The actors had known each other for some time and had worked together previously. There is a great deal of physical and psychological intimacy in the play—kissing and fondling, and the powerful imaginary circumstances of sexual molestation. These actors understood the demands of the play and what they could expect of each other. They performed the required behavior without hesitation or apology, freeing them to concentrate on the more challenging psychological aspects of the play. These actors had a very high level of trust, and the playing was very effective.

> **The failure to trust—the audience, your partners or yourself—is perhaps the** *biggest obstacle* **to effective playing. The willingness to trust is perhaps the** *crucial ingredient* **to ensure effective playing.**

Before work can begin on playing, the environment in which you can most effectively play must be prepared. There are two environments to prepare—internal and external. The internal environment is, of course, you. The external is everything else, but practically speaking the external environment refers to the relationships between you, your classmates and your teacher/coach.

Commitment

The full participation on the part of each actor in the ensemble, including the teacher/coach, is required to optimize the creative environment. Each activity, exercise, improvisation, and scene demands the fullest commitment of which you are capable. Acting can and should be engaging, provocative, and fun, but each actor is directly responsible for the level of concentration, the quality of engagement, the depth of provocation, and the amount of fun. You must commit to your own development as well as the development of everyone else in the room. One of the hallmarks of a good team, or ensemble, is that the whole is often greater than the sum of its parts. That is, despite varying levels of skill and talent, the commitment of the players to each other raises the level of play for everyone. This is true in theater as it is for a jazz band or a baseball team. Some of the greatest examples of theater have come from ensembles, dedicated to each other and to the work (see Text Box— **Excellent Ensembles**). These ensembles all have in common a solid foundation of trust and an abiding commitment to the group, to the work, and to their artistic ideals. For the classroom, the following five guidelines will help you and your fellow player forge an effective, and successful, ensemble.

"(S)uccess will depend upon five factors:
1. The actors' sensitive response to each other.
2. Their honesty and openness to each other (this requiring courage).
3. The daring and inventiveness with which they have solved the problems they have set themselves.
4. The relevance and interest of the problems themselves.
5. The actor's skill in presentation."
      —from *Group Theater* by Brian Clark. Theater Art Books, New York; 1970

Excellent Ensembles

The King's Men—The final name for the company that first performed many of Shakespeare's plays. Though there are thousands of books and even more websites about Shakespeare and players of the day, we do not know a great deal about the acting style or even how they rehearsed. But the plays, and the actors who first performed them, have left an indelible mark on theater throughout the world.

The Group Theatre—An American group formed in 1931 by Harold Clurman, Cheryl Crawford and Lee Strasberg. The Group has had a profound impact on acting in the United States and abroad.
　　See www.pbs.org/wnet/americanmasters/database/group_theatre.html for a good introduction, and Clurman's *The Fervent Years* for a personal history of the Group.

Steppenwolf—Founded in 1976 by nine actors (many now famous), this ensemble is characterized by its vigorous and visceral acting style—a sort of theater of "big shoulders" (to modify Carl Sandberg's description of Chicago, where this ensemble is based). See www.Steppenwolf.org.

Theatre de Complicité—A British group founded by former students of Phillipe Gaulier of the L'ecole Jacques Lecoq—a master of mask and theater. This ensemble is characterized by inventive use of the actor's body and the integration of design elements in the performing. See www.complicite.org for information about this company.
　　Other groups: San Francisco Mime Troupe, Mabou Mines, Theatre de la Jeune Lune, the Open Theatre, and see http://dir.yahoo.com/Arts/Performing_Arts/Theatre/Theatre_Companies/Professional_Companies/

Risk

Acting involves risk—physical, imaginative, and emotional. To risk requires trust. To trust requires respect. To respect requires care. You must care about your work and your fellow players. You must take risks, but you must also know your limits. *You* set the risk level. Acting is by its nature an intimate activity, but personal boundaries must be respected. *You* have the responsibility to know your boundaries and acknowledge those of others. Sometimes you will not know yours or your partner's boundaries until you smack up against them. There are numerous exercises that develop trust and clarify the boundaries between you and your fellow actors, and between you and the teacher/coach. It is useful at the early stages to take care to debrief, allow discussion, and reflect upon an activity in writing. A journal can be very helpful in assimilating the work (see Text Box—**Journaling**).

The Group Contract (G).　This preliminary exercise can be an effective way to begin creating ensemble and fostering a creative environment. The goal is to state clearly and out loud what you need to play your best as well as offering your best to

Journaling

Journals are used by many actors and teachers of acting as a place to reflect on the creative process. Sometimes these reflections are more formal, such as Colley Cibber's *Apology for Actors,* or Anthony Sher's *Year of the King* (about his year-long investigation and performance of Richard III). Joseph Chaiken's book, *The Presence of the Actor* reads like a series of journal entries, as does Jon Jory's recent *Tips for Actors.*

Your journal, should you choose or be required to write one, can take many forms. Unlike a diary, where random thoughts about the day are perfectly acceptable, a journal is a more organized attempt to think about what you have done, what you are doing, and what you will do.

Journals ought to be completely confidential!

help others play. By doing so, you and your fellow players will understand that almost everyone needs the same things, and that each individual has something unique to give to the group.

Complete the following statements in one or two words

1. "What I need from the group to perform my best is . . . "
2. "What I can offer the group to perform their best is . . . "

Record the responses and type them up or post them online in a discussion board. At the next meeting, everyone should sign (or have read) the contract. This is a promise between you and your fellow actors to honor the needs and provide the offerings indicated in the contract. For example, you may say to the group that you "need constructive feedback and can offer a sense of humor." Someone else might "need patience and can offer enthusiasm." These "contracts" are present in all our interactions with groups, although most are unspoken. But the unspoken nature of our social contracts often leads to misunderstandings and poor communication.

In the professional world there are actual contracts that control the business transactions of actors and producers, clearly delineating rights and responsibilities of both parties. However, this is not so in the subtle interactions of rehearsal where unspoken assumptions can lead to miscommunication and divisiveness. A contract clarifies the working relationship, setting the terms and describing the processes of the interactions. When the terms are clear, everyone involved can let down defenses. When the terms are not clear, then you have to spend a lot of time negotiating meaning—decoding what has been said and done.

Commitment can be instantaneous—decide to commit and it is done. Trust is built over time—but it does not necessarily have to be a long time. Through shared experiences involving personal risk, sufficient trust between players can be built fairly quickly. The willingness to risk grows as trust grows. But whereas once established trust is a given (until shattered by misbehavior or accident), risks must be faced each time anew. Each time you encounter a risky situation, you must overcome the fear that always accompanies awareness of risk—whether it is walking down a strange, dark street, auditioning for a part, or doing an exercise in class. Like jumping into a pool, your willingness to overcome your fear, and the beginning of all your playing, starts with breath.

Breath

Life begins and ends with a breath. Your impulse to breathe is the primary and central life-sustaining impulse. This basic impulse—you need only exist to have it—is similar in structure to any impulse you have. Breath is the essential act. Its shape is the shape of all acts—initiation, growth, peak, decline, and end. Learning to breathe provides all the essential knowledge you need in preparing to act. As Hollis Huston says in *The Actor's Instrument,* breath is *inspiration* and *expiration* (22). With each cycle you are inspired and you expire—life and death in one simple act.

You have an instinctual need to breathe. Yet to breathe optimally, you must relearn to breathe, to take a full breath, to allow a full breath to occur. You can control breath to some degree. You may choose when to breathe, to hold your breath, and when to exhale.

In /Expire (G)

1. Allow yourself to expire. Feel the impulse to inhale, but do not inhale. Nurture the need to breathe until you can wait no longer and allow the breath to fall into your lungs. Note your physical sensations and the emotions. Repeat this step five or so times, refining your sense of emptiness and fullness, and discerning the optimal time to take a breath—when you are neither in dire need, nor before you truly need. In Chapter Five we will explore different impulses that lead to different breaths.

2. Find the shape of your breath—what is it? Take a breath and see. Yes, in and out, but what else? Breathe in and out five times, slowly. Note the shape of your breath, focusing on step one with breath one, step two with breath two and so on.

   1) Initiation (Where does the breath begin in the body? How does it grow inside?)

   2) Growth (How does the breath fill you up? Where does it go—front, back, sides?)

   3) Peak (How do you complete inhalation? Where does it finish—top of the chest, lower back, the sides of your torso? What is the change between inspiration and expiration?)

   4) Decline (How does exhalation begin? How does breath leave the body? Where do you feel the breath being released?)

   5) End (How do you know a breath is completed? Where is the last of your breath leaving your body—lower lungs, top of the chest, the sides of your torso?)

The smooth operation of breathing may be hindered by numerous factors, both external and internal. External obstructions to breathing include the quality and quantity of the air. If the air stinks, you will not want to breathe. If you're underwater, you will be unable to breathe. Internal obstructions to the smooth operation of your breathing are far more numerous. Your capacity for breath may be limited, especially if you smoke, are terribly out of shape, or suffer from asthma or other inflictions affecting the lungs. The way you carry yourself may impede breathing. If you slouch, carry unnecessary tension in your shoulders, hold in your stomach, hitch a hip to the side, if you can't stand still—all these things will hinder the smooth operation of breathing.

While these things may be addressed physically, there is often a psychological element involved as well. You may slouch because you're depressed, your shoulders may be tense because you are afraid, you hold in your stomach because you are self-conscious, you hitch your hips because . . . who knows? These are issues you must address, in your own time and way. But the physical solution to the obstacles to your breathing we can address right now by finding the optimal alignment of your body.

Actor Ready (**F**).   Actor Ready is the balanced and aligned psychophysical place from which the actor is ready to respond naturally and organically to an impulse. Actor Ready is unprejudiced in any way, but active and alert. The ready actor is aware, available, and articulate in the application of energy to a task. There are many imaginative and prescriptive ways to align, but in whatever manner this is done, it is a **process,** not a **product.** You never arrive at alignment; you are always aligning.

1. Feet are in full contact with the floor. Move side to side and back and forth to find your "plumb line," or balanced position, in which you use the least amount of muscle to maintain your position. Feel your energy go into the ground.

2. Allow your awareness to travel up from your feet, through your ankles, knees, thighs to your pelvis, releasing any unnecessary holding.

3. Allow your awareness to travel up through your spine. The spine is the central conduit of your energy, the natural alignment of which is a slight curve. The spine extends up from the pelvis (the sacrum) into the head, the head resting lightly atop the spine on a ball joint, as if a balloon on a string. The eyes should float in the center of the eye socket, neither cast up or down. You may feel the neck and facial muscles release—there is very little sense of holding alignment, but rather of continual adjustment.

   (A good example of this is trying to balance a dowel rod or yardstick on a finger. You must continually adjust; otherwise the stick will fall to the ground).

4. Through your awareness, inventory your sensations and feelings. Release or place to the side of your mind any concerns or distractions. Acknowledge their presence then let them pass through you until your mind is also afloat.

5. Breathe. Allow the breath to fall in and out. Breath is *inspiration* and *expiration*. With each half of the cycle you live and die.
6. Tune in to the energy of the room without judgment.
7. Stay with it. See how long you can maintain readiness. Each day try to go a bit longer until you can stand for 10 minutes without losing focus or allowing tension to creep in.

Giving/Taking Over (**T, E**).   The exercise works directly on trust. By physically giving control of parts of your body to your partner, you will develop self-trust and build your partner's trustworthiness. In pairs, give over the weight of a body part to your partner.

1. Head—place the hands so as to cup the neck and base of the skull and gently lift the head off the ground slightly (an inch or less). Gently turn the head left and right, encouraging your partner to release, release, and release.
2. Arms and shoulders—standing behind your partner, lift the arms and allow them to fall back to your partner's side. If your partner is holding the arms at all, the arms will not be dead weight, and the fall controlled. Encourage your partner to release, release, and release. Try the same with the shoulders, lifting them up and letting them drop.
3. Legs—with your partner lying down, lift a leg into the air, encouraging your partner to give the full weight of the leg over to your control. Switch to the other leg. Provide feedback to your partner about any differences or changes you notice.

Trust Circle (**F, T, E**).   This is a traditional trust exercise that you may have encountered before. If you have, keep yourself open to a new experience with it. By bringing your full awareness to the exercise you will deepen your trustfulness and trustworthiness—a task that is required for each new exercise, scene work, play rehearsal and performance. If this is new to you—allow, dare, and find the fun!

1. Four to six people (supporters) form a fairly close circle around you
2. Cross your arms at your chest, placing your hands on opposite shoulders
3. Supporters may place a hand lightly on your torso to give you a sense of security. (At a more advanced stage of trust, you may choose to be free of that reassuring touch.)
4. Keeping the body fairly rigid, fall backwards into the hands of the supporters
5. Supporters then pass you around the circle, forwards, backwards, side-to-side, etc.

Ki *Points*

■ It is imperative that the supporters be sensitive to your trust boundaries. You should notice almost immediately in which direction you are most or least comfortable to be passed. Supporters should gently encourage you to work through your discomfort, but only as far as you are willing to take the risk.

- Work together to *build* trust. This is *not* an exercise to scare, but to dare.
- At a very advanced level, supporters may move quickly along the outside of the circle and exchange places with other supporters while you are falling. This is very exciting, but only for an ensemble that is physically adept and very comfortable with one another.
- Falling tips—think "stiff as a board, light as a feather." Notice where and when you seize up and see if you can allow yourself to fall past that point.
- Supporting tips—be vigilant and help those who have trouble supporting the weight of the actor alone (or get help if you are having trouble).

After the exercise, describe how it felt to fall. Describe how it felt to support people falling. How trusting are you? How trustworthy?

***Trust Falls* (F, T, E).**   There are several ways to do this traditional trust exercise, but playing safely is imperative.

1. Find a table, ladder, or platform from which you may fall—four to six feet is plenty high.
2. The group lines up so as to catch you, grasping each other's wrists with their hands. Their feet should be placed one in front of the other, knees bent. It is important when catching to "give" a little as the weight of the body falls into the arms but you must be sure to "give" straight down—otherwise catchers may bump heads.
3. Climb up the platform, turn your back to the group, and place your heels near the edge. Cross your arms on your chest and close your eyes.
4. The teacher/coach speaks "stiff as a board, light as a feather, one, two, three," and you fall back into the arms of the group.

Ki *Points*

- You need *not* fall, but only *imagine* falling.
- It is the decision to fall or not that compels our attention. What will you do? In this one simple exercise, you go through nearly the entire performing process. Learn how to be "in" the decision. Like the "Land of I-Don't-Know" this is a powerful place to be.

***Getting to Show You* (T, E).**   Pair up and interview each other, doing the following in two minutes:

1. Exchange names and basic data
2. Teach each other a phrase from a favorite song
3. Teach each other a move from a favorite sport/activity (not sleeping or sleeping with)
4. Teach each other a favorite noun (person, place, and thing)

5. Share your information with the group together, but you must introduce and talk about your partner, not yourself. After the exercise, sit in a circle and consider these two questions—how well did you listen? How well were you heard?

These are just a few trust-building exercises. You and your fellow players and teacher/coach may come up with many more. Throughout your time together, whether it is for a few weeks, months or even years, it is wise to return to these kinds of exercises as a way to "check-in" on the ensemble and see how it is functioning. Trust can be fragile initially. It can be broken easily by simple carelessness, and only mended with time and attention. However, the stronger the trust, the more it can withstand. Doing the next exercises, and indeed, working together on playing, will probably deepen the trust you and your fellow actors have established.

Once you and your fellow actors are "ready," you may more effectively begin the process of generating, focusing, transforming, and exchanging (assimilating and emitting) the energy to act.

Freedom is a necessary condition for playing. Your energy must be free to move through you, be released from you, and to play between you and your fellow players. Energy must freely flow within the structural demands of the form (that is, the style or genre of the play/scenario), and it must flow between the actor and audience. These are large demands, the weight of which often can bind you. Judgments— internal and external—will also bind you (see Text Box—**Evaluating Acting**). The optimal creative environment is one in which you are free to make choices and take risks.

Evaluating Acting

When an athlete in a particular sport is described as good there are usually facts to support it—batting averages, points/game, yards gained, etc. But determining whether or not an actor is good is a little more elusive. For one thing, "good" is a judgmental word and is not very useful. When someone says, "That was good," about your performance, there is little you can do with that information, except say "thank you." Judgmental words like "bad," "terrible," "that stinks!" are also useless and can only damage any trust built between you and your fellow players and your teacher/coach. "Effective" is most apt when talking about acting. Understanding the task and harnessing the specific energy to accomplish the task for the perception of the audience are the primary concerns for the actor. Acting is effective if the task is clear and the energy sufficient to accomplish the task. Acting is wonderful when the energy sufficient for the task is produced with ease and grace (that is, when the acting appears as if little or no effort were required). Great acting occurs when, in addition to ease and grace of the application of energy to a task, the energies of the actors and audience create a communion in which both actors and audience are transformed (if only briefly) into a whole, living entity.

CHAPTER

3

Ki: Energy for Playing

"There is a vitality, a life force, an energy, a quickening, that is translated through you into action . . . "

—Martha Graham

In this chapter we will:

- Explore the concept of *Ki*
- Investigate the play of energy through you, and between you and a partner

Imagine you are watching a baseball game—your favorite team against their arch rivals. Your team is down by two runs, with two outs, bottom of the ninth inning, runners on first and second. The clean-up batter is up, facing the ace reliever. Fans scream, horns blare, drums beat. The pitcher stares at the batter, awaiting the sign from the catcher. The pitcher winds up, delivers. . . . crack! You may supply your own ending.

In this scenario, what is most important? Is it the action of the pitcher? Is it the action of the hitter? Or is it what happens to the ball? The ball reveals the energy exerted by the players through their attempts to accomplish various tasks—hitting, throwing, and catching—all designed to win the game. We know how the game is going by what happens to the ball. Be it an object (such as a ball or puck), a touch (as in fencing, wrestling, boxing), a limit (such as a bar in the high jump, or time in a race)—all games are measured by some expression of energy. Then what is the "ball" in theater?

Name Toss **(F, E).**   This exercise is an effective "getting to know you" game as well as a demonstration of the concept of the play of energy.

1. Gather in a circle and throw a ball back and forth among all the players.
2. As you throw, call out the name of the individual to whom you are throwing.

3. As a group, keep the ball going as quickly and efficiently as possible and try not to repeat throwing to a player until everyone has caught and thrown the ball.

Ki *Points*

■ Throw the ball so it may be caught easily. Catch the ball with a minimum of fuss.

■ When the ball is dropped, it is like when a line is dropped in a play, or a cue missed—the play stops until the players recover and get the audience back into the play.

■ When the ball flies around the room easily and smoothly, it is like when a performance is playing well. It appears effortless and feels thrilling, as in "how long can they keep this up!"

Advanced level

4. As you throw the ball, follow it and exchange places with the person to whom you threw it. The person catching the ball should try to throw it and run before you reach his/her place.

5. Add a second and then a third ball, continuing to exchange places as you throw. Work for ease and grace in throwing, catching, and running.

    Variation—instead of running through the circle, run along the perimeter to your new spot. This requires a good deal of space and is best played outdoors or in a very large room.

    Initially, this all can be quite chaotic (and fun), but by focusing on the task at hand, the group will improve. You will eventually feel the energy change from tense and chaotic to easy and joyful—just as in the rehearsal process of any play.

6. Speak a line of text (from a sonnet or any memorized text) after you name the catcher. For example, "Heather, Let me not to the marriage of true minds admit impediments!"

Theater is made of actions, revealed to an audience in the interplay of actions performed by human beings. The actor's primary task is to make perceivable the play of energy. In the game of theater, the most important thing is the play of energy between actors, and actor and audience. The actor reveals energy by attempting to accomplish various tasks—achieving a goal, satisfying a need, obtaining power—all designed to maintain or regain equilibrium.

Before you attempt to accomplish these and other tasks, you must first free and focus your energy. The fact is you are already an energy, or *ki,* master. You have spent your entire life generating, focusing, transforming and exchanging energy. But, by drawing your *attention* to what you already do, you may increase your *awareness* and more effectively do it. Your effectiveness in doing will facilitate your *availability* to the play of energy, and thereby you will become more *articulate* in the application of energy to the task.

The Four *Ki*-Posts

The following concepts are the *mental* directions for Actor Ready, adapted from Aikido practices (see Text Box—**Martial Arts/Theater Arts**). These directions encourage the *free* and *balanced* play of energy between you and your partner. Once you have found your physical alignment and your breath is falling in and out with ease, these four directions align your energy for playing.[1] The exercises included are designed to give you the experience of the directions as clearly as possible.

Keep One-point

Imagine that the universe is infinite. Now imagine the center of an infinite space. It is nowhere or anywhere. If anywhere, why not make it you, the center of you? A human's center is just below and a few inches into the navel. In Aikido this is known as the "one-point," and the master always maintains that sense of centeredness, of one-point. This *is* the center of the universe. It is the *source,* the wellspring of all your energy, your *ki.*

Center of the Universe (G)

1. Imagine you *are* the center of the universe and take a walk around the room. As you move, so too does the universe. Notice how your energy does (and does not) flow through you.
2. Pick someone from the group at random as the center of the universe. Adjust your walking so that as the new "center" moves, you move and revolve about the center.
3. Go back to being the center yourself and note the difference. Continue to shift from a single individual as the center to everyone in the room being the center. Note any change in the flow of energy.

Extend *Ki*

Ki is the flow of energy through the self. The effective application of energy requires that it should be focused and yet flows freely. To focus, or extend *ki,* one must first allow it to flow. Every effective actor knows he/she must be **available** to his/her

---

Martial Arts/Theater Arts

Aikido is a purely defensive form of martial art, invented in the late nineteenth century by Morihei Ueshiba out of a number of samurai martial arts traditions. Sensei (an honorific title for the teacher of any martial art) Ueshiba said Aikido is "the way of nonviolence, blending and harmony." In essence, rather than block attacks, Aikido practitioners learn to move with the attack. For example, if someone pushes you, the typical response is to push back. The way of Aikido is to *blend* with the attack; that is, allow yourself to be pushed until the energy of the attack is sufficiently diminished so that you may redirect the energy of your assailant, usually to the ground.

own imagination, feelings, etc. as well as to other actors and the audience (not to mention the affect of set, lights, sound, costume). You must get out of the way of the energy; you must not impede it through tension, fear or doubt. In Aikido the extension of *ki* begins with the open hand.

Extending **Ki (G, F)**

1. Begin with a hand at your one-point, standing in Actor Ready.
2. Imagine your energy is water or light. Allow your arms to rise into the air from your sides. See and feel energy flow out of your arms and hands into the space you are in. You may feel the tips of your fingers tingle as the blood flow quickens and moves into your extremities.
3. Breathe easily and deeply. Allow the arms to come back to your sides, but maintain that sense of energy flowing freely through your body—extend *ki*.
   Ki may be extended through objects (useful when handling props).
4. Pick up any object and extend your *ki* through the object and out into space.
5. Imagine the object being carried or held not by your hand, but by the energy.

Ki may also be extended to and through another. The practice of shiatsu massage is based on the idea of passing *ki* through the hands into the body of another. However, extending *ki* to another does not require actual touch, only the exertion and focusing of energy. Recall a heated exchange or an exciting flirtation—certainly *ki* was flowing in those situations. Recall an attempt to overhear a conversation you were not meant to hear. Your entire being—and energy—became focused on your ear. This is all that is meant by "extending *ki*." Usually, we do not extend *ki* specifically, only generally. As stated previously, we tend to walk around in a kind of energy swamp and often our playing is mired in that swamp and is vague or general. But effective playing is marked by the specific application of energy to a task—by the focused extension of *ki*.

Maintain Your Ground

Your feet are fully on the ground; you have a sense of your weight going into the earth. It is a stable stance that says "I own the space I'm in." In stressful situations we move up and forward on our toes—in order to fight or run away. But because this is behavior that is preparing you for another behavior, it is inherently unstable. In a culture that emphasizes being on the move constantly, many of us have lost our ground. In a culture that devalues some of us, many of us feel little right to the ground on which we stand. But life is not all about fighting or driving or moving. You needn't *keep* nor *hold* your ground, but rather nurture it, and when it is time to move, move. When you stay, stay.

Allow *Ki* to Flow

Tension is a sign that energy is blocked or obstructed. Many of us have been taught to chase that tension around and out of our bodies but it is a Sisyphean task (see Text Box—**Try Hard to Relax**). Tension maintains structure, like the cables on a

---

Try Hard to Relax

Many of us receive mixed messages about effort. The first is usually, "try harder!" But what is meant is "work more effectively" (although neither gives you much guidance about how to proceed). We internalize this message to try harder, and it soon becomes, "I worked so hard" (as if exertion is the only thing necessary for success, or an "A"). To try is to test (as in trial)—to see whether or not an action will work. Trying comes out of fear—either of success or failure. It is like hedging your bets. In the movie *The Empire Strikes Back*, the character Yoda said, "Do or do not . . . there is no try."

The other message we receive is, "just relax!" We try so hard that our bodies turn into knots of tension. These knots tie up the optimal flow of energy. So, we are told to relax. But again, this admonition provides no clear way to proceed. There are a number of ways to help the actor relax—meditation, guided imagery[2], massage, yoga, simply shaking the body. However, relaxation is not an end—it is a *means* to the end of allowing *ki* to flow. There are many ways to facilitate the flow of energy. Relaxation is merely *one* way.

---

suspension bridge. Without tension you would simply collapse. Flow is a *quality of engagement*—the easy and graceful application of exactly the appropriate energy to accomplish a task.

Allowing *ki* to flow is to act with maximum efficiency and minimum effort. Allow and trust and your *ki* will flow.

Once energy is flowing, the next step is to focus it. First, you will learn to focus energy within yourself, and then send focused energy out from yourself.

The Unbendable Arm (**G, F**).   Actors of relatively similar size and strength pair up.

1. Extend your arm, palm up. Let your partner place one hand between your bicep and elbow, and an open hand beneath your wrist (see Figure 3.1).
2. Your partner tries to bend your arm by pushing up the wrist and pushing down just above the elbow. Resist as best as possible. You will *not* be able to resist long (unless quite strong).

Ki *Points*

- Your partner should *not* pinch the elbow or wrist (this breaks the energy meridians, or pressure points, at those locations and makes it very difficult for you to resist).
- You should register how it feels to engage the muscles to resist the bending.

3. Extend *ki*—imagining light or water (or whatever image seems effective) pouring from your one-point through your fingertips.
4. Your partner will try to bend your arm again, only this time your partner will exert a small amount of pressure on the arm, increasing it gradually, thus testing your *ki* flow. Your partner will give you feedback on whether or not the

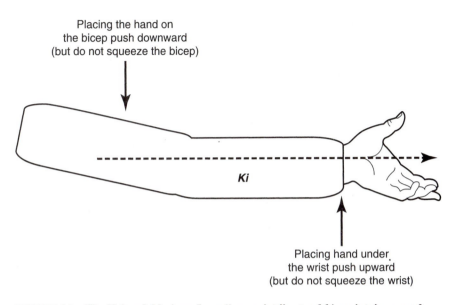

Placing the hand on
the bicep push downward
(but do not squeeze the bicep)

Ki

Placing hand under
the wrist push upward
(but do not squeeze the wrist)

FIGURE 3.1   The Unbendable Arm (keep "one point," extend *ki*, maintain ground, allow ki to flow).

muscles are being engaged (there will be some of course, to maintain the arm in space, but the muscles should not be engaged to resist your partner's attempt to bend your arm).

Ki *Points*

- Extending *ki* effectively does not occur immediately—indeed it takes a long time to master this "trick."
- The point is not to become an Aikido master, but rather to experience the sensation of energy being focused, and that it *can* be focused. Some may be skeptical of this initially, but it opens the mind to the possibility of channeling energy in a specific way without strain or "working hard."

5. Switch, with you now attempting to bend your partner's arm, following steps one through four above.

Your effectiveness as an actor will depend upon the grace and ease with which you can generate and focus your energy. Equally important, however, is your sensitivity to the energy of others.

Now! (F, E)

1. Face your partner within arm's reach, focusing on just each other's eyes.
2. One at a time, attempt to touch each other's sternum with the index finger.

3. When you perceive or sense that a touch is coming, say "now."
4. Continue the game until you can almost sense a move *before* it occurs.

Ki *Points*

- Focus on the eyes, not the hand. You can see the movement begin with a thought to move.
- Keep your mind clear. Do not try to stop the touch, just sense it coming. Allow your gaze to soften. You are not defending against the touch; you are opening yourself to the play of energy.
- Give feedback about the accuracy in assessing the attempt to touch. So, if your partner anticipates and guesses too early, you can claim a point. But if your partner does sense you are about to move, even if you haven't initiated a movement, you must acknowledge that your partner was correct and concede the point.

Initially, you should attempt to touch several times before switching, but after you get the hang of it, switch after each attempt.

Now! works on sensing the flow *ki* in the other. When played well, *Now!* exercises your ability to pay attention and stay "in-the-moment." If you give over to the game, you will find yourself in tune—sensing when an attempt will be made and letting go of trying to trick the other (see Text Box—**Two Samurai**).

Catch (F, T, E)

1. Play catch with an invisible ball. Attend to the size of the ball and the energy exerted by the thrower, and catch the ball that was thrown.

   The class and your teacher/coach can evaluate whether or not the energy exerted to catch the ball is consistent with the energy exerted to throw the ball. If the ball caught seems like the ball thrown, you may throw it to another person.
2. As you throw, call out the name of the person you are throwing to. This engages the voice with the physical activity.

Two Samurai

There is the famous story of two Samurai who meet on a road in the rain. Each expects the other to make way; each refuses to give way. Simultaneously, the Samurai assume an en garde position. They remain absolutely still for a long time. Then, simultaneously, they release from en garde, bow deeply to one another and gently pass each other and continue on their way. This is the ideal battle of ideally matched opponents. For either to initiate an attack would make the attacker vulnerable. The ideal game of *Now!* would be motionless— only the word "now" uttered by each actor in turn as they sense the *ki* of their partner flow toward pointing.

As the group becomes more efficient at playing the game, you may choose to transform the ball's size, weight and even shape. The essential task is to catch the object thrown.

Catch is a simple way to get you to attend to your partner and to the energy playing between the both of you (and the group). Without stopping the game, proceed directly to the next exercise.

Casting Spells (**T, E**)[3]. This is a paradigm for the acting process, because it imitates the play of energy within and between organic systems. The game requires both *exchanging* (emitting and assimilating) and *transforming* energy. You must blend with your fellow players, catching the ball of energy thrown to you. You must be in the moment, keep open, grounded, free. You must be aware, available and articulate to play effectively (see Figure 3.2).

Set-up: Five to 10 players in a circle. For fun, you might imagine that you are a sorcerer, witch, warlock, or other magical creature. It is quite important to find the fun (see **The Practice of Practice** in Chapter One) in all games and exercises, but especially this one.

1. Form a circle and using movement and sound, send out, or "cast a spell," upon another actor (**emit** energy). For example, you might shoot out your arms and cry, "bla-ah" towards someone across from you.
2. When a "spell" is cast on you, receive the "spell" as it was sent to you with sound and movement (**assimilate** the energy). For example, you might feel the "spell" hit you in the chest, sending you slightly backward with a yelp.
3. **Transform** the energy with sound and movement—that is, allow the energy received to travel through your body and voice, like a bolt of electricity or a shiver, and **let it change.** For example, you might begin with a shake and a high-pitched whine that transform into waving and a low growl.
4. Send out a "spell" to another actor, using your full voice and body. For example, you might fling out an arm and leg and shout "aiiieeee!"

Ki *Points*

- There are three parts to the exercise—taking in, sending out, and transforming energy. Each is equally important, but you may find that you are more comfortable with one part over another. For example, some actors will tend to be very effective at sending out and not so effective at taking in. Others will transform quite well, allowing energy to travel through the voice and body and letting the energy change into a new sound and movement quite organically.
- Be sure to focus on each part of the exercise as well as utilizing your full range of sound and movement.
- Concentrate on using different parts of your body (legs or hips instead of arms and hands) and different parts of your vocal range (high instead of low, consonants instead of vowels, for example).

Advance levels

- Oppositional spells—Receive an "evil" spell and transform it to a "good" spell, focusing on the transformation phase of the spell.
- Spells in rhythm—instead of random vocalization, actors cast spells using rhythm, as in scat singing. The actor receiving the spell must then modify the rhythm without abandoning it completely.
- Spells with text—using words, phrases or whole sentences from a text. At this level the task is to maintain the energy of the full body/voice spell, but moder-

Send out

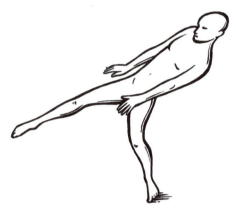

Take in

Transform

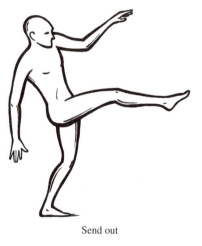

Send out

FIGURE 3.2   Casting Spells.

ate it to a more commonplace behavioral repertoire. Initially, use any text you are working on, but later whole scenes may be played in casting spells (all scenes already are a series of spell castings).

If there is time, casting spells for longer than 10 minutes may result in full, unpremeditated releases of sound and gesture. Grotowski spoke of the actor "resigning from *not* doing," when the actor would stop resisting the exercise and give over to it. Once this happens, new behaviors emerge and the unconscious or intuitive faculties are engaged. *Casting Spells* is one of those exercises that benefits greatly from the actor "resigning from not doing."

Casting Spells makes perceivable the play of energy that occurs between people all the time. It is a paradigm for the acting process, and works simultaneously at all three levels. That is, you must be **aware** of the energy being sent, **available** to the energy (allowing it to change you), and you must be **articulate** in sending the energy back out again. It also deals with all four aspects of practice—generating, focusing, transforming and exchanging (emitting and assimilating) energy.

The following traditional game is deceptively simple, but it offers a number of opportunities to explore focusing and exchanging energy. It also adds a competitive element that heightens the **playing energy,** which is essential for effective playing in performance.

Zip-Zap-Zop (F, E)

1. Form a circle. Hands are clasped together as in prayer—this is your zip-zap-zopper.
2. Aim your zopper *precisely* at someone and say, "Zip." That person aims his zopper at someone and says, "Zap." That person aims at another and says, "Zop," and so on.[4]

The object of the game is to maintain the flow of energy, represented by clarity of physical and vocal action. Keep alert and maintain a peripheral awareness. Shut off your mind and trust the game. Like *Casting Spells, Zip-Zap-Zop* is a model for the actor's work for it imitates the play of energy in organic systems.

Level One: The zopping travels around the circle in one direction. Actors are to arrive at and maintain a rather quick tempo.

Level Two: The zopping still travels in a circle, but anyone at anytime, may change the direction (clockwise to counter-clockwise, for example).

Level Three: Zopping happens randomly across the circle. At this level, actors can be eliminated if they fail to keep the words in sequence or if they miss being "zopped." If two people respond to a zop, the *sender* is eliminated for lack of clarity. Individuals are eliminated until only a single person remains. This adds a competitive edge to the game that can be helpful in generating greater energy.

Variation. In a culturally diverse group it can be quite useful to exploit language differences. After the game is understood, speakers of different languages should offer nonsense syllables of their own as substitutes for zip, zap, and zop. Every language has sounds that will be unfamiliar to those who do not speak the language. This requires everyone to listen very carefully and to speak very clearly. For example, some Asian languages have sounds that are unlike anything in English. Playing the game with these sounds not only adds to the challenge for some, it levels the playing field for those whose native language is not English.

The Weave **(F, E).**   This exercise works on the direct and indirect levels as well as requiring you to focus and exchange energy. In addition, it is an excellent training tool for developing a sense of spatial relationship to the space and to others.

Set-up: Boundaries are identified to delineate a rectangle. It should be large enough for the entire group to move freely, but small enough to create the possibility of collisions.

1. Walk in a constant, regular movement, keeping a 1–2 foot "field" around you. Walk in a straight line until "repelled" by the presence of an oncoming actor or the perimeter of the rectangle. "Bounce" or deflect in another direction until once again encountering a person or perimeter—like a ball on a pool table.
2. At a signal from someone in the ensemble, try to stop completely in unison. You will hear when that has or has not occurred. Keep working until the ensemble is stopping and starting in unison. If the ensemble is working effectively, there will be no extraneous sounds, just the stopping and starting in near perfect unison. Work until the ensemble has reached that near perfect unison.
3. At a signal from someone in the group, jump up and down three times in unison. Keep working until the group is jumping in unison. If the ensemble is working effectively, there will be three distinct thuds as the jumps land. Work until there are three thuds in perfect unison.
4. Stop in unison. Close eyes. Sense an empty space near you and where other players are. On the count of three, step to an empty space with awareness of others moving around you. Open eyes. The goal is to balance the space so that players are spread more or less evenly about the area. Repeat until the group moves efficiently to balance the space.
5. Stop in unison again. Close eyes. On the count of three, step to an empty space you sense near you, but this time choose a level—high, middle, or low. High means filling the area above you, reaching up into the air as high as you can. Middle means filling the air around you—reaching out, bending to the sides and extending your body (legs as well as arms) into the space between your waist and head. Low means filling the air below you—crouching or lying on the floor. The goal is to balance the space in three dimensions instead of just two (as it were).

   Variations. Add a small object such as a ball to the game. Once the ball is in play, actors must pass it off as they make eye contact. Actors should neither seek to get the ball, nor seek to avoid it. The goal is to pass the object smoothly from one person to the other.

- Add this imaginary circumstance—the object is desirable. If you have it, try to keep it. If you don't have it, try to get it. If eye contact is made, the ball must be passed. All other rules must be followed—you must follow your direct path until deflected from it by another, you cannot go out of your way to get the object. Neither can you reach out and grab the object; it must be given.

- Reverse the imaginary circumstances: the object is undesirable, like a hot potato. If you have it, get rid of it. If you don't have it, avoid it. You must accept it if you make eye contact with someone who possess the object. You cannot move out of your path to avoid it, nor can you reach out of your path to give it away.

  In both instances, adding a time element will heighten the energy, particularly in the "hot potato" version. Limit the time one may possess the object, with the added consequence that should the time pass, the person with the object is eliminated from the game.

Discuss how the variations affected the playing of the game. What happened to the ensemble's ability to move as one? Did the added elements hinder or facilitate ensemble playing? Can the ensemble play the game and maintain the connection with each other?

***En Garde* (E).** *En Garde* is a great exercise in focusing and processing the exchange of energy. It is also an apt metaphor for the rehearsal experience— excitement followed by confusion followed by frustration followed by breakthrough. The exercise may be adapted to include three or more people, two or more groups of people, and to incorporate selected text.

1. Face partner in Actor Ready and without speaking, move one step at a time so as to maintain a constant spatial relationship—that is, if you move forward, your partner moves back, if you move to your right, your partner moves to his/her left.

2. After each move, the initiator of the movement changes—for example, *A* first, then *B,* and so on.

3. Add a sound or word as you or your partner initiate a move.

4. Make a sound/speak a word when you or your partner *follows* the move. Level four is quite difficult, but it is exactly what happens on stage in performance— and often with more than two people!

Ki *Points*

- Begin with simple utterances (vowel sounds), and then try a series of connected words such as a list of countries, states, colors, car makes, etc. As you become more proficient you can improvise entire dialogues, an open scene, or a scene from a play.

Intention

So far, we have explored *ki* through various games that imitate how energy plays within and between organic systems. The various ground rules set for you in these games have been, for the most part, without a goal beyond playing by the rules. You have been enacting, or acting out, the energy process. But acting is not just the play of energy; it is *the application of energy to a task.*

- The task gives direction, or intent, to the energy.
- The intention is always to manage change—to recover or maintain balance.

This next game has a clear task—to tag the other player's tambourine before your tambourine is tagged. This task provides a direction (or intent) for your energy. Since two people play it, the intentions necessarily collide. This collision creates the "drama" of the game—who will win?

In order to win, you must keep your focus on your opponent to protect your tambourine, while alternately looking for openings for you to tag your opponent's tambourine. The tambourine is the object of your intent, but it also provides a *means* to accomplish your task and gain your intent.

The means by which you attempt to accomplish your task will necessarily generate characteristics— the *kind* of player you are **emerges** from *how* you play. That is, you do not play a character; you simply play in a specific way. Character assessment occurs **outside** of the action *by the audience* (and by you, after the task).

Thus, in this game you play with two primary elements of theater—action and character.

***Tambourine Tag* (F, E).**   Set-up: Two tambourines and space sufficient for a large circle

1. Make a circle for two "contestants" to enter, each with a tambourine.
2. Each contestant attempts to touch the other's tambourine first, using the free hand.
3. The contest is over when someone's tambourine is touched. Then two new contestants enter the circle and begin to play.

Ki *Points*

- The tambourine is your "voice" and is to be used to have a "conversation" with the opposing actor. Resist the urge to continually shake the tambourine. Use it when you must, to lure, distract, entice or otherwise engage the attention of the opposing actor.
- Set a time limit of two to three minutes, otherwise the game could go on indefinitely. Count down the final 10 or so seconds and note what happens to the energy of the actors.

- If you let go of the need to win and defeat, some interesting things can happen.
- When you watch a contest, cheer on one player. Note any differences you see in their playing.

After a few rounds, ask two questions for each pair of players

1. Who are they? What relationship seemed to be evoked by the playing—siblings? Parent-child? Lovers? Rivals? What observations did you make that leads you to your conclusion? Allow yourself to imagine what *might* be the relationship.
2. What was going on? What do you imagine the two were contesting? If siblings, was it an attempt at domination? If lovers, was it a mating ritual? Allow yourself to imagine what *might* be going on.

For example, two aggressive but silly players might be characterized as siblings fighting. Play that is sly or coy might be characterized as a lover's spat. Action reveals character. We'll come back to this in Chapter Eleven—**Playing Character.**

At its essence, theater is created by the play of energy between people, revealed in the resistance to change, and is about how certain changes feel. The preceding ideas and exercises are designed to increase your awareness of, and your ability to make perceivable, the process of change—take in, transform, send out. The actor's job is to nurture to full expression the impulses we all have to act, and to perform the act so that an audience may perceive it. In order to provide maximum clarity for an audience, the actor must have an expressive instrument capable of clarity. This means that to be an effective actor, you must develop your instrument, or your acting tools—your body, voice, imagination, and your feelings. We now turn our attention to that task.

NOTES

1. Craig Turner (University of North Carolina) introduced me to these concepts and several exercises that follow. Robert Cohen writes of "alignment" in *Acting Power* (13), and the use of "align" here is similar. More specifically, to align your energy actually means that the direction of force/energy applied to a task is focused, unified—going in the same direction.

2. Guided imagery usually entails focusing on a part of the body and visualizing the release of tension. For example, you can imagine your body being a series of sandbags which empty, or you can imagine your body melting. Guided imagery works quite well for some people, not so well for others. Your task will be to discover the most effective means by which you can achieve optimal flow of energy.

3. I was taught *Casting Spells* and *Tambourine Tag* by Norma Bowles, coauthor of *Cootie Shots* (New York: Theatre Communication Group, 2002).

4. I have found that speakers of languages other than English sometimes have difficulty hearing or pronouncing the difference between the "a" sound in "zap" and the short "o" sound in "zop." In practice, any series of three nonsense words will do, and I have found it useful to let the students choose the sounds themselves.

PART TWO

The Tools for Playing

Since a performance is a series of acts designed for perception, it is necessary that the means by which the acts are perceived are optimally functioning. *The means of the actor are the body, voice, imagination and feelings.* These are the **tools** the actor employs to perform actions determined by theatrical conditions to accomplish a task. Your voice, body, imagination and feelings must have **power, depth,** and **range** in order to respond to theatrical conditions and to accomplish the task with ease and grace. Acting class is where you begin to explore your tools, to develop range, power, and depth, and to put them in service to accomplishing a task. The next few chapters will help you begin your investigation and exploration of your tools for making theater.

The physical, vocal, imaginative, and emotional choices of the actor are essentially **pathways of energy.** Innumerable influences and obstacles create the path through which the energy travels, finally emerging as behavior, as **acts.** The action begins deep inside you as an impulse. It travels through you (the pathways of energy) beginning with feelings (urges and drives) developing into thought and emerging as behavior. The job of the actor is to **facilitate** that journey by **optimizing** the energy pathways.

Workouts and Warm-ups

If you ever played a sport at the organized level, then you know that before every practice or game, you warm-up. If you have ever wanted to increase your strength or change your shape, then you know that you had to workout. Acting is no different. Before each class, rehearsal, and performance you warm up your body and voice, stimulate your imagination, free your feelings and focus your energy. This is fundamental to preparing to play. Between classes, rehearsals and performances, most professional actors go to the gym, voice and/or singing lessons, and acting class to develop their skill and craft.

Central to development of the actor's tools is a clearly structured and progressive warm-up. A regular discipline of exercise and practice leads to **power** (strength and focus), **depth** (endurance and consistency), and **range** (flexibility and capacity). An effective workout and warm-up forms the basis for using the tools in the acting process—it is like the scale or barre work of the actor. The warm-up provides you with a method of developing and maintaining your body, voice, imagination and feelings over an entire career.

4 Body: The Actor's First Tool

"Our own physical body possesses a wisdom which we who inhabit the body lack."

—Henry Miller

In this chapter we will:

- Examine our ability to move
- Define fitness
- Describe an effective routine of physical development and maintenance
- Introduce a vocabulary of movement

There are few sights more spectacular than a human being flying through the air performing some intricate feat of physical strength, dexterity, and grace. Think of your favorite basketball star slam dunking the ball, or a figure skater pulling off a quad, a gymnast dismounting from the high bar or a tennis player diving to save match point. Athletic stars are usually endowed with natural gifts and an intense desire to excel that keeps them practicing and practicing. The same, of course, is true of performing artists. Perhaps you've seen a gifted dancer seemingly defy gravity, or heard a singer release a note of impossible beauty. But the actor's use of body is a little different. The actor must be adept at behavior in a variety of spaces and conditions, both real and imaginary. Every character and/or role demands specific behaviors. Sometimes a clown, sometimes a warrior, a lover, king, fool, the actor must create ordinary behavior under extraordinary circumstances or extraordinary behavior whatever the circumstances. So, your body must be adaptable to a tremendous variety of behaviors.

Over time, you have developed a number of behavioral preferences—the walk you walk, the way you stand, your handshake. Along with preferences, you also have limitations—how fast you can run, how high you can jump, how far you can stretch. There is nothing inherently wrong with preferences or limitations, but they may not give you access to the tremendous variety of behaviors that effective playing demands.

> **The primary challenges in developing the player's body are *identifying preferences* and *overcoming limitations*.**

Walk the Walk

1. As a group, simply walk around the room for a minute or so. Just walk naturally, as you normally do.
2. Upon a signal from your teacher/coach, secretly decide to imitate the walk of another person in the room. You need not follow this person, but try to match their gait, the motion of their arms, the alignment of their head and neck—everything you can to imitate their walk as exactly as possible.
3. After a few minutes, stop and identify the person you were imitating. Describe the basic behaviors you focused on in creating their walk. Then the person you followed should say who they were following, and so on. (It doesn't matter if two or more people imitated the same person or if two people imitated each other.)
    - What behaviors were commonly focused on? What was the chain of imitation—did everyone end up walking like one person?
4. Individually, walk across the floor and have another person follow and imitate the walk. Observe and note the basic behaviors that characterize the walk.
5. Pair up and stand facing your partner. One at a time, imitate each other's stance. Walk around your partner so you have a 360 degree view of "yourself."
    - One at a time, go before the group and stand like one of your fellow players. Can the group identify the person?
6. Walk around as a group again, in your normal walk, and shake everyone's hand. Note three distinct handshakes. With your eyes closed, see if you can identify a person simply by their handshake.
    - Imitate the handshakes and see if others can identify the individual you are imitating (For instance, you imitate Joe's handshake. Can your classmates identify Joe's handshake as performed by you?).

This exercise exposes some of your preferences. We will explore those in more detail later in this chapter, and again in Chapter Eleven—**Playing Character.**

Human Motion

One remarkable evolutionary change from primates such as apes and chimpanzees to humans is that we walk on two legs. This may seem like a little thing. You may take for granted your ability to move on two legs until that ability is taken from you.

But from that change, it has been proposed that no less than the human mind was made possible.[1] Upright, the human brain grew larger, and the arms, hands and jaw grew smaller and more refined. The spine changed to hold the head up and allow the legs to project down nearly 180°. All of this has a tremendous impact on how you move, starting with the relationship between your head and neck, and moving down through the spine, the shoulders, torso, pelvic girdle, and the legs. You do not have to have an intimate knowledge of your body to play effectively, but a general knowledge will increase your awareness and thus enhance your ability to make changes and choices—always an artist's chief ability.

The Body at Play

The body knows first. If you can focus energy and nurture the impulse and ability to change, you can generate an effective performance. Many approaches to work on the body are techniques—prescriptions for how to more effectively use the body (see Text Box—**Physical Techniques**). These techniques are useful, but they are not the ends. They are only a means. What is finally wanted is a *vocabulary of movement*. The larger your vocabulary, the more choices will be available to you when acting. Expanding that vocabulary is your mission. The journey takes many forms—as many forms as there are actors.

Fitness

Fitness is defined by what *you* want to be able to do. If you want to be able to do a show without collapsing with exhaustion at the end, unable to take your curtain call—you're going to have to work on conditioning. If you want to be able to lift

---

Physical Techniques

The following is a partial list of major movement techniques and the individuals who created them. A good place to start your exploration of movement studies is at the website for the Association of Theater Movement Educators—www.atme.org.

Laban Movement—www.lims.org

The Alexander Technique—www.alexandertech.com, www.directionjournal.com (an online journal of the technique), www.ati-net.com

Feldenkrais—www.feldenkrais.com, www.feldenkrais-resources.com

In addition to the movement techniques, physical practices that you may find useful include yoga, Tai Chi, martial arts (particularly Aikido), any kind of dance, fencing, and gymnastics, to name just a few.

everyone in the company and you can't—you'll have to work on strengthening yourself. Ask yourself these three questions:

- What do I want to do?
- Can I do it?
- If not, what must I do so I *can?*

An effective physical workout should

1. Stretch—to increase flexibility (range).
2. Articulate—to increase capacity (range).
3. Strengthen—to increase power and depth.

> **An effective warm-up should free the body—to allow you to amplify an impulse and respond to change clearly, with ease and grace.**

Following is a description of elements that make up an effective warm-up. Your teacher/coach will have preferences as to how to go about creating the warm-up, but eventually (should you continue) you will construct your own. Once you are familiar with the elements of the warm-up, you will know best what you need to work on. Today you might need to give more attention to your neck. Tomorrow, perhaps your hips will need a little more time. A warm-up must be performed with great awareness, otherwise it is empty rote, just like memorized lines rattled off without thought and action is an empty performance. Explore, note, and turn your attention to what your body can do and how it does it.

Stretches/Articulations (T).   It is often useful and more fun to warm-up to music, but it is not necessary. Music provides a rhythm and a count, but it also has its own energy that you may respond to, filling the music with the particular movement.

1. Head/Neck—be sure to differentiate between head and neck, and don't crunch the vertebrae in your neck as you rotate it back
2. Scapula/Shoulders—twisting forward and back, and rotating in opposition
3. Arms, wrists, hands, fingers—rotate and flex
   - hand wave—a ripple of the hand beginning at the first knuckles, and moving into the wrist
   - arm wave—a ripple of the arm, beginning with the hand and moving through the elbow and shoulder
4. Torso—forward/back, side to side, and rotating in a circle (this is primarily a movement of the spine)
5. Hips—rotation, ab/adduction (side-to-side and up and down)
6. Legs—open hip sockets, rotating forward and back
7. Knees—pliés
8. Ankles/Feet—rotations, relevé

Body Wave (T).   As a rope moves when snapped at one end, the body wave travels from the toes through the head and essentially involves a large undulation of the spine. It begins with a bending of the knees and the head dropping so the chin rests near the chest. As the knees straighten, the hips roll forward, followed by the stomach, chest and finally the head. The undulation should be smooth rather than discontinuous; that is, the entire body is moving as the "wave" travels through it. As the hips roll forward, the head begins to rise from the chest. As the chest rolls forward, the head begins to tip up just slightly, and as the head tips back at the end of the way, the hips roll back slightly.

Stop the wave any time along the way and walk, allowing the body part most forward to lead the movement. There are any number of places the wave may stop, but there are five major places: a) head down, knees bent; b) hips forward, chin up a bit; c) stomach forward, head up; d) chest forward, nose up; e) bottom out, head up. The body wave provides a nice finish to the physical warm-up as it, like the vocal range, extends the body through a series of movements and also may be utilized in creating specific pathways of energy (see Figure 4.1).

Yoga

The word "yoga" comes from the Sanskrit root *yuj,* which means "to join" or "to yoke." There are a number of yoga forms (such as mantra, rahja, or tantra) but hatha yoga is the one most of us associate with yoga. Hatha yoga is primarily aimed at freeing through physical means. The use of asanas, or poses, is offered here as simple and effective means to freeing your body (and mind) to play.

| Actor ready | Knees bent, chin down, back bowed | Hips forward, chin level, back slightly arched | Stomach forward, chin up slightly, back arched | Chest forward, chin up, upper back arched | Chin tipped up, pelvis tipped back |

FIGURE 4.1   The Body Wave.

Yoga Resources

There are numerous reference materials on yoga and asanas (poses). A quick internet search will yield thousands of sites devoted to yoga with clear instructions and illustrations of many poses. Of course, your library will have books that will also provide instruction, illustrations, and also some of the philosophy of yoga practice. In addition, there are many instructors available, perhaps even at your school, and you might try a class or two or invite a teacher to come to your acting class for some basic instruction. It is important to remember, however, that you determine the depth of your involvement. Yoga can be used purely for the physical benefits it provides. Should you wish to explore it more deeply, that is your decision. If you feel that some of the spiritual aspects of yoga contradict your own beliefs, then certainly you should not feel compelled to participate. Consult your teacher/coach on how best to fulfill the warm-up through other means.

   http://yoga.org.nz/postures: This free site out of New Zealand offers clear instructions and moment to moment development of many poses.

Essentially, yoga is a practice of stretching and breathing. While its means are physical, its true aim is to free the mind and spirit (see Text Box—**Yoga Resources**). Our concern is primarily the stretching and breathing aspects of yoga. By moving to and through the poses, and connecting the in- and expiration of your breath to the movement, you will stretch and free your body—two of the aims of an effective warm-up. The poses should be thought of as developmental rather than static. As in alignment (see **Actor Ready**), a pose is a process, not an achievement. It follows then that there is no perfect way to achieve a pose; there is only the pose you achieve today, moment to moment. While ideally your teacher/coach or yoga instructor will guide you in finding a pose and connecting your breathing, it is not necessary. Really, any stretching and breathing will warm you up. But yoga offers a particularly effective approach to the warm up and is proposed here as an example of how you may begin to construct your own discipline of preparing the body for playing.

Sun Salute (**F, T**).   This is a yoga practice that moves through specific poses with coordinated breathing. The basic breath pattern is on a four count*—inhale for four, hold (full) for four, exhale for four, hold (empty) for four. Inhale as you initiate each pose and complete the pose by the fourth count (see Figure 4.2).

1. Begin in Actor Ready. Inhale and bring your hands together as if in prayer (Prayer pose) Hold. Exhale. Hold. (#1)

---

*Note: Instructions on the exact form and progress of any pose vary from teacher to teacher. The sun salute in particular has a number of slight variations, depending on who is doing the teaching. Any discrepancy between what is in this book and what your teacher/coach or yoga instructors say is to be expected. As always, you ought to heed your own teacher.

FIGURE 4.2 The Sun Salute.

2. Inhale and reach your arms up and arch back as far as comfortable (Half Moon). Hold. Exhale. Hold. (#2)
3. Inhale. Reach up and bend over, touching your hands to the ground and bringing your head to your knees, if you can (Forward Bend). Hold. Exhale. Hold. (#3)
4. Inhale. Jump or step back so that you end in a push-up like position (Plank). Lower your body to the ground (Crocodile), then Hold. Exhale. Hold. (#4)
5. Inhale. Arch your back, hands flat on ground, arms extended, shoulders down (Cobra) Hold. Exhale. Hold. (#5)
6. Inhale. Pressing back with your hips, hand flat on floor, make an inverted "V" shape, head between the arms (Downward-facing Dog) Hold. Exhale. Hold. (#6)
7. Inhale. Raising your head and shifting your hips down, bring the right leg forward, hands on either side (Lunge). Hold. Exhale. Hold. (#7)
8. Inhale. Bring feet together and bend over, touching your hands to the ground if you are able (Forward Bend). Hold. Exhale. Hold. (#8)
9. Inhale. Stand and reach up and back. (Half Moon) (#9)
10. Inhale. Return to Actor Ready (Prayer pose). Hold. Exhale. Hold. (#10)

Repeat sequence, but in step 7, lunge with the left leg.

***Triangle Pose* (F, T).**   This is an excellent horizontal stretch, especially useful after performing the sun salute, with its more sagittal (forward and back) orientation. The breathing pattern is the same as in the sun salute (see Figure 4.3).

FIGURE 4.3   Triangle Pose.

1. Begin in Actor Ready. Jump your legs apart wider than shoulder width, but not so wide as to lose balance or overstretch. Simultaneously, extend your arms out to the sides, level with your shoulders.
2. Reach out with your right arm and allow your torso to lean directly over your hips. As you continue to reach out, allow your torso to bend toward the ground until you may grasp your right shin with your right hand. If you are able, you may place your hand on your ankle or on the ground in front or back of your ankle. Your left arm is raised directly above you so that your arms form a line up to the ceiling (or sky).
3. Turn your head and look at your left hand. Maintain your hips in line with your torso and arms. Feel as if you are continually turning toward your hand. Hold for several breathing cycles.
4. Repeat to the left side.

Dancer Pose (**F, T**).   Also known as the King of the Dance pose, this is an especially effective asana for balance. The level of difficulty is a bit higher than the triangle pose, but you set the limit of the stretch. Remember, with all acting exercises, you need to play within yourself while safely stretching your limits (see Figure 4.4).

1. Begin in Actor Ready. Inhale. Bend the right leg and grasp your left foot with your left hand (either on the inside or outside of the foot) while simultaneously extending the right arm straight up.
2. Pull your left leg up behind you as high as you can and reach out in front of you with your right arm at about a 45 degree angle. Your torso will bend forward slightly. Hold for several breathing cycles.
3. Repeat on the other side.
    Alternating how you grasp your foot (on the outside or inside) will provide a good stretch for your scapula (shoulder blade).

FIGURE 4.4   The Dancer Pose.

Stretching practices from athletics or dance are effective alternatives to yoga. When any stretching coordinated with breathing is practiced regularly, along with regular loosening and articulating the joints and limbs, you will begin to increase your range of motion. But an actor with the most expansive range of motion is uninteresting without an effective means to put that range to use in service to the theatrical material. As learning the alphabet is but the first step in making words, learning to move is but step one in creating a fully embodied presence on stage. In both cases, a vocabulary is needed to communicate ideas, feelings and intent.

Laban Movement

Rudolph von Laban (1879–1958) was an artist and scientist who discovered basic movement principles of form, sequence, and dynamics as he searched for a way to capture movement in writing. He called these principles Effort-Shape and Space Harmony. He also developed a symbolic system for recording movement called Kinetography, or Labanotation. What makes Laban Movement Studies (LMS) so useful to actors is that it provides a vocabulary of movement—it describes what we do and therefore provides a means by which you can change how you move. It is a highly evolved way of thinking about movement and teachers of LMS must be certified. However, some of the basic concepts can be explained here and put to use in your work, in class, and on stage.

The Dimensional Scale (**F, T**).   This multilevel exercise created by Laban is based on martial arts defensive maneuvers. It travels along the three dimensions: vertical (door plane), horizontal (table plane), and sagittal (wheel plane). The scale is to be done on both the left and right sides of the body. Once the scale is learned, it is useful to have some memorized text (a nursery rhyme or tongue twister, for example) on hand (see Figure 4.5).

1. Stand in Actor Ready and initiate a movement from one-point that *lengthens* the spine and moves the body *up,* as you *rise* on the toes and reach up with the hand to the highest vertical point *lightly,* as if you are placing a teacup on a shelf just within reach.

   Again, initiating from one-point, draw yourself in, *shortening* the spine, coming *down* off the toes and *sinking* into a squat, placing the hand on the floor with *strength,* as if pushing down on a can to crush it.

2. Initiating from one-point, allowing your torso to *widen,* reach *out* to the side, balancing on one foot to extend your reach, allowing the body to *expand,* keeping your eyes front with an *indirect* focus, as if you're taking in a magnificent view.

   Gather in from your one-point, allowing your torso to *narrow,* reach *across* to the side with your arm and hand, *enclosing* your body, eyes following your hand to a point about 10 feet *directly* off your shoulder, as if spying a spot of dirt on a white wall.

3. Initiating from one-point, allow the torso to *bulge* and the hand to reach *forward,* as you step on a leg to *advance* the body ahead in a *sustained* manner, as if steadily tracking your target.

   Initiating from one-point, allow the torso to *hollow* and the hand to reach *back,* taking a full step as you *retreat quickly,* as if avoiding a punch to the stomach.

The scale works on five components simultaneously and helps you inhabit your body and the space around you. Most importantly, it provides you with a basic vocabulary of movement to manifest a variety of changes.

The *dimensional* component works on placing energy (extending *ki*) in a single dimension and plane. After some regular practice with the scale, try to "place" your energy in front, back, or in the middle of the plane. This can lead to some striking effects in performance. For example, placing energy in front of you in the vertical (door) plane seems to create a sense of control, while placing energy behind you creates a sense of being pursued. Of course, as you experiment with this component, you will discover the effect of the specific placement of energy for yourself.

The *body* component works on creating flexibility in the spine and is connected to breath and emotion. For example, when assuming a high status, there is generally a lengthening of the spine and for low status a shortening. We tend to bulge when on the attack, and hollow when afraid. Although widening and narrowing the spine or torso is less apparent externally, the effect upon the inner feelings is clearer. Again, experimentation will reveal the nature of the affect for you.

Take a Walk (F, T)

1. Begin by walking casually around the playing area, focusing only on moving freely. Change directions now and then, avoiding walking in circles or in the same direction as your classmates.

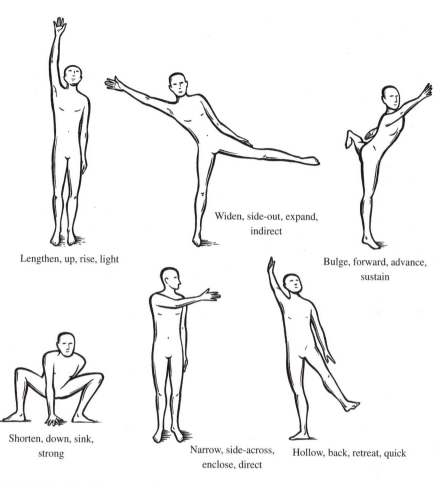

Lengthen, up, rise, light

Widen, side-out, expand, indirect

Bulge, forward, advance, sustain

Shorten, down, sink, strong

Narrow, side-across, enclose, direct

Hollow, back, retreat, quick

FIGURE 4.5   The Dimensional Scale.

2. **Bulge.** As you walk let your torso bulge forward as your spine bows. Allow yourself to change—the tempo (speed) of your walk, your intent, and note how it makes you feel.
   - Speak to someone on your way, either improvisationally or with prepared text. You may stop and speak or keep going—whatever you feel like doing.
3. **Hollow.** As you walk, let your torso hollow back as your spine arches. Allow yourself to change tempo, intent and feeling. Even let yourself walk backward.
   - Speak to someone on your way, either improvisationally or with prepared text.
4. **Widen.** Feel as if your torso is widening (you might take a deep breath to increase your sense of widening). Allow yourself to change tempo, intent, and feeling. Let the progress of your walk change as well.

- Speak to someone on your way, either improvisationally or with prepared text.
5. Repeat with a sense of lengthening and shortening.

    Combinations: hollow and shorten, lengthen and widen, bulge and shorten, narrow and hollow, etc. Note how it changes your tempo, intent and feeling. Be sure to interact with someone and connect the exercise to your voice.

A simple movement of the spine can change every aspect of your playing and is the beginning of fully embodied presence on stage and the creation of character.

The *directional* component extends the range of mobility and allows practice in losing and recovering balance (behaviors fundamental to a great deal of theater). As part of a daily warm-up, the directional demands ought to become greater, requiring you to stretch higher, squat lower, reach out further and enclose more tightly. This takes you out of the comfort zone of habitual behavior and into new physical territory. It will quickly become clear with which direction you are most and least comfortable. The dimensional scale has great value as a diagnostic tool, allowing both you and the instructor to see and experience limitations in mobility and then structure exercises to actually move beyond those limitations.

Which Way Home? (F, T)

1. Pair up and in turns tell each other how to get from the classroom to your home. As your partner speaks, begin to imitate the gestures employed— *pointing, arcing* (waving), *spoking* (arms jutting out directly from the torso), or *shaping/carving* (hands and arms cutting through the air or making shapes out of the air).
   a. Pointing—one-dimensional
   b. Arcing/Spoking—two-dimensional
   c. Shaping/Carving—three-dimensional
2. Note you and your partner's preferences. Then choose one of the above that is different from the way you gestured initially and give the same directions home using only that way (pointing, arcing/spoking, shaping/carving only).

Laban noticed that people generally gesture in three ways or combinations of three ways. Each of us has a preference in gesturing. By naming what we do, we can change what we do.

The *shape* component works on moving three-dimensionally from one-point. There is a tendency with many beginning actors to move only the arms and the head, creating a somewhat disembodied appearance in performance. Rising, shrinking, expanding, enclosing, advancing, and retreating can only occur with the entire body engaged.

Funhouse Mirrors (F, T)

1. Pair up. Move in three-dimensional opposition to your partner, as if you are both mirrors in a funhouse, continually distorting and changing shape.

    a. Rise and shrink
    b. Expand and enclose
    c. Advance and retreat
2. Go through each pair several times, then mix it up:
    a. Rise and expand, enclose, advance, or retreat
    b. Enclose and rise, shrink, advance, or retreat
    c. Advance and rise, shrink, expand, or enclose
3. Speak improvisationally or with some prepared text as you move. Note how the movement changes your tempo, intent, and feelings.

Changes in shape found their way into our speech long ago. When Shakespeare described Cassius as having a "lean and hungry look," Elizabethan playgoers knew what he meant. Laban might describe Cassius as narrowing and lengthening, rising and enclosing. Someone who is described as a "shrinking violet" might be also described as hollowing and shortening, shrinking and enclosing. Either way is descriptive, but LMS gives you a specific thing to do. A metaphor may stimulate your imagination and thereby create the physical presence you are seeking. Or you can change your body using LMS descriptors and see how it affects your imagination and feelings.

The *effort* component is a major aspect of LMS. Effort describes our inner attitude toward four elements of movement—Weight, Time, Space, and Flow. Each effort exists on a continuum characterized by two extremes.

Flow is our attitude "toward goingness, the quality of continuity of movement" (Bartenieff 53). The range of Flow goes from free—kinetic, continuous movement—to bound—potential, restrained movement.

Don't/Go with the Flow (F, T, E)

1. *Weave* about the room (see *The Weave* exercise in Chapter Three). As you walk, never stop moving. Every change should flow into the next. Nothing abrupt should occur. If you encounter an obstacle, spin away. You may feel as if you are under water or in outer space. You might imagine you are lightly floating or swimming. You are going nowhere in particular.
2. Decide to go in certain directions. Choose to go to your right, left, forward or back. Take a quick second to stop, and then choose a direction. Let your decision take two seconds, then five, then ten.
3. Stop completely and consider which direction to go, but never decide. Keep changing your mind—Right? Left? Forward? Back?

Another effective way to practice Flow is through the children's game "Red light, Green light." Red light is bound flow, full of potential to move. Green light is free flow, fully realized movement.

Free flow is fully realized energy. You are doing everything you can. Bound flow is full of potential energy. You might do anything, but you are not doing anything yet. Free is not sloppy or without intent—there simply is no impediment to movement. Bound is not tense or tight—there is simply the unrealized potential to move.

Space effort refers to how one approaches space—either directly, such as pinpointing, or indirectly, such as addressing a large group or taking in a tremendous view.

Searching/Finding (F, T, E)

1. Begin to *Weave*. As you move, take in the whole group. Keep your focus wide and open as if you are searching a crowd for someone you know.
2. Continue to weave. As you move, find a point or object and move toward it. Once you arrive, change direction and find another object or point toward which to move. It is as if you think you've found the person you are searching for, but once near, discover it is not them at all.

Another imaginary entry into the Space effort is visualizing different environments. For example, you might imagine you are at the Grand Canyon or standing before a mountain range. Indirect Space effort is usually how people take in these vistas. Then imagine you are looking for a coin or contact lens on the ground. Direct Space effort describes how people usually perform this kind of task.

Weight effort refers to our "attitude toward the use of body weight." (Bartenieff 55). Weight falls between strong, such as picking up a heavy object, or light, such as holding a newborn baby.

Two games that may help you find the feel of light and strong weight respectively are the egg in a teaspoon relay race and tug-o-war. In the former, you must employ light Weight effort in order to carry the egg (and also *direct* Space effort and *quick* Time effort). In Tug-o-war, you use strong Weight effort as you use the whole weight of your body (and strength of muscle) to move the rope in your direction (but the Space effort in this case is usually *indirect,* and the Time effort is *sustained*).

Time effort refers to our attitude in time. At one extreme we take our time, there are few changes and they occur regularly or in a sustained manner. At the other extreme we are quick, with many changes occurring rapidly. "Time as an effort is not to be confused with time as duration. Duration is the amount of time that a movement might take. Time as an Effort describes the attitude toward how one approaches whatever the duration of time is" (Bartenieff 56).

Early/Late (F, T)

1. Weave. Walk as if you are early for a date, or have all the time in the world to get where you are going (notice your Weight and Space efforts as well).
2. Walk as if you are late for a date or important appointment. You have no time to spare! (Note your Weight and Space efforts.)

In *As You Like It,* Rosalind has a speech about how time feels to different people under different circumstances. Time "trots" for a maiden between her vows and her wedding night, "ambles" with a priest who lacks Latin ("he sleeps easily because he cannot study"), and "gallops" for a thief "for though he go as softly as foot can fall, he thinks himself too soon there" (III, ii 300–314). This is an apt expression of the Time effort.

The chart details the action for each level of movement involved in practicing the Laban Dimensional Scale. To reinforce the vocabulary, you can speak the word as you perform the action:

- Lengthen, up, rise, light (as if grasping a china teacup).
- Shorten, down, sink, strong (as if putting down a bowling ball).
- Widen, out, expand, indirect (as if taking in a magnificent view).
- Narrow, across, enclose, direct (as if pointing at a spot on a wall).
- Bulge, forward, advance, sustain (as if about to swat a fly).
- Hollow, back, retreat, quick (as touching a hot plate).

Dimension	*Body*	*Direction*	*Shape*	*Effort*
Vertical	Lengthening	Up	Rising	Light
Vertical	Shortening	Down	Sinking	Strong
Horizontal	Widening	Out	Expanding	Indirect
Horizontal	Narrowing	Across	Enclosing	Direct
Sagittal	Bulging	Forward	Advancing	Sustained
Sagittal	Hollowing	Backward	Retreating	Quick

Since LMS is a description of how we move, the components of the scale are really nothing new. You already do them all. What LMS does is provide a vocabulary, a name, for what you do physically, and thereby gives you the ability to change how you do what you do. The beauty of the scale (and other scales devised by Laban) is that it provides an explicit exercise that develops mobility and flexibility, and takes you out of habitual behaviors, thus providing a larger vocabulary of movement upon which to draw in creating a performance.

Two more exercises that are more directly theatrical are included to put your movement vocabulary to use.

Freeze Tag Improvisation (G, F, T, E)

1. Form a circle; two players enter and face each other in Actor Ready.
2. **Player 1** chooses a relationship to **Player 2,** and an action. For example, **2** is **1**'s fiancée, and **1** will propose.
3. Using only the word "red" or "blue," **1** begins the improv, **2** blending along. (Following the example, **1** might say, "Red, red red red-red red?" Meaning, "Darling will you marry me?")

4. At the point of highest energy (when the conflict is at a peak), or when it seems as if there is no further development likely, you should shout, "Freeze!" Step in and replace either **1** or **2,** assuming **exactly** the body position of the individual you are replacing.
5. Allow the body position and the spatial relationship between you and your partner to suggest a new relationship and new action, and the entire improv begins again.

Ki *Points*

- Note what is happening on a body, shape, space, and effort level and recreate the body you are replacing.
- Trust the body and the spatial relationship between you and your partner to suggest a new relationship.
- Call freeze at the moment of greatest potential energy. As you watch the improvisation, focus on when the relationship has clarified—when both players know who they are and what they are doing the energy of playing will necessarily soon decrease. Call "freeze" as soon as you sense the energy begin to dissipate.
- Take the body with the greatest potential energy. A body that is arcing or spoking, twisted, bent or otherwise out of Actor Ready is the body to take on. The bound Flow of the frozen and specific body will give you all the energy you need to proceed. Trust it!

***Three Feelings Dance* (T).**   This is a high-stakes exercise, involving physical and emotional risk. It is important to commit fully to the exercise and to fully support the work of your fellow actors. Discussion in class or reflection in a journal is recommended to help process what occurs.

Choose three current feelings, for example, hungry, tired, and happy.

1. For each feeling, create a movement or series of movements that is an expression of that feeling. The movements ought to be more abstract than literal.
2. After creating three movements (and/or series of movements), find a way to make a physical transition from one feeling to the next.
3. Rehearse the movements for about 10 minutes until the dance is known and fully embodied.
4. Perform the dance as a solo for the class.
5. After everyone (or almost everyone) has performed, talk about what you observed. Stick to nonjudgmental statements, such as, "The movement had a strong weight effort to it," or "The transition from one movement to the next was not always clear to me."

Movement studies are imperative for any actor with a desire for greater command in performance. However, for the individual interested in simply being a more effective actor, greater awareness of the body and what it can do is a good starting point. Whatever exercises are included in a course or which you discover on your own, the primary questions remain: What do you want to do? Can you do it? What will it take so you can?

Your Body, Your Self

How fit are you and for what?

1. Explain your gestures/posture—where they may come from physiologically, socially, culturally.
2. What aspect or part of your body and/or physical ability are you most/least proud? What does that hide? What does it reveal?
3. Describe your movement in terms of your attitude toward Time, Weight, Space, and Flow.
4. Describe someone else's movement in those same terms.

NOTES

1. There are a number of works on this subject. The works of Stephen Jay Gould are a recommended start for those interested in the evolutionary development (and place) of human beings.

5 Voice: The Actor's Second Tool

"Speak properly, and in as few words as you can, but always plainly; for the end of speech is not ostentation, but to be understood."

—William Penn

"Human speech is a cracked tin drum on which we pound out tunes to make bears dance when we long to reach the stars."

—From *Madame Bovary,* by Gustave Flaubert

In this chapter we will:

- Describe the human voice and the "active" voice
- Propose an effective warm-up format
- Examine the major elements of the voice—breathing, sounding, vibrating, and articulating

A baby can scream and cry for hours and never lose its voice. Speaking normally, the average healthy person almost never runs out of breath in the middle of a sentence. Yet, these are fairly common occurrences for the beginning actor. Losing your voice before opening night or running out of breath in the middle of a big speech are *symptoms* of a voice ill-used.

The major factors in ineffective use of the voice are *habits and inhibitions* that impede the vocal process.

But if you can relearn to use your voice (and you can) and allow the natural process of vocalization to occur (and you may), then your voice won't be a cracked tin drum, but a magnificent expression of human feeling and action.

Origin of Human Speech

As much as we know about who we are and how we function, there is still much to learn. The origin of human speech, like art or the evolution of human beings, is not fully known. However, there are some things we do know and things we may infer that you may find useful in your study of acting and the work you will do on your voice.

Unlike legs, which were meant for mobility, the larynx was probably not originally meant for speaking. Current research indicates that the pieces of cartilage that form what we call the vocal folds were originally designed to protect the air passage (trachea) while eating.[1] They also assist in respiration and in the elimination of waste. (A block of air pressure is created upon intake of breath and the closing of the larynx, which pushes waste down through the bowels.) An organ that began its existence protecting animals from choking on food evolved into an instrument of communication, due to the shift from *quad*ruped to *bi*ped (see Figure 5.1 on page 63).

> The shift in performance comes from using the structures of the feeding apparatus, which is an input organ, for use in speech, which *transforms* it into an output organ . . . In man, the hands were freed from locomotion so that only one pair of limbs serves this function. The forelimbs changed as they became wholly used for the new function of food getting, food preparing, and feeding. In so doing the forelimbs freed the oral structures for speech . . . (DuBrul 85, 89) [note: author's italics]

All creatures are adaptive, and human beings are perhaps the greatest adaptors. We make use of our endowments to maintain systemic balance. Thus, early humans discovered their ability to make sound, nurtured and cultivated that ability and, linking it to our capacity for symbol making, speech arose. *You learned to use sound to get what you want*—from your first cry calling for mother as a baby to the sophisticated negotiating you do now as an adult.

Developing Your Voice

You may have learned to use your voice, but you probably do not use it optimally. Thus, we have vocal production and speech classes, singing and elocution lessons. Since before Demosthenes[2] ran up and down the Grecian hillsides, mouth stuffed with pebbles to render his speaking more articulate, actors have worked on their voices. The human voice can be a most sensitive, expressive, and beautiful mode of communication. Or it can be like a bad cell phone connection. Fortunately, because speaking is learned, the voice can be trained.

Work on the speaking voice is imperative, but is in some ways the most challenging. When discussing the voice, there is a tendency to ascribe qualities to an effective voice rather than to factors that may be tested. When we say an actor has a sensitive voice or a truthful one, we may feel this to be accurate, but it does not provide you with the means to achieve these qualities. An effective voice is in the ear of the listener. Whereas in singing most of us can tell when a note is in tune, it is less certain when a speaking voice is in tune. There are, however, some descriptors that are useful: range, power, resonance, and articulation—these things are measurable to a degree.

Range	variation in pitch from lowest to highest, usually designated by singing range: bass, baritone, tenor, alto, mezzo soprano, lyric soprano
Power	volume and stamina, usually measurable in decibels and endurance over time
Resonance	access to overtones, usually described in terms of "richness"
Articulation	clarity of speech, usually described as distinctiveness of vowels and consonants

The development of your voice and the specific goals you have for your voice will probably mean that some changes occur and some choices will be made. It is your responsibility to decide for yourself about changing your voice and speech, with your teacher/coach as a resource of knowledge to facilitate the choice-making process. All choices have consequences. It is your job to make the choice, and the teacher/coach's job to ensure that it is an informed choice (see Text Box—**Finding Your Voice**).

The issue is not only how we speak, but also how we hear. Ears not tuned to the rhythms and inflections of a particular accent or dialect will not hear the words as well as someone whose ears *are* tuned. Communication is a two-way street. You must do your best to be understood. As listeners we have a responsibility, too—to tune our ears to hear a world of voices. Decide for yourself (in consultation with your teacher/coach) what you want to do, whether you can do it and, if not, what you need to do to achieve your goals.

Finding Your Voice

A student from Haiti wished very much to work on Shakespeare and requested to take my advanced acting class in performing Shakespeare. He was a good actor with a wonderful presence and ambitions to be a professional in the United States. However, his accent made it quite difficult to understand his English. Together, he and I worked on the text, sometimes word by word, for pronunciation. We made no attempt to eradicate his accent, but rather tried to work with it. He was just beginning to take on this task, so he spoke only some of the text in a way that most people could understand him. However, given his ambition to work professionally in this country, he understood that learning to speak English clearly would help a great deal in realizing his ambition.

The Active Voice

No matter the speech issues of a particular actor, one thing is certain—the voice connected to the action, to the task at hand, compels attention. A voice that is true or good, full or energetic—as desirable as these attributes are—are *judgments* about a voice, not a *description* of it. A more useful term is *active*. An active voice is directed at accomplishing a task. The central challenge for the actor is always clarity of task. If the task is clear, the voice will do its best to serve the task. Difficulties arise when the best the voice can do is garbled, strained, and/or muted.

The primary goal of vocal work is optimizing the production and the articulation of sound. To prime the voice to respond organically and fully to impulses, the actor must have a flexible and strong instrument. Achieving flexibility and strength requires exercising the voice in a programmatic way. Initially, you must free the production of sound. Then you must optimize that production. Finally, you must address specific demands made upon the voice by different material. You and your teacher/coach should be clear about the purpose of each and every exercise, and then you must practice it regularly. Like every acting tool, you must attend to and nurture the development of the voice. It doesn't happen by magic, but when the voice is working effectively, magic can happen.

There is a tendency for beginning students to be a bit shy with the voice, which is understandable. The voice is a delicate and quite sensitive tool and, although we may talk a lot, we rarely tap into our full vocal capacity. Vocal exercises usually employ indirect means to achieve results. The risk element of the exercises may seem high to some. Therefore, it is important to take your time, be patient, have fun and most of all, suspend judgment as you work on the voice.

There are many approaches to vocal training and over the course of your life you may explore several (see Text Box—**Vocal Technique**). Serious students should commit themselves to one or more approach and study arduously. That said, here are areas of the voice to work on and exercises for those areas.

The Vocal Warm-up **(F, T).**   A good warm-up should include work on the following areas:

1. Breathing—inspiring and expiring (power)
    Exercises should include developing breath capacity and control, but must begin with finding your natural breath (and eradicating obstacles that impede it).
2. Sounding—releasing and opening (range and resonance)
    Exercises should encourage the full engagement of the vocal cords and develop the vocal range.
    Muscles inside the throat bring the chords together as air passes between them. The chords vibrate, setting up sympathetic vibrations in the skeleton and in the sinus cavities, thus amplifying the sound, which travels up through the throat over the tongue and teeth, past the lips and out of the mouth.

Vocal Technique

The following is a list of some of the major practitioners and leaders in the field of vocal production and speech. A good place to start your search is at the website of the Voice and Speech Teachers Association, www.vasta.org.

- Kristin Linklater—*Freeing the Natural Voice,* http://ci.columbia.edu/ci/subjects/ arts/facinter.html (an interesting interactive site where Ms. Linklater talks about voice and acting)
- Cecily Berry—*The Actor and the Text*
- Patsy Rodenberg—*The Right to Speak*
- Catherine Fitzmaurice—www.fitzmauricevoice.com
- Arthur Lessac—www.lessacinstitute.com

Two useful sites on the vocal mechanism:

- The Greater Baltimore Medical Center, Milton J. Dance Head and Neck Rehabilitation Center site, www.gbmc.org/voice, is a good primer on the vocal mechanism as well as providing useful information about the care and repair of the voice.
- The University of Pittsburgh Voice Center also has some excellent references on the mechanics and care of the voice: www.upmc.edu/upmcvoice

---

3. Articulating—channeling and focusing

The muscles responsible for forming vowels and consonants require exercises in strengthening, conditioning, and flexibility in order to deliver speech with maximum effectiveness and minimal effort.

Although the phonation process is actually quite complicated, Kristin Linklater has simplified it into six steps (Linklater, 6):

1. Impulse—the need to communicate.
2. Breath—inspiration, the intake of energy necessary and sufficient to effectively communicate.
3. Oscillations—air passes over the vocal cords, which oscillate, creating a tone.
4. Vibrations—the oscillations create sympathetic vibrations in the body, primarily in the facial cavities, but also in most major bones throughout the body.
5. Amplification—via resonating chambers of the pharynx, nasal cavity, and sinuses.
6. Articulation—by the cheeks, teeth, tongue and lips.

Working on your voice facilitates and optimizes this process. Along the way, of course, there may be obstructions, usually of either a physical or psychological

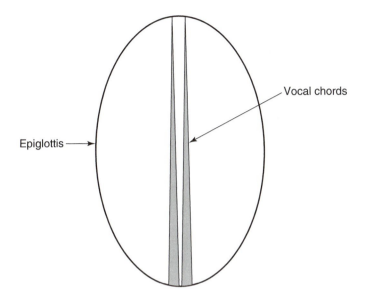

FIGURE 5.1   The Vocal Cords.

nature. Particularly when performing (acts designed for perception), you may encounter difficulties. Speech itself is a performative act; that is, it is meant for perception. Speaking and vocalizing in a play make additional demands on the voice in order to be heard and understood by a group of people in a theater. We will examine how to facilitate and optimize the phonation process in breath, sound, and articulation.

Breathing

Hold It (F, T)

1. Inhale deeply, filling your lungs from bottom to top, as full as you are able.
2. As you reach your air capacity, choose to hold your breath. Draw your awareness to your throat and feel the larynx close off the trachea.
3. Release your breath in a puff of air.
4. Inhale deeply again. Hold your breath, maintaining your awareness of the functioning larynx. *Shift* the air down from the upper to the lower lungs, as if you were about to push your bowels. Your stomach may push out as your diaphragm moves it out of the way.
5. Release your breath on an unvoiced "hah" as if you are about to deliver a long speech.
6. Inhale as before. Shift the air to lower lungs. Maintain your awareness.

7. Release your breath in a fully voiced "ah." Let the sound glide out. Maintain your awareness of what is happening in your throat.

   You ought to have felt the vocal folds come together in your throat. Most of us tend to prepare to hold our breath by filling the upper lungs. This is natural, as the upper lungs oxygenate the blood more quickly and in greater capacity. Whenever we prepare to hold our breath (to swim or to exert physical energy), the body automatically channels the air into the upper lungs so that as much oxygen may be supplied to the blood as possible, to keep the muscles working effectively. When speaking, however, you need greater control of your breath. The muscles around the lower lungs are better able to control the release of air than the upper lungs. Also, by placing the air in the lower lungs, there is less air pressure on the upper respiratory tract, including the vocal mechanism. Did you notice any difference in your throat as you exhaled with a puff, an unvoiced "hah" and the voiced "ah"?

8. Fill your upper lungs again as if you were to take a dive underwater, then change, as if you were about to make a long speech. What differences do you notice?[3]

9. Release the breath on a voiced "ah."

10. Inhale again, this time as if you were about the make a long speech, shifting the air to the lower lungs. The diaphragm may move your stomach out of the way. Note the feeling in your throat, your jaw, and tongue.

11. Release on a voiced "ah." Note your sensations.

Inspired Breath[4] **(F, T).**   The need to speak generates a breath exactly enough to fill the impulse. In everyday speaking we rarely run out of breath, but that sometimes happens with prepared text, such as from a play or speech. Breath is *inspiration*. What inspires you? What makes you take in and expel breath?

1. Inspire yourself by imagining an event or occurrence.
   a. a pinprick
   b. an ice cube down the back
   c. an insult
   d. a kiss (one you want, one you don't want, a peck, a smooch, a deep passionate three-day variety)
   e. caught doing something wrong (a little wrong, a lot wrong)
   f. about to propose
   g. about to break up
   h. about to jump out of an airplane
2. Let your partner inspire a breath through behaviors
   i. Hand raised to strike
   j. Arms raised to hug
   k. Fingers up to tickle
   l. Playing the fundamental actions (see Chapter Eight)

Note the nature of the breath and the impulse to sound. Which imaginative stimuli were effective? Follow the breath with a sound, then a word, and a phrase. See how much speech the breath can sustain. How does your energy seem to focus (push-pull-hold-release) in different imaginary circumstances?

Sounding

The sound of a human voice can be thrilling or horrible, beautiful or grating, clear or choked off. Your task, in developing your sounding capacity, is to stretch, strengthen and free your vocal mechanism so it may respond organically to an impulse. Your voice should sensitively reflect even the subtlest change in action. Yet, it must also be clearly heard and understood. Like a well-trained dancer makes seemingly impossible leaps appear effortless, the finest speakers and singers make complicated speeches and demanding arias flow with ease and grace. Naturally, this takes *years* of training. However, there is much you can do, right now, to develop your sensitive, flexible, strong and active voice.

Loose Lips, Dropped Jaws, and Tripping Tongues (**F, T**).   Before work on sounding may begin, you must loosen and stretch the pathway of sound.

1. After a thorough physical warm up and some breathing exercises, return to Actor Ready.
2. Massage your face, giving special attention to the jaw and the hinge by which it is attached to the skull. This hinge is a bundle of tendons, nerves, and tiny muscles and is often full of tension. Give some gentle attention to your lips, too.
3. Drop your jaw as you continue to massage. The jaw is hinged so that it drops down *and* back, not just straight down.
4. Clasp your hands together and quickly shake them back and forth, allowing the shake to move your jaw. The movement of your hands and arms should be quite quick and short. This will loosen the jaw, but keep your teeth from knocking together. If you do feel your teeth knock together, shorten the stroke and quicken the pace.
5. *Gently* shake your head left and right, allowing your jaw to sway.
6. Blow air through your lips so they flap. Shake your head gently, but firmly enough to feel your lips move back and forth across your face.
7. Open your mouth wide as if about to take a bite of a big apple. Bring your lips together as if you are about to give someone a little kiss. Repeat several times.
8. Stick your tongue out as far as it can go (be sure to allow the jaw to drop down and back). Wiggle it between your lips as fast as you can. Stick your tongue between your lips and blow air through your lips and tongue.
9. Massage your face once again. Note any differences. Return to Actor Ready.

Sighs of . . . (G, F, T)

1. Begin with a yawn. Stretch, open your mouth, and allow a yawn to come out. Indulge in the sound and let the sound release any tension you may feel throughout your body (including the throat).

2. Imagine something to stimulate a sigh of relief, such as falling into bed after a long day, or plunging into cool water on a hot day. Allow your imagination to stimulate the impulse to breathe, allow the breath to fill the lungs and release over the vocal folds, through the resonating chamber (pharynx, nasal cavity and sinuses) and finally out through the articulators (cheeks, tongue, teeth and lips). It may come out as an "ah."

3. Imagine something to stimulate a sigh of resignation, such as watching your team lose a game, seeing that your lottery numbers did *not* win (again), or picking up the phone, hoping to hear from that special someone, but it turns out to be a sales call. This may come out as an "aw" or an "oh."

4. Imagine something to stimulate a hum of pleasure, such as tasting a delicious piece of chocolate or smelling a fragrant rose. This may come out as an "ummm."

Ki *Points.*   This is just a brief sample, but incorporated into a warm-up over time, you can explore a great variety of imaginative stimuli that provoke many sounds. Your imagination is the method by which you generate energy that results in sound.

Vocal Range

Sound, of course, is vibrations in the air. These vibrations are measured in number of vibrations, or cycles per second, and correspond to a pitch on the musical scale. An orchestra is usually tuned to the note A above middle C on the piano, or A 440, (440 are the number of vibrations per second that correspond to A above middle C). Less energy is required for lower pitches because there are fewer (and longer) vibrations. Greater energy is required for higher pitches because there are more (and shorter) vibrations. This is all fairly common knowledge, but nevertheless is useful to understand. For optimal phonation (the making of sound) lower notes (fewer vibrations, less energy) require a smaller opening, higher notes (more vibrations, greater energy) require a larger opening. Your mouth opens to let out sound—the louder and higher the sound, the more open your mouth will be. This occurs organically—that is, you will usually do this without thinking about it.

Try this experiment.

1. Imagine you are about to yell to a friend you see 100 yards away. Take a breath, but don't shout. Notice the opening you created preparing to shout. Probably it was large. That is because it takes a good deal of energy to make yourself heard over 100 yards.

2. Whether or not you consider yourself a singer, imagine you are about to sing the "Star Spangled Banner" and you are approaching the highest note in the song ("the land of the *free*"). Take a breath. Don't sing. What kind of opening did you generate to sing that note? Probably it was pretty large. It takes a good deal of energy to sing that note. (If you have any doubts, the next time you watch a sporting event, watch the singer's mouth as she gets to that famous note.)

The human voice typically has a range of about two octaves or so on the standard musical scale. Each person's range falls within certain parameters, commonly identified in singer's terminology as bass (low), tenor (medium low), alto (medium high) and soprano (high). There are a number of ways to classify a person's voice. What is important is that you have a feel for your range and may begin to expand it. Most of us use only a small portion of the vocal range available to us. No matter the reason, however, the actor is wise to have the greatest range of options available, as any visual artist would wish to have the greatest number of paints available.

Sliding Scales (**F, T**).   Every approach to vocal work, whether speaking or singing, employs some exercise that moves up and down the vocal range. This one is a hybrid of the bel canto approach[5] to singing and standard vocal production work for the actor.

1. Begin in Actor Ready. Using the vowel "ah," start a low pitch sound. "Ah" is one of the most, if not the most, open sound you can make. (Other vowels engage the tongue or jaw a bit more. We'll play with vowels later.) If you feel tension in your throat, or you hear a garbled sound, you may be starting too low. Allow the sound to slide up the slightest bit on the scale (the smallest number of vibrations per second). Take a breath. Start at the same pitch, and then slide up again. Take a breath. Continue making your way up through your range. Allow the jaw to drop down and back as you ascend in pitch. If you feel any tension in the jaw, lips, or tongue, stop and shake or massage it out. When you reach the top note you can go without straining (although you may be quite loud), slide down the scale in the same manner—pitch, slide, breathe, same pitch, slide, etc. The first time you do this, it may take quite a long time for you to accomplish. Take all the time you need and then some.

2. Slide through your scale again, but this time do it twice as fast. Breathe when you require breath and not in between each pitch. Allow the jaw to drop down and back as you ascend your scale. Stop and shake/massage out any tension you encounter.

3. Slide through the scale again, but twice as fast as previously. Note any differences in what is happening in your voice, in the vocal mechanism, in your body.

4. Slide through the scale at the same speed, but choose a different vowel sound. Note differences in your sound and vocal mechanism. Draw your awareness to what is happening in your jaw, tongue, lips as well as the sensations in your throat.

Variations

- Add consonants before the vowel, such as la, la, or ma, ma, or ba, ba. If this is part of your daily warm up, you might experiment with all vowels and consonants. Note which sounds are easier or more difficult.
- Work with a partner, sliding through your scale simultaneously and one after the other. Be sure to work with someone who has a different vocal range than you as well as with someone who shares your vocal range.
- Work in groups of three or four, simultaneously and one after the other.

Ki *Points*

- Play. There is really no substitute for an entire course (or better, years) focusing on the voice, but at the beginning it is important to play around and find the fun.
- Take it easy. Let the sound flow out.
- Explore. Discover your voice as if it is a new thing. Investigate each sound and how it affects your body, imagination, and feelings.

The next exercise takes it a step further, from simple vocal releases to more complicated sounds, but still prior to speech.

***Primal Sounds* (G, F, T).**   This is similar in structure to the *Three Feelings Dance* exercise.

1. Choose three current feelings, for example, hungry, tired, and happy.
2. For each feeling, discover a sound (using vowels and consonants) that is an expression of that feeling. The sound ought to be more abstract than literal.
3. After creating three sounds (and/or series of sounds), find a way to make a vocal transition from one feeling to the next.
4. Rehearse the sounds for about 10 minutes until the "song" is known and fully voiced.
5. Perform it as a solo for the class.
6. After everyone (or almost everyone) has performed, talk about what you observed. Stick to nonjudgmental statements, such as, "The sound was fully released," or "You used a wide range of pitches."
7. Begin again, but this time, use the actual word for the feeling you're vocalizing but maintain the journey of sound you created initially. So, "hungry" might initially have started as a low grumble, transformed into a chattering sound, and finished with a release on an open vowel in the upper register of the voice.

Follow the same journey using the word "hungry," something like:

                    REEEEE!
          gra-gra-gra
      n-n-n-n
huuuu

A Scene at the Opera (**F, T, E**)

1. Working in pairs, actors set up a basic improvisation—Who, What, and Where.
2. *Sing* the scene, as if it is an opera.

The main objective is to explore vocal range, not to sound good. For those who feel they cannot sing, approach speaking by elongating everything you say. Again, you must "dare to fail gloriously" in this exercise. If you do, you will find it a truly wonderful and often hilarious experience.

Articulating

Speaking clearly is essential for understanding. The lips, tongue, and jaw shape the sounds into consonants and vowels—if these are clean and clear, the words will be clear. That is at least half way to understanding.

Vowels.   First we cry, and then we coo.[6] The first sounds we make as human beings are vowels. Vowels are our most primitive utterances and therefore appear to be more directly connected to our feelings. It is important to remember that words and speech are a later development. First are feelings and sensations; language comes later.

> All our sounds, no matter how fluent and complicated our words, begin in how we feel.

In exploring your sounds, keep in mind that although the origin of speech is unknown, the making of sound is a very primitive act, deeply connected to our most basic and unrefined self. What you are working toward releasing, then, is that unique and pure sound of *you.*

It is a well-established fact in the study of linguistics that a normally functioning infant of any race or culture can make *all* the sounds necessary for *any* language. Over time, as a particular language is acquired, that ability is limited. As the ability to speak matures, sounds begin to accumulate bits of meaning. So, for example, "o" is no longer a meaningless sound, it becomes associated with the word, "oh." All sounds accumulate bits of meanings within a language, a culture, and in each individual. "Oh" may be associated with surprise, for example, or warning, or trouble. "Ah" may be associated with understanding or relief. There is no rule to this, except that you already associate sounds with meaning. As you explore sound, note how you are predisposed toward a meaning or feeling when you make a certain sound. A sound has imprinted itself on your body, your imagination, and your feelings. If you are aware of the imprint a sound has made on you, then you may change your habitual response to the sound. You may find this useful in making speaking choices when you act.

Vowel Play (**F, T**).   *a, e, i, o, u,* and sometimes *y.* These are the letter representing vowels in English, but the actual sounds to say "I," for example, includes at least two vowel sounds for most people: "ah" and "ee." Vowels are rarely pure. They usually come in packages of two or three—diphthongs and triphthongs.

1. Say each vowel as slowly as possible and note what is happening inside your mouth. How do the jaw, the tongue and the lips change the shape inside your mouth?
2. Say "ah." Say "ee." You should be able to make both sounds by only moving your tongue. Place your fingers lightly on your jaw and say "ah" and "ee." The tongue should move forward, the tip behind the bottom teeth, arching up to meet the upper teeth on either side of your mouth.
3. Cycle through the vowels, beginning with "ah" and changing to "oh," "oo," etc. Then, begin with "ee" to "oh," "ee" to "oo," etc. until you have cycled through all the combinations.
4. Repeat, but create packages of three vowel sounds, such as "ah—ay—ee." Cycle through the vowels, altering the first vowel, then the second, etc. Simply note what is occurring inside your mouth as the jaw, the tongue and lips shape the sound.

This exercise is introductory, of course. At the beginning of your study of acting, just playing around and becoming aware of what happens during sound-making is sufficient.

Consonants.   Like vowels, consonants began as primitive utterances. A baby's babble is playing with sounds, and consonants are good fun because of the funny way they roll around the mouth. As with vowels, as language is acquired, consonants begin to accumulate meaning and make an imprint on your body, imagination, and feelings. "L" may make you feel like skipping. "T" (unvoiced, just the release of air from the tongue behind the upper teeth) may feel aggressive. "F" (unvoiced, just the release of air from the lower lip contacting the upper front teeth) may feel exasperated. In your exploration of consonants, note how you are predisposed toward a meaning or feeling when you make a certain consonant sound. It has imprinted itself on your body, your imagination, and your feelings. If you are aware of the imprint a consonant has made on you, then you may change your habitual response to the consonant. You may find this useful in making speaking choices when you act.

Constant Consonants[7] (**F, T**)

1. Walk about. Beginning with "b" repeat the consonant over and over, playing around with the feel of the sound in your mouth. Let it change you. How does it make you feel? What impulses arise as you make the sound? How does it alter your body and alignment? Your walking tempo and rhythm?

Where does it take your imagination? Who might you be, or what kind of person?

2. Meet another person and exchange sounds. You may greet or confront or simply acknowledge the other person. It doesn't matter as long as you allow your impulses to affect your body, imagination, and feelings.

3. Go through all the other consonants in the same manner. Follow your physical and imaginative impulses. Note how the sound makes you feel.

Vowel/Consonant Gibberish (F, T, E)

1. Either alone or in pairs, choose two fundamental actions to play (see Chapter Eight).

2. Play the action, vocalizing on a single vowel or consonant.

3. Go through the entire series of vowels and consonants in this way, altering the verbs and experimenting with different combinations of verbs and sounds.

4. Note in your journal what (if any) feelings are evoked by the sounds, and the connections you make with sounds and action. For example, you might find that *push from* and an open "ah" sound are aligned in the nature of their energies. Or, *hold to* may align with "oh." More specific actions may align with more specific sounds, but try to stay with gibberish rather than finding actual words.[8]

This exercise can be introduced during exploration of the voice, but rather than exploring all the sounds at once (which can get tedious), different sounds may be incorporated into the daily warm-up (see end of Part Two) during the action exercise. Over time, the entire range of sounds should be explored.

More advanced articulation exercises might include any number of tongue twisters, passages from poems or plays, or memorized text. There are plenty of resources for these, and your teacher/coach will undoubtedly have favorites. But you may also attempt tongue twisters in other languages. There are sounds in Chinese, for example, that speakers of English do not make. If you or any of your fellow players speak a language other than English, share the tongue twisters or nursery rhymes of that language. Note how challenging it can be to even hear the unfamiliar sound, let alone pronounce it! Play around and see how it affects you—body, imagination, and feelings.

Your Vocal Heritage

What is revealed and hidden by your voice and how? Observe, analyze, and draw conclusions about your voice in the following categories:

1. Genetic/Physiological—for example, gender, physical capabilities (small/large mouth, deviated septum), vocal range (soprano/alto/tenor/bass or other descriptors of your vocal range).

2. Ethnicity—for example, "my voice reveals my heritage as a Caribbean-American in the way I pronounce certain words, such as . . . "; "But I sometimes try to hide my ethnicity when I . . . "

3. Regional dialect—for example, "As a Long Islander, everyone can hear the addition of the vowel 'u' to practically everything I say, such as 'b-oo-all,' for 'ball.'"

4. Socio-economic/Educational status—for example, "Growing up in an upper-middle class environment, my parents demanded correct usage of language at all times, to my great annoyance. However, to this day I cannot bring myself to say 'ain't' or 'anyways' or use 'jealous' when I mean 'envious.'"

5. Personality—for example, "My voice reveals my self-confidence in my habitual high volume talking, but I often hide my real feelings by using a small part of my vocal range."

N O T E S

1. See DuBrul, E. Lloyd. *The Evolution of the Speech Apparatus*. Charles C. Thomas. Springfield, MA. 1958. Also, Trask, R.L. *Language: The Basics*. Routledge. London 1995.

2. See Plutarch, *Lives of Noble Grecians and Romans*, translated by John Dryden, edited by Arthur Hugh Clough. Modern Library Series. Reprint 1992. Or at http://classics.mit.edu//Plutarch/demosthe.html

3. Your throat may feel tighter; the muscles around your jaw more tense, the tongue swallowed a bit. Or it may not. The important point is to draw your awareness to what is happening.

4. Hollis Huston inspired the exercise in his book, *The Actor's Instrument: Body Theory, Stage*. (University of Michigan Press, 1993).

5. Bel Canto means "beautiful singing" in Italian. This approach emphasizes a smooth and effortless vocal line and was taught to me by Jana Pivacek. The Bel Canto approach and vocal production work that emphasizes free and organic sounding seem to work well together.

6. "Naturalistic observations as well as acoustic studies indicate that there are two distinct types of vocalization and that each has its own developmental history. The first type includes all sounds related to crying . . . the second type of vocalization [are] sounds which eventually merge into the acoustic productions of speech. This second type of sound emerges only after about the sixth to eighth week. It begins with brief, little cooing sounds that fairly regularly follow the smiling response." Lenneberg, Eric H. *Biological Foundations of Language*. (New York: Wiley & Son, 1967), 276.

7. This exercise is derived from an exercise in Kristin Linklater's *Freeing Shakespeare's Voice*. New York: Theatre Communications Group, 1992.

8. In the *Four Actions* exercise (see Chapter Eight—**The Names of Action**) you are encouraged to find a word or phrase (a mnemonic) to connect speech with the action. The mnemonic is to act like a "hook" to facilitate aligning your energy. In this exercise, the objective is to explore sound and the action is more a means to that end.

6 Imagination: The Actor's Third Tool

"Imagination is the beginning of creation. You imagine what you desire, you will what you imagine and at last you create what you will."

—George Bernard Shaw

In this chapter we will:

- Examine the nature and function of the imagination
- Explore the imagination and its application to the acting process

What are you doing tomorrow? Review your schedule in your mind. When do you have to get up? What will you eat for breakfast? Where do you have to go? Will you meet friends? Do you have things to do? How do you feel about tomorrow? What about next week? Next year? Five years from now? Where will you be? What will you be doing? What if you're rich? What if you're poor? What if you win the Oscar? Can you imagine? Yes, of course you can. Just as you can imagine the love of your life, your dream job, dream home—you can imagine anything. Stanislavski called this process "the Magic If" (56). It seems like magic because effective use of your imagination will *transform* you physically, vocally, and emotionally.

The imagination is the center of creativity and the most powerful of the actor's tools.

There is a wealth of material on developing the imagination—games, improvisations, and exercises that your teacher/coach will no doubt have experience in and/or access to. We will not reiterate all that here. However, we will discuss the structure of the imagination, suggest an effective working attitude, and then offer a few exercises that will begin developing this most important actor's tool.

The Nature of Imagination

It is not an overstatement to say that the imagination is what makes us human. Our ability to think, communicate, and create all proceed from the imagination. Somewhere in our prehistory, this ability arose—perhaps out of dreams, the residue of psychic overload discharged during sleep, recalled the following day—to sense within the mind a vision, a sound, a smell, a touch, a feeling that is not related to the moment in which we find ourselves. Instead this vision, sound, smell, touch, or feeling is part of some past, or at least not part of the present. With the imagination we can take ourselves out of time and the world all together to imagine what *might be, not just what is.* As you can imagine, this turns out to be a key survival trait. Without the keen senses of other animals, humans needed to develop another method to deal with threats and take advantage of opportunities. Our ability to imagine threats and opportunities in the environment enabled us to be proactive and reasonable, rather than merely reactive and instinctual. Primitive humans could not easily smell a bear waiting inside a cave. But they could, upon seeing the dark cave and imagining what might be in it, determine a course of action. Modern humans are no different. We are presented each day with dark caves of one sort or another, and by imagining what might be we decide what to do.

Love or Death

1. Begin walking about the classroom. Imagine you are walking down a street and see someone who does not see you. S/he is the love of your life. What do you do?
2. Sit in a chair. Imagine you are at home when you hear a strange noise. It is the violent burglar who you've heard about on the news plaguing the area. What do you do?
3. With a partner, get as far apart as possible and begin walking toward one another. Imagine that you are old friends, you haven't seen each other in a long time, and you cannot remember whether you parted on very good or very bad terms. What do you do? Approach and say hello.

Discuss these imaginary events. Did you feel as if your actions were effective or did it feel phony or faked? Did your fellow players find it believable? What might you have done differently if this situation had been real? What is the difference between imagining threats or opportunities in real life and imagining threats or opportunities in play?

The Active Imagination

Like all human functions and perceptions, the artist employs that which is useful for the making of the art. Although originally a mental process necessary for survival, the imagination is employed by the artist to concoct what might be. In a way, each play presents a dark cave, really a whole world for the audience to imagine. The actor is a cipher for the audience—the means by which the invented world is experienced. If the audience is offered a dark cave, the acts you perform to accomplish a task are determined by the imaginary theatrical condition of a dark cave. As with all your acting tools, the imagination is engaged to generate, focus, transform, and exchange energy. But the specific function of your imagination in acting is to *maintain the direction of your actions.* Your imagination keeps you, and the audience, in the cave, in the world of the play.

Using the Imagination

Working with your imagination carries some risk—when freely playing, you never know what might come up. A young child delights in living in an imaginary world full of silliness, rude noises, and such. But once school begins that kind of behavior is not encouraged and we soon lose the aptitude for imaginary play we once had. By the time you reach adulthood, your imaginative impulses are *mostly* successfully repressed. While this is arguably good for the social order, it is anathema to your work as an actor. Much of the work in the acting studio is relearning how to use your imagination, to releasing the inhibitions, built up over time, that impede the free flow of your imaginative energy. The attitudes that best promote exploration of the imagination are *delight* and *discovery.* Like a young child, you must find pleasure and joy in discovery and delightedly throw yourself into the work. But as an artist, you must discriminate between trying to *make* things happen and *allowing* them to happen. As you work on your imagination, it is important to let things occur naturally and organically. It is delightful when your imagination stimulates a psychophysical response, but it is deadly to force or fake a response. Like "Morales" in *A Chorus Line,* if you feel nothing, do nothing. Your attitude ought to be "actor ready;" and when something does happen, the discovery will be delightful!

Instant Acting (G)

1. Imagine you are brushing your teeth. Just taste it. You needn't remember the taste or smell of your toothpaste. Call it forth from your imagination onto your tongue.
2. Take an imaginary glass filled with liquid in your hand and drink up.
3. It's orange juice.

Perhaps you went "yuck." Or, if that didn't do anything for you, cast your mind back to junior high when the best joke was, "Imagine you're sliding down a banister and it turns into a razor blade." Or imagine fingernails on a chalkboard, foil on the teeth, or Styrofoam rubbing together. Probably one of these images will arouse a psychophysical response—a sound, a movement, a feeling. And this response arises merely by exercising your imagination.

This is the basic procedure for using your imagination to maintain the direction of your actions. The challenge is to allow the full manifestation of your psychophysical responses and then to build a vocabulary of imaginary stimuli to assist you in maintaining the direction of your actions. Your imaginative vocabulary will be developed via two primary sources:

1. Sensations
   - energy generated by imagining different sights, smells, tastes, sounds, and textures
2. Inventions
   - energy generated and focused by imagining various conditions, situations, relationships

***Sensation Exploration* (G, F)*.**   In the first part of the exercise, you create a written report based on the sensory activity below. This becomes the basis for building a vocabulary of stimuli you may employ to maintain the direction of your action. It will also increase your awareness and heighten your sensitivity, which becomes quite important for the free flow of your energy when playing—as we shall further explore next chapter.

- Smell—Get a good whiff of your closet, roommates, bathroom, dorm/apt, notice all smells anew. What associations do you make with different smells? What smells are evocative for you? What feelings do they evoke?
- Hear—Try not to talk all during dinner or some period of time when you normally talk. Listen for as long as you can. What happens? How do others behave toward you? What sounds are evocative for you? What feelings do they evoke?
- Taste—Have a partner or roommate blindfold you and give you a taste test. Can you identify foods? How is it to be fed by someone? What tastes are evocative for you? What feelings do they evoke?
- Touch—Rediscover touch. Investigate how your skin senses. You sense touch with your whole body. Notice as if for first time and list as many textures as you can between now and dinner. What feelings does touch evoke?
- Sight—See things that aren't there. At a meal or any idle moment imagine the person you're talking to has an ugly wart or a bug crawling on them, or is bleeding. Try to see it and note your response (and theirs). Also, try to see without composing, that is, try to deconstruct an image into mere shapes, color, and light. Do it; it's weird. What sights are evocative for you? What feelings do they evoke?

***Walk-about* (F, E).**   You will need to recall and have ready a nursery rhyme (and eventually any text) to speak when called upon to do so.

---

*We will return to this exercise in the next chapter, so keep your report on hand.

1. The group walks about randomly, changing directions, tempo, etc. in a mobile "actor ready."
2. The teacher/coach calls out a Where and Time (both day and season), such as "the beach in winter-midnight."
3. One sense at a time, each actor smells, touches, sees, hears, and tastes something in the suggested environment. For example, you might say, "I smell chestnuts roasting," or "I see a snowman."
4. Speak the nursery rhyme, while maintaining the sensory stimulation.
   -or-
   allow a movement to arise out of the sensory stimulation.
5. After evoking the sense requested, walk about again under new imaginary circumstances (called by the teacher/coach or by various people in the class) until "freeze" is called and another sensory stimulation is suggested.

Variations

■ **Walkabout in Pairs.** Collaborate with a partner as you imagine new circumstances. See, hear, taste, smell, and touch things together. For example, you might say, "Look at the snowman!" and your partner might reply, "What a great carrot nose!" Focus on evoking a world together, so that you both are cold to the same degree (approximately, of course), both walking through the same depth of snow, both in the same place and time. This variation can also be done with threes, fours, or fives.

■ **Team Walkabout.** Split the group into two or three teams. Devise several sets of sensory stimulations and write down each set on a separate piece of paper. As in Charades, each team must play the set devised by the other team. Evaluate each other on the effectiveness of creating a world as a team. Is everyone focused on the task? Are they working together or individually?

The objective is to connect sensory stimulation to some kind of action. As has been discussed and will be further explored under the next actor's tool (Feelings), the imagination may provoke a psychophysical response. This exercise is designed specifically to nurture the connection between imagination and action. The connection is there naturally, but for many, years of negative conditioning and other cultural/social barriers have stifled the connection, corroding it so that the impulse does not pass into the body to find its clear manifestation in action.

The Walkabout may also be usefully employed in make-believe, or invented, conditions and situations. Some examples include (but are limited only by your imagination)

■ Walking through **conditions** such as molasses, ice, in outer space, on a cloud, or through environments such as the forest, beach, city, mountains
■ Walking in **situations** such as being late for an appointment, being followed, or having to urinate

Like You/Loathe You (**F, E**).   This is a variation of a Keith Johnstone improvisation.

1. Three actors choose one of the other actors they really like and one of the other actors they loathe.
2. Improvise a scene in which a simple decision must be made—where to eat, what movie to see, what clothes to wear, etc.
3. Move toward the person you like and away from the person you loathe.

The relationships will probably be immediately clear to everyone—actors and audience. You are encouraged to make a big choice to really, really like one person and really, really loathe the other. Remember, this is not about being nice; it is an exercise to develop your ability to imagine and play with relationships.

Variations

1. Instructor calls out "switch" and you immediately change who you like and loathe
2. Two or more actors with two or more objects—each of you choose which object you like and which you loathe. Get the object you like and get rid of the object you loathe. This game can be "switched," too.

As If . . .

The *as if* is an imaginary operation, but also operates in daily life. To pretend that something has a value other than it actually has for you is to *endow* that thing. In daily life, we continually endow things, people, feelings, everything with some value. Value is simply energy. The more energy you engage in with something, the greater the value. This is the beginning of a relationship—"X means Y to me,"or "She means the world to me!" How the relationship is fully realized is in the *return* of some value to you: X means Y to me, and I mean Z to X. "She means the world to me!" you might say. But she might say, "You mean nothing to me." This is the game of *Like You/Loathe You.* This improvisation usually only lasts for a short while because it is static in nature, that is, the value does not change. In a play, the central relationship is usually not static. In fact, the dynamic of the central relationship in a play *is* the play. We will return to this in Chapter Nine.

Who, What, and Where (**F, T, E**).   Generate three lists: people, places, and activities. For example, your people list might include professions and relationships such as doctor, the president, a construction worker, sister, husband, and son. But it can also include types, such as obsessive-compulsive or lothario (a sexual predator). Places might include the Laundromat, a bar, a castle, a lake, and a ship at sea, as well as places under certain conditions of time, weather, etc. Activities might include shopping, an operation, a hold-up, a job interview, and giving birth (a perennial favorite). Generate a list of 10–20 of each.

1. *Where* Improvisations

   Group Where: Someone will choose a *Where,* enter the playing space, and **silently** begin an activity that can only occur in that *Where.* As soon as you understand the *Where,* join in with the activity or begin another activity specific to that *Where.* Continue until everyone is playing. Once everyone is in, your teacher/coach can signal for you to speak. After a minute or two, stop the game and discuss where you were, what you were doing there, and who you were. Were your activities consistent with the *Where?* Did you establish relationships with those around you? What was the source of your dialogue—the place, what you were doing, or the relationship you created with others?

   Solo Environments: Alone or individually with the whole class, begin a simple imaginary activity such as brushing your teeth or getting dressed. Your teacher/coach will call out different places, times, and conditions. Focus on the situation and allow your activity to be altered. For example, you might brush your teeth in a museum, in the Arctic, first thing in the morning, or in a rainstorm. Let your imagination guide your energy through the activity.

   As a solo activity this game can effectively develop your ability to change quickly. It can also be played competitively, with two players at a time, the winner being the one who reacts most quickly and effectively to the changing situation. (Some reactions may not exactly be appropriate, but they might be effective. Effectiveness will be assessed by the daring and freedom with which you play.)

   Team Where: In groups of three or more, play either game above. In *Team Where,* the places are offered from the opposing team to one person on your team (as in Charades). You will start an activity specific to the *Where* and your teammates join in as soon as they determine where you are. Once all on your team are in, time is called. Then your team offers a player on the opposing team a *Where.* After a few rounds, the winning team is determined by the shortest amount of total time taken to get everyone on the team playing. If someone on the team performs an activity that is not specific to the *Where,* a time penalty can be assessed.

   In the *Team Environments* game, everyone in the group plays at once, but each with a different activity (for example, if there are four players, there must be four different activities). The opposing team calls out environments and your teacher/coach will rate the effectiveness of playing on a scale of one to ten (or any other manner of assessment—it doesn't actually matter).

2. *Who* Improvisations

   Who am I? Choose a *Who* from your list. Your partner will await you in the playing space. Enter as your *Who,* doing things that the *Who* would do to your partner. Your partner's job is to determine who s/he is based on your behavior.

The focus is on specificity of behavior so your partner will know quickly who he/she is to be.

Who are We? In pairs, groups or teams, choose an association of *Who*—accountants, a baseball team. As in *Group Where,* enter into the space when you understand the *Who* and choose who you might be—either a part of the group or someone related to the group. For example, if the *Who* is a baseball team, you might be a reporter, if accountants, you might be a disgruntled client with a poorly prepared tax return.

Changing Who with What. Choose a simple imaginary activity. The class or your teacher/coach will call out a different *Who* every 10 seconds or so. Adjust your activity based on your understanding of the imaginary *Who.*

3. *Who, What,* and *Where* Improvisations

    You and a partner come out to play. The audience will provide you with any combination of Who, Where, and What from their lists. For example, the president and a barber fishing. Any combination will do. Your task is to maintain the direction of your energy by focusing on the demands of the improvisational elements: Who, Where, and What. These improvisations create scenarios much like those in more formal dramatic structures. However, the objective of the exercise at this point is the development of your imagination and not script development. In other words, your focus should be on playing and not writing.

    Changing Where with Who and What. The class or your teacher/coach will choose a Who and a What for you and your partner, then call out various places, times, and conditions.

    Changing What with Who and Where. The class or your teacher/coach will choose a Who and a Where for you and your partner, then call out various activities for you both to perform. The most effective activities are those that require you and your partner to work together.

Fairy Tales.   This is a long form improvisation requiring some reflection and rehearsal, although an hour is probably more than sufficient. It brings together a number of elements introduced in this chapter, as well as making significant demands on your body and voice. Teamwork is essential, as is risk-taking and a dare-to-fail-gloriously attitude. The basic guidelines are that at some point during the piece, everyone must a) play a character, b) narrate, c) portray a thing, d) create the world (sounds, sights, even abstract elements such as moods, desires, magic).

1. In a group of four or five, choose a fairy tale you all know. Retell the story to each other, and have someone write down the basic Who, Where, When, and What. For example, in the "Three Little Pigs," you have the pigs and the wolf (Who), the three houses and the land (Where), long, long ago (When), and the pigs learning to outsmart and defeat the wolf (What).

2. Assign roles and begin to develop the story. Determine what ought to be narrated and what may be enacted. Each Where and When must be created by the

group. For example, in the "Three Little Pigs," the group must somehow create the houses of straw, sticks, and brick.

3. Once you've worked out the basic plot and use of narrative and character dialogue, rehearse the transition from scene to scene. The idea is that everyone is always doing something—there is to be no standing around while the narrator describes an event or relates the passage of time. *Something must be acted out by everyone all the time.*

4. Rehearse it once or twice then perform for the group.

Ki *Points*

- There is nothing you cannot act out somehow. You can be the big bad wolf, but you can also be his big bad breath knocking down the house of straw. How? Figure it out!
- Two is better than one. You and partners ought to collaborate on creating a character, environment, sounds or whatever. Find ways to use your bodies and voices together to create the tale.
- Move it along. Use as much of the playing space as possible, and keep the pace fairly quick. Stable and static is boring!

Evaluation. Did everyone participate at all times? Did everyone play a character and narrate? Was everything acted out that could have been? Was every opportunity to use two or more people to create things exploited?

The imagination is a powerful tool. Using it you can alter not only your behavior, but also your very physiology. There are numerous examples of people who simply believe in something and are changed by that belief—simulated surgery that relieves pain, auto-suggestion that induces relaxation, placebos that cure illness, or hypnotic suggestion that triggers cravings or desires. We encounter the world through our imagination. Some say that the world itself, our reality, is a product of our collective imagination. But the imagination itself is a higher order of something even more primitive and basic—your feelings. In the next chapter, we will examine how you can use your feelings in playing.

7 Feelings: The Actor's Fourth Tool

"I don't feel, they do!"

—Fanny Brice

In this chapter we will:

- Examine the nature of feelings—sensations and emotions
- Examine the place and function of feelings in acting
- Explore feelings through some exercises

Imagine you are in an unfamiliar city. You are on your way to an important meeting, but you are late. You take a turn down a quiet street and realize you do not know where you are. You look for signs, but find none. You approach a street you believe will lead you where you want to go and peer down it. It is dark and empty, narrow and long. In the distance you see a crowded, sunlit avenue that appears to be your destination. However, every doorway in the alley seems to promise danger. Eyes seem to be watching you from the windows above. Your heart begins to race and you feel a mixture of fear and anger. What do you do?

If you have ever had an encounter similar to the one described above, then you know that the feelings you had were quite real. Fear, anger, anxiety—prompted not by what was actually happening, not by a memory of what once happened, but prompted by what *might* happen. You imagined the possibility of danger and your body responded in a complex and very real way. We are feeling creatures. There is purpose to our feelings, and every moment of our existence is filled with feelings—even when we play.

Actors have very likely been arguing about feelings and their necessity in acting since human beings told stories around the fire hundreds of thousands of years ago. There are some who may find this very chapter irrelevant or even dangerous. Others might wonder why there is so little examination of feeling in the book. But a few have begun a thoughtful and interesting examination of the place and use of feelings in theater and acting. With advances in neuroscience, genetics, and in imaging technology, our understanding of feeling has developed tremendously in the last decade or so. As the nature of feelings begins to unfold, the mystery of how feeling functions in art, theater, and acting is beginning to unravel as well. This chapter attempts to summarize current thinking about feeling, and the relationship between feeling and actor training.

The question is not *if* we feel when we act (we do), but *what* are we feeling? And are our feelings *relevant* to effective acting? If so, in what way are feelings relevant to acting? And finally, how ought (if at all) the actor proceed in utilizing feelings in acting? First, let us examine the nature of feelings—what we know so far about what they are and what they do.

The Nature of Feelings

The fact is that we do not yet fully understand what feelings are or just how they work. There are several dominant theories (see Text Box—**Emotional Intelligence**), but the ideas presented here are based on the cognitive model and recent discoveries in neuroscience as to the physiological changes that occur in the brain as we feel. All needs of any organic system arise from the basic law of homeostasis; that is, maintaining balance in the face of change. Feelings are the moment-to-moment psychophysical events that we register at both the conscious and unconscious level as change occurs. Our feelings prompt action, and are in fact a source of energy. Feelings behave like transformers—they take a charge and channel it for use by the organism to maintain systemic balance. You see a dark alley, your emotions are stirred, you have feelings of fear, and you act.

Feelings are elusive. We name them—anger, sadness, happiness—but these names are merely convenient markers for processes that defy categorization. Feelings are part of a *phase* of the continual psychophysical process of living (see Figure 7.1). The following is a simplified, but accurate, set of steps that outline the psychophysical process we call feeling.

Emotional Intelligence

There are several major theories—Social, Cognitive, Behavioral, Physiological—that have a number of adherents. The theory this book utilizes is the cognitive model, as articulated by Nico Frijda in his book, *Emotions* (University of London, 1989). But, recent work by Elly Konijn *Acting Emotions* (Amsterdam University Press, 2000) and Antonio Damasio *The Feeling of What Happens* (Harcourt, 1999) and *Looking for Spinoza: Joy, Sorrow, and the Feeling Brain* (Harcourt, 2003) also inform the ideas in this chapter.

See The Salk Institute site on emotions—http://emotion.salk.edu/emotion.html for a good start and a number of links on the subject, and G. Scott Acton's site—http://www.personalityresearch.org/basicemotions.html.

1. At the beginning of the process are your **sensations**—all the input you gather from the external world and your internal monitoring system. You *see* the dark alley.
2. This sensory input induces an emotional response particular to the nature of the sensory input that readies your body to act. Your energy is excited in patterns that correspond to urges to avoid or approach, fight, feed, flee, or procreate, for instance. You see the dark alley, your energy level jumps up, readying you to run.
3. You become aware of this readiness to act, and "feel" the sensations and emotional stirrings. The dark alley means something to you, the emotions preparing you to run have pumped you up, you perceive the urgings to run, and you feel a unique combination of nervousness, fear, and perhaps anger and other emotions.
4. Based on the feeling, you evaluate the circumstances and decide to act. You feel the urge to fight or flee, and you think, "Hey, it's the middle of the day, what can happen? You're late for the meeting. Go on and walk! But, who do you know here? You don't know if this neighborhood is safe. Those doorways look like a great place for a maniac to hide. Maybe you should ask someone for directions. No! Just go. Don't go! Come on! Are you crazy?"

And all of this happens almost instantly (except the last part that includes the internal dialogue—that can take seconds to minutes of hemming and hawing). The implications of this process for actors are tremendous. At each step, the process can be impeded or facilitated. We will examine each step in the process and suggest ways to facilitate the process for the purposes of playing.

Sensations

All living things have sensations that assist in managing changes that occur internally and externally. We sense two things: energies and qualities. The forms of energy we sense include light, sound, and temperature. The qualities we sense are taste, smell, and touch. These are very complicated reactions, quite elaborate, but rarely do any sensations rise to the level of awareness—we do not usually feel the light by which we see, unless it is too much or too little. Most sensory activity occurs below the level of consciousness. However, when the energy is sufficiently great or the quality sufficiently rich, then the impact on our senses push the sensation above the threshold of awareness—we feel it. So, a flash of light in the darkness causes us to react—to blink, wince, cover our eyes and say (with annoyance) "Hey! Do you mind? I'm trying to sleep!"

Our senses are dulled by lack of use and abuse. Dulled senses will impede the feeling process. If all you listen to is hard rock, country music may sound more or less the same to you. If all the music you listen to is loud, it is likely that you will be unable to hear quiet sounds well. *Our senses are enhanced by variety and awareness.* Enhanced senses will facilitate the feeling process. Listening to many forms of

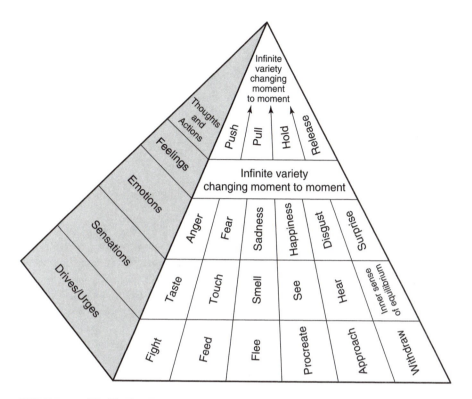

FIGURE 7.1   The Feeling Pyramid.

music allows you to hear the nuances of that music. Westerners are often hard pressed to hear the microtonal differences in indigenous music from Asia; but exposed to this music with some consistency, your ears may be trained to hear those nuances and subtleties. Exposure to a greater variety of foods will sensitize your palate. Exposure to a greater variety of color will enhance your ability to discern color (even if you are color-blind). The same holds true with all your senses.

When you employ imaginary sensory input in your playing, you increase your sensory sensitivity, and it also facilitates the feeling process. Sensitive senses will make you feel better!

Super Sense (G)

1. Refer back to your *Sensations Explorations* list you compiled with a group. Imagine in the fullest detail each sensory stimulus. Imagine each smell, taste, sight, sound, and touch explorations. For instance, imagine silk on your fingers or back of your arm. Or imagine yogurt on your tongue.
2. What does the imagined thing make you feel? Anything? Nothing? For example, does imagining the taste of something good stimulate saliva in your

mouth? Does imagining the sound of fingernails on a chalkboard give you the shivers?

3. What does the imagined thing make you want to do? Does imagining food make you want to eat (approach)? Does imagining a horrible sound make you want to get away (avoid)?

4. Share your list with a partner from a different group and make suggestions to each other. Observe any changes in behavior upon making the suggestions then briefly talk about what feelings or actions the suggestions may have prompted. Remember, it is possible that you feel nothing different and that you do not feel prompted to do anything at all.

Emotions

Emotions appear to be predetermined patterns of excitation that prepare people for certain acts. An event occurs (internally or externally) that impacts a person—the sight of a dark alleyway. An impulse to deal with this impact rises from the visual stimuli and develops into a general excitation with a general direction—to avoid or approach, fight, flee, feed, etc. Emotion is energy with a shape; it has *tendencies* toward an act, but is not yet an act. Emotion is the movement of energy through the system, but not manifest as an act. It is the second *phase* of the feeling process.

Emotions are generally categorized into six to ten types—anger, sadness, happiness, surprise, disgust, and fear, for example. Each gets you ready to act in a certain way and they do so time after time. Since these emotions are hardwired into us, they are *always* and *immediately* ready to be set off by the appropriate set of conditions and/or stimulations. If you are generally healthy, *there is nothing that you have to do to have emotions*. They are there; ready to go, when you need them. It is what happens *after* you have emotions, when they rise to the level of feeling that problems may occur. Inhibitions, learned or systemic, may impede the flow of energy so that your feelings and the urge to act is suppressed. You see a dark alley. The fear response is triggered. You suppress the feeling and the urge to run. "Be reasonable," you may say to yourself. "Nothing to be afraid of." Then, someone touches you from behind and you yell or exclaim something. It should be fairly obvious, besides being well documented, that over the years, through socialization and simply living life that many of your feelings and urges to act are suppressed, repressed, or sublimated (redirected). Naturally, this will have some consequences in your acting when you hope that your feelings will be available. But the good news is that your emotions, the predecessors to feeling, are still there, strong and active as ever. They reside as a kind of background in your felt life, always at least faintly buzzing and hovering just below the surface of your awareness. As you live, different emotions will rise to the level of feeling, while others subside. But, just as your muscles ache after significant use, the buzz of an emotion will linger after an outburst of anger, a flush of happiness, or a rush of fear.

This exercise is designed to tune you in to your background emotional levels. There is no display required (quite the opposite, in fact). It is simply for you to recognize that something is always going on emotionally.

TABLE 7.1 **Emotional Levels**

Emotion	Your Levels	Partner's Levels (your guess)	Group Guess	Group Average
Anger Happiness Fear Surprise Disgust Sadness				

Emotional Levels (F, E)

1. On a scale of one to ten, one being practically nonexistent and ten being practically overwhelmed, rate your emotional levels. How happy, sad, angry, surprised, disgusted, and fearful are you, right now? Using Table 7.1 as a guide, write it down on a piece of paper.

2. With a partner, go through the six basic emotions together, and simply state your emotional level to each other. However, guess for yourself where you think your partner is. For example, start with happy. Write down what level you think your partner is. Then simply share the levels you determined in step one. Go through the basic six in the same way. How are the two of you in comparison? Was there any large differences? Were you aware, or could you sense, the level of your partner?

3. Go through the exercise with the whole group. First, go through the basic six and see if you can guess the "mood" of the group on your own. Write down a level for each emotion. Then, with someone recording everyone's level, go around the group and share the emotional level you wrote down in step one. Find the average for each emotion and compare to your guess. Were you close? Were your answers skewed by your own current levels? Did anyone guess the mood of the group more or less correctly?

This is not to be taken too seriously or accurately. It is just an awareness game. But the implication is that if emotions are always present and ready, we may, by providing the appropriate imaginary stimulus, tap into our emotions and bring them to the level of feeling for our use in playing.

What Are We Feeling?   We feel what we feel based on the sensory input, the emotional response triggered, and our evaluation of what is going on. We are always feeling something. Sometimes, we simply feel fine—this is the basic default setting for a balanced person whose primary needs are all met. When you act, however, the basic setting is often pumped up a bit, due to the excitement, fear, and elation of playing. Meanwhile, the feelings imputed to the character you are playing may be something else. Sometimes our feelings seem to match the circumstances of the theatrical event and sometimes not. In acting it is quite usual for an actor to have feelings that are uncorrelated to the theatrical event. When acting you may feel nervous or calm or disembodied, or the feelings *may* seem consistent with the imaginary circumstances of the play. In *Acting Emotions,* Elly A. Konijn theorizes that the feelings actors experience are actually related *not* to the emotions imputed to the character, but to the emotions that arise as a result of the actor doing the job—or what she calls "task emotions."

> According to current emotion psychology, emotions are now considered having a function in satisfying the individual's concerns. The actors' concerns during performance relate to the acting tasks. Actors therefore use task-emotions to flesh out character-emotions, transforming task-emotions to support their characters. **Task-emotions do not have characteristic facial expressions and cannot be recognized by their appearance, but they are accompanied by increased action readiness.** In this way the outwardly 'empty' behavior of characters is sustained by the actors' own relevant emotions, which creates or strengthens the illusion of spontaneous character-emotions for the audience. (154) [author's boldface]

We feel all the time, but only certain feelings rise to the level at which an act is engendered. Those certain feelings (and all the others filtered out) may be useful in acting effectively. For we can shape the emotional energy we have access to into behaviors that appear to be related to the feelings the audience imagines the character is experiencing.

Are Feelings Relevant to Effective Acting?   Fanny Brice, famous singer and comedienne of the Ziegfield Follies used to say, "I don't feel, **they** do!" ("they" meaning the audience). You may be nervous and still get through the performance without a hitch (even if every moment feels like impending doom). You may feel powerful emotions but nevertheless perform ineffectively—either through poor diction, ill timing, or any number of factors. You can feel almost emotionally free and yet move an audience to tears. Or you can feel those same powerful emotions and deliver a tremendous performance. Instead of getting bogged down in which is better, to feel or not to feel, the question really is, *"Are the feelings that inevitably occur helping or hindering effective acting?"*

Too much or too little energy necessary to accomplish the task will result in ineffective acting. A voice too loud or soft, a body too stiff or ceaselessly moving, an imagination empty or overactive, and feelings too controlled or too wild will lessen the effectiveness of your acting. The challenge is to discover and then apply the energy necessary to accomplish the task, and allow the feelings that naturally arise to be shaped by your natural response to the imaginary circumstances.

It does not matter so much *what* we feel. But, generally speaking, it is *useful* to have access to a range of feelings available simply because it is another source of energy. It isn't *necessary* to feel anything in particular, but it can be very useful to have particular feelings. Given a choice of having a tool at your disposal or not, why not have the tool? But can feelings be a tool? Can they be used for specific purposes? Called upon at will? Yes.

But let us be clear. Feelings you may experience in playing are different than the feelings you feel in daily life for this simple reason—there are no actual consequences to your actions. If you really push someone, they will fall down. You cannot do this playing on stage or in any media (well, you *can*, but you'll get in big trouble). Metaphorically, your push has the *tint* of a full push, but not the complete saturation of color. Similarly, the feelings you may feel in playing are a tint or shade of the real feeling and are not to be confused with "real" feeling.

As you may know, when we perceive color, what we actually perceive is an absence of certain spectra of light. When you look at a red shirt, most other wavelengths of light are absorbed by the material—only the red spectra is not absorbed, only the red is released. So, too, with feelings.

Feeling Exercises

The actor's job is to make perceivable changes in action. The channel is the voice/body. The method is the imagination. The means are playing actions. Just as you wish your body, voice, and imagination to be flexible and strong, you also want your feelings to be flexible and strong. You may already have a wide range of feelings available to you, just as you may already be endowed with a strong and flexible body, voice, and imagination. However, many people do not. For one reason or another, you may have learned to suppress your feelings or limit yourself to a less than full range of feelings. The following exercises are designed, like any other exercise, to expand your expressive range, in this case, to open your feelings.

When you repress, sublimate or suppress feelings, just as when you limit your physical or vocal range, you have impeded the natural flow of energy through you. If you don't use your hips much, they won't shake on cue. If you don't use the upper register of your voice, you won't have access to the high notes when needed. If you don't allow yourself a certain set of feelings (for example, if you suppress most angry responses), it will be more difficult for you to shape your task emotions into signs of anger. The bar for expression has been raised, so to speak. You want to lower the bar, the threshold where feelings are manifest. By doing so, it will require less energy from a source (the imaginary circumstances of a play, for example) to prompt a reaction. Lowering the threshold is the same as increasing sensitivity. Exercises for your feelings are designed to *sensitize* you to the impact of energy—whatever form it takes—and to *generate* energy for action. There are two fundamental ways to generate energy from feelings—through some external event that generates the requisite energy, or some internal act that does the same. So, we have things we can *do* or things we can *imagine*, to stimulate a felt response.

If you are doing everything else involved in acting effectively, feelings will *usually* take care of themselves. If energy is flowing freely through your voice and body and if you are playing clear and strong actions, feelings will necessarily arise and will be manifest in your behavior. For example, if you are warmed up and actor ready and you are *pushing from* in a scene (see Chapter Eight), your facial muscles and vocal cords will be involved and will convey the signs consistent with *pushing from*. It is only when feelings seem blocked or the theatrical event demands a specific felt behavior that you need to be concerned with feelings. The difficulty is that feelings are inherently unstable, so they tend to dissipate quickly. Work on feelings is most effective when linked to an action of some sort.

Exercises that work on your feelings primarily deal with five tasks:

1. Develop sensitivity
2. Generate felt energy for playing
3. Focus energy specifically for a task
4. Transform energy from one kind to another
5. Facilitate the exchange of energy

If you and your coach determine that work on feelings is useful and necessary, there are many ways to work on feelings through your imagination, through your body and/or voice, and through action. You will find a preference as to how best to access your feelings, but that will undoubtedly change as you change, mature, and live. Certainly, as you become more secure in yourself, psychological inhibitions to allowing feelings to manifest will lessen. As in all aspects of acting, the more experience you have the better you will play—if the foundation upon which you have built your art and craft is solid. But it is important to keep in mind that manufacturing some resemblance of some emotion is not the goal of feeling exercises. The goal is simply to encourage access. Just as with your imagination work, if a feeling is there, it is there. If it isn't there, do not manufacture something. In the process of working on your feelings, feelings may arise. Let it happen, but don't make it happen.

Helen Keller (**T**).   Like the *Three Feelings Dance* and *Primal Sounds,* this is a high-risk activity. It is important to provide plenty of time to prepare and process the exercise.

As many of you may know, Helen Keller was an extraordinary human being who, despite being unable to hear or see from an early age, developed into a highly articulate speaker and writer. Prior to her being taught by Anne Sullivan, Helen had developed her own "language"—gestures and sounds that meant something to her and her family. Of course every infant does this as well until they acquire language. What made Helen Keller a bit different is that she maintained these gestures and sounds well beyond infancy and developed them into a kind of language of her own invention. This suggested the following exercise, in which you are asked to create your own "language" to express a thought and/or set of feelings.

1. Complete the following phrase in their minds—"what I want you to know about me is . . . . What I don't want you to know is . . . "
2. For each phrase, work out a series of gestures and sounds that express the thoughts/feelings of the phrase. The gestures and sounds ought not to be com-

posed of any formal language (verbal or sign), but rather they ought to arise out of the feelings inherent in the phrase.

3. Rehearse the piece and present before the ensemble.

It is a simple exercise, but one which demands the utmost commitment and willingness to risk, to dare to fail gloriously.[1]

The Exchange (E, T).   This is an exercise created from combining a Strasberg-like exercise and the children's game, *Mother, May I?* Pair up, standing about five or six feet from your partner and go through the following sequence, one after the other, maintaining eye contact throughout.

The Single Exchange

1. Actor A: "I feel _____." (*whatever you are feeling, including sensations such as hunger, aches, and emotions; for example, "I feel tired, hungry, jumpy, silly, and my back itches."*)
2. "You seem to be feeling _____."(*whatever you perceive your partner is feeling at that moment; for example "You seem unhappy, bored, embarrassed, tired." It is never a judgment about your partner, just an observation.*)
3. "And that makes me feel _____." (*as before, this time acknowledging any change that may have occurred in time and due to the encounter; for example, "And that makes me feel calm, sleepy, and my back still itches."*)
4. You then ask your partner, "May I?" requesting to take a step toward them.
   - If your partner says "yes", you move one step towards them.
   - If your partner says, "no", they didn't believe you about your own feelings, so you must stay where you are.
   - If your partner says, "go back" that means you were mistaken about their feelings or made a judgment about their feelings (such as "you're mad at me"), so you must take a step back.

> **Evaluation is placed outside the actor—the test is in the other actor.**

5. Your partner then goes through the same sequence—"I feel . . . You seem to be feeling . . . that makes me feel . . . "

You must be aware of your energy as well as your partner's—and how that energy affects you. In effect, the transaction is like a little play or scene. The energy (in this case in the form of feelings) changes you and how you will behave in a given moment. Like *Casting Spells, The Exchange* essentially breaks down what occurs in any moment between two people. In between the impressions received and the expressions made, a moment of reflection is inserted to help you become more aware of, and attend to, what is happening. We all are always playing the exchange, casting spells on one another, and this energy is often felt as a psychic impact.

This exercise is primarily aimed at developing your awareness—self-awareness first, then awareness of another. But it also develops your sensitivity to the play of energy between you and your partner—the **exchange** and **transformation** of energy. *The Exchange* may include more than two actors, so that you must take in more and let it affect you.

The acting process is no different from the living process. We are all actors and we interact in fundamentally similar ways. In order to recreate this process, we must deconstruct it, become aware of its structure, be available to the change elicited, and then become articulate in reconstructing it.

Name and Bow[2] (F, T)

1. Walk into the playing area from offstage to center.
2. Scan the group, making eye contact, and allow yourself to be changed by the energy of the group.
3. Speak your full name.
4. Bow. (Your fellow players applaud.)

Ki *Points*

- The exercise begins with four clear steps, so they should be done clearly. Come in as if you belong, as if you deserve to be there. Eyes up, an easy and graceful gait—no apologies implicit in a downcast eye or slumped posture are to be permitted. You may have to try and come in several times before you may proceed to the next steps.
- Take in the group; allow yourself to change. This change may be quite subtle or it may be obvious. You may sense the group rooting for you and that may cheer you up or it could intimidate you. You may sense inattention from the group and that may feel threatening or it may be a relief. The point is to be aware of the feelings arising and to allow yourself to be changed by those feelings. Release, release, release. Your teacher/coach may make some observations such as, "You seem to be holding some unnecessary tension in your neck. Allow your neck to release unnecessary tension." You may be shifting from side to side or sticking a hip out or holding tension in your wrists. Just send a message to release any unnecessary tension, using breath to encourage your *ki* to flow. No need to fuss or fidget. Just "get out of your way."
- Speak your name as if it means something. It's your name, after all! This does not mean shout or show off, but simply allow the simple, unaffected "you" to be released and revealed.
- Allow yourself to take in the applause. It's fun. It feels good. There's nothing like a little applause—and in this case it is simply for coming into the room and saying your name!

■ If you are watching your fellow actors, applaud as you would be applauded. The energy of the applause assists in drawing out feelings for it signals encouragement and support (and this exercise requires a great deal of both).

5. Stand in actor ready and make eye contact with your teacher/coach, who will simply ask, "how do you feel?" (Maintain eye contact throughout the exercise.)

6. Respond in a simple, efficient manner, such as, "I feel tired, calm, stiff, fidgety." Similar to *The Exchange,* this step is purely an examination of what you actually feel at that moment.

7. Release those feelings through a sound—an "ah," for example. Allow the sound to emerge, never force a sound. You will feel when the sound is true, or connected, to what you feel. If you are unsure, check with your partner or coach. They can tell you if the sound has engaged your vocal mechanism fully or not.

8. When you feel that you are releasing your feelings through sound as fully as you are able, speak a nursery rhyme or any other nonsense, and then proceed to some prepared text or speech.

Ki *Points.*   The teacher/coach may provide feedback to help you maintain a connection with your feelings, asking you to alternate between the vowel sound and the rhyme or text whenever they sense you're manufacturing results. If it appears that you are showing some feeling (i.e., *indicating* your feelings rather than simply releasing it), the teacher/coach will call out, "Sound!" Vocalize on the "ah" until you feel reconnected or your teacher/coach calls out, "Rhyme!" at which point begin the rhyme or text again.

This exercise may be expanded to include any text from a sonnet to a monologue. Initially, sense and meaning are not important. The purpose of the exercise is to release your feelings through the sound, to voice the connection between text and feelings. The exploration is simply to become aware of feelings. The use of sound is a means by which you become available to the full range of feeling that is continually present. As the exercise becomes more familiar and feelings more available, you may then *choose* a particular feeling to allow, in order to articulate various emotions. So, for example, you might explore the depth of sadness, happiness, anger, or fear you have available that day. There is no reward for big displays of feeling—you will feel what you feel. Your teacher/coach and fellow players are there to provide feedback and foster your awareness of when you are indicating/showing feelings and when you are simply allowing your feelings free play.

Name and Bow requires a very high level of trust between you, your teacher/coach, and the entire class. Sometimes the exercise may feel manipulative or coercive because the teacher/coach continually asks how you feel. This can be provocative. A typical response a minute or two into the exercise is "I feel annoyed!" Often an angry response is a sign of impending release of other feelings—feelings you may not wish to reveal. As in every exercise, you set the risk level and may choose to stop at any time. The teacher/coach should stop the exercise if it appears that the feelings are becoming overwhelming.

Cooling Down

Work on feelings can be very powerful and great care must be taken. Acting class is not psychotherapy, and most acting teacher/coaches are not qualified to deal with the release of volatile emotions. But your feelings and emotions may be released during any exercise, in rehearsal, or in a performance. After any intense physical activity, it is common knowledge that you should spend some time "cooling down." If your heart is racing and your breath is short, naturally you need to slow down until your heart rate and breathing returns to normal. You must recover your equilibrium. The same is true of any work that stimulates the intense release of energy. So, when working in class or rehearsal, or after a performance, it is important to take some time to recuperate, to ease away from the heightened expenditure of energy and calm down. There are a number of ways to achieve this, depending on the circumstances.

- Shake it off. After an exercise that stimulates a felt response, the simplest and quickest way to begin to recover equilibrium is by vigorously shaking your arms and legs, rolling your head, and lightly jumping up and down. You may have seen this sort of behavior exhibited by athletes after a race or a fall. In the course of an intense activity, your energy is directed in a highly focused way through your body. By shaking, you actually redirect your energy to its normal flow.
- Break it off. When working with a partner, you may find that you both are engaged so intensely that it is necessary to break away from each other. Once the break occurs, you and your partner might acknowledge the intensity, shake hands or hug, laugh it off, even walk about to give your energies a chance to return to their normal flow.
- Meditate. Sometimes the intensity is so high that the most effective means to return to equilibrium is by isolating yourself and getting quiet. There are a number of ways to meditate and recover. Simply sitting and breathing in and out on a four count may be useful. You might focus on a point or close your eyes. You might hum or repeat a calming phrase. You might imagine a pleasant place, such as the beach, that feels calming and relaxing.

However you return to equilibrium, it is important that you do. Energy expended by intense activity requires what Laban called recuperation. You need to recoup the loss of energy and this is often accomplished by acting in opposition to the effort employed. So, if you were working with a strong weight effort, you would recuperate using a light weight effort. The same principle applies to action and tasks (see next chapters) as well as feelings. Feelings, however, do not actually exist in opposition (they only seem to). The recuperation from a **high** level of feelings, whatever those feelings may be, is a **low** level of feeling. In some schools of thought (Zen Buddhism, for example), this is called "detachment." But, this is a judgment, not a description. A more accurate term might be "affectless." *All the proposed* *methods of cooling down essentially reduce internal and external stimulation.* To quiet the mind, you might focus on breathing or some other task that is detached from your feelings. To quiet the body, you might reduce your sensory input—close your eyes, find a quiet place, lie on a uniform surface. This will reduce your sensory input, and thereby lower your feeling energy.

The actor's tools—body, voice, imagination, and feelings—are the channels through which your playing is revealed. The tools are employed to channel pathways of energy *through* you, and are perceivable as patterns of energy *between* you, your collaborators, and the audience. Your flexible, open and strong body, voice, imagination, and feelings will reveal the energy you apply to a task.

Now, in the conclusion of your preparation for playing, we turn to the exact nature of the energies applied to accomplish tasks.

NOTES

1. As such, I never make anyone perform—but like the *Three Feelings Dance* and *Primal Sounds,* there are always several who go, and that often leads to many others going, too.

2. Derived from the Strasberg exercise, *Song and Dance,* I have adapted this exercise I learned from Gillian Goll, an acting teacher/coach in New York City.

8 The Names of Action*

". . . life consists in action, and its end is a mode of action . . . "
—Aristotle

In this chapter we will:

- Identify and explore the fundamental actions and their variants
- Take a timeout to examine the nature of theatrical illusion
- Construct an example of an effective warm-up to prepare for playing

Acting Is Doing

Now it is time to conclude our Preparation for Playing by examining what "acting is doing" exactly means and how you can do it. This is the central aspect of the actor's art and what makes theater, theater. In fact, you have been applying energy to tasks all along. But now we will look at the specific and fundamental actions that underlie *all* acting, and begin to develop your vocabulary of action.

The Fundamental Actions[1]

In nature we find four fundamental forces—electromagnetism, gravity, and the strong and weak nuclear forces. Essentially, a force either repels or attracts. In some cases, the two forces balance each other, for example in the earth's orbit around the sun (more or less). The sun's gravitational pull on the earth is balanced by earth's mass and motion, and the combination of these forces hold the planet in its orbit. In

---

*Portions of the ideas and exercises in Chapter Eight were originally published in *Theatre Topics* (V9, #2). The Johns Hopkins University Press. Baltimore, MD. 1999.

some cases, distance and motion overcome the forces and an object is released from the forces' influence. All energy systems—from stars to human beings—follow the same basic physical laws.

In order to maintain homeostasis, you are always acting upon the environment with force (energy, *ki*), either attracting things to you, repelling them, holding them, or letting them go. Initially, of course, these acts are instinctual, impulsive and beyond your will. However, quite early in infancy, you began to act upon the world in a willful manner. First, you instinctually sucked at your mother's breast or from a bottle, you automatically grasped objects placed in your hand, and you eliminated waste without a thought.

But within months you began to seek nourishment. You felt a need (hunger), you had learned the fulfillment of the need (caregiver), and you employed whatever means available to meet that need (sucking), and when you were satisfied, you let go of the bottle or breast. You reached out to touch and hold things, and then let them go. You felt an urge to move your bowels and you chose to push, and when relieved, you released the muscles you engaged.[2]

> It is the central thesis of this book and approach to acting that these intentional actions—push, pull, hold, and release—are the root of all behavioral actions.

These fundamental actions and combinations of them, like primary colors, make up all the other actions. *Everything* you do is essentially a push, pull, hold, or release (see Table 8.1—**Action List**). By learning to focus your energy in each of these four fundamental ways, you will have laid the foundation upon which you may build a large vocabulary of action, and act more effectively.

Each of the actions has two variants—*to* and *from*. Your basic vocabulary of action is:

1. push to, push from
2. pull to, pull from
3. hold to, hold from
4. release to and release from

Imagine that "push" and "pull" occupy opposite ends of a continuum, with "to" and "from" variants above and below the continuum axis (Figure 8.1). Variations of actions, such as tug or poke, exist somewhere along the continuum. Push and pull make up the bulk of our behavior, particularly in a play, improvisation, and

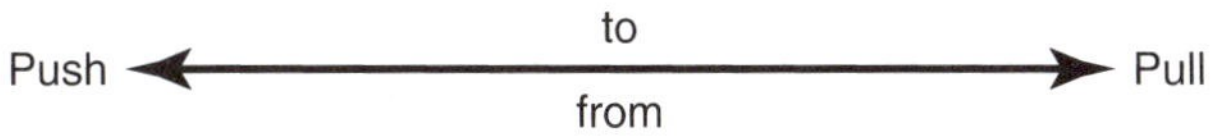

FIGURE 8.1   The Push-Pull Continuum.

other types of theatrical performances. These actions are *assertive* and the task to which these actions are applied is typically to prompt or enforce change in the environment (which might include another person or your surroundings). When conflict occurs in a scene, play, or improvisation, what you probably perceive are people pushing and pulling each other around.

At critical moments in every task—from the simplest transaction to a scene or an entire play—when change occurs or is imminent, we find two more actions at play. When two assertive forces meet (push versus push, or pull versus pull, for example), a moment occurs when energy is flowing but *change has not yet occurred.* This is often called the **crisis**—the critical juncture when a choice is about to be made, but has not yet been made (see Chapter Ten for a more detailed discussion of dramatic structure). The action at this moment is **hold** *to* or *from.*[3]

The moment when change occurs—the **climax** of a moment or scene—there is a cessation of the *hold* energy, or a *release.*[4] The release is usually the end of a task, but it also allows the next task to occur. Energy is built up during the hold (potential energy—what **might** happen), and then released (kinetic energy—what *does* happen).

In a play, tasks are never performed without resistance of some kind. There is always something that inhibits the completion of a task. Usually, but not always, the source of resistance or inhibition is another person, performing his own task. It is the resistance that reveals the action to an audience. You have a need, you encounter resistance to meeting that need, and then you take action to manage (overcome, remove, etc.) the resistance. Perhaps you accomplish your task, perhaps you do not. That's the play.

For example, you want your love to give you a kiss. You approach. Your love moves away. You approach again. Love moves away. You offer your hand to your love. Love hesitates. Love accepts.

Such a typical interaction might go something like this in terms of our vocabulary of action:

Pull-push-pull-push—hold—release

As we have discussed, you only use enough energy sufficient to accomplish a task. If, in taking action to meet a need you encounter resistance, then the level of energy increases sufficient to manage the resistance. As energy increases, new behavioral acts are taken. In our example, perhaps the simple movements are not sufficient to gain the kiss. You might take further or stronger action, which might take the form of speech. As discussed in Chapter Five, speech is a highly developed form of action. In many plays (although not all), speech is *necessitated* by resistance to accomplishing a task. You speak because you must in order to accomplish your task and meet your need.

The dialogue for our scene might be:

YOU: Come here. [pull to]

LOVE: Go away. [push from]

YOU: Come here! [pull to]

LOVE: Go away! [push from]

YOU: Please? [hold to]

LOVE: OK. [release to]

This is the basic pattern of energy that is recreated in a play, scenario or improvisation.

The Action Mandala

For your conceptual convenience, consider the "Action Mandala" (see Figure 8.2). Pick any action and see if you can locate it somewhere on the Mandala. For instance, "shove" could be generally seen as a push, but you can both shove someone away and shove that person to something. Nudging someone is a gentler kind of push, and so is located near release. Shake might be considered a kind of shove that is more a push-hold combination.

The usefulness of the Mandala is to simply demonstrate that any action you play can probably be boiled down to one of the four actions and their variants. The power of these actions is that you already know them and do them. You need not learn them anew, but rather harness them to your will.

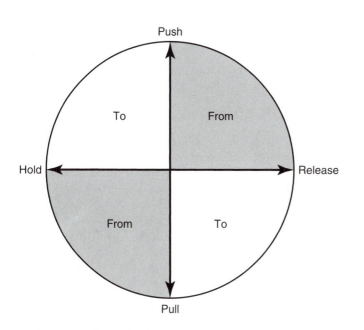

FIGURE 8.2   The Action Mandala.

Four Actions Exercise (**G, F, T, E**).   This exercise develops your ability to form your energy and to transform the energy of the action into behavior.

1. Pair up and begin to physically push against each other, hand to hand, engaging your whole body (see Figure 8.3). Be sure to push from a stable position but in such a way that your partner must push back in order for you both to maintain balance. Feel your energy align into a push throughout your whole body—like metal filaments drawn toward a magnet.

2. When you feel the push is stable, balanced, and your energy is aligned, vocalize on an "ah" vowel. The "ah" is a vocal manifestation of push. This connects the voice and body to the action—a *kinetic* expression of the action.
   It is critical not to *indicate* or force the "ah;" rather, *allow* **your voice to align with your intent.** If your voice is free and open, a sound will emerge naturally. However, even though most of us have limited vocal freedom, a clear, strong action will help free it.

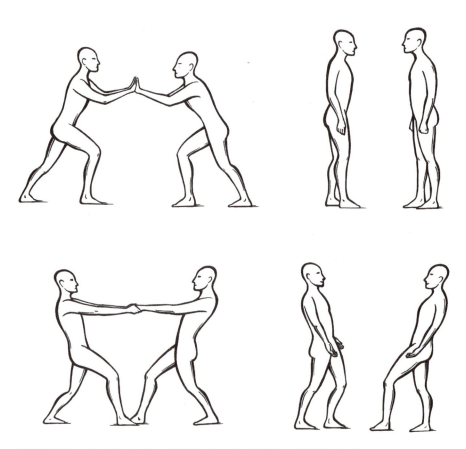

FIGURE 8.3   Push, Push Potential (top), Pull, Pull Potential (bottom).

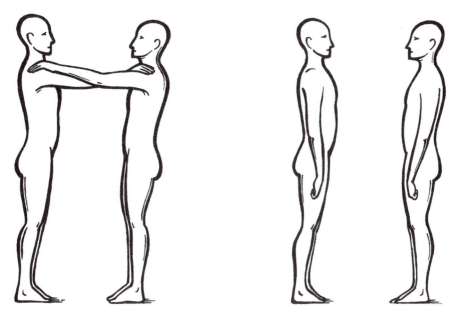

FIGURE 8.4 Hold, Hold Potential.

3. Maintain the alignment of your energy, separate from your partner, take a breath as you are about to push, then *pause*. This is a "push" about to be realized—a *potential* push.

   As in the game, *Now!,* you want to feel the **potential** for action before you actually do something. The evidence of the action is revealed only in your eyes. Of course, minute changes will occur in the musculature of your face and throughout your body, but at this time you are limiting those behavioral signs to the slightest manifestation.

4. While maintaining the "push potential," vocalize again, but this time use gibberish, a nursery rhyme or any automatic text. (The idea is to progress one level of articulation at a time.)

5. At your teacher/coach's signal ("dialogue" or "text"), begin a monologue, sonnet, improvise a dialogue, or begin the text of a scene on which you are working.

6. At a signal, stop, and begin the whole process again, this time proceeding to "pull," "hold," (see Figure 8.4) and "release," also including the variants of "from" and "to."

As you practice, find a word or phrase that helps you connect vocally with the action and which acts as a "hook" that may quickly engage you in the action. For example, *push from* may suggest "get away," *pull to,* "come here," *hold,* "stay," and *release,* "O.K."

There are four important lessons in the exercise.

1. **Behavior arises out of action**
   Anything you do (movement), anything you say (text or improvised dialogue) on stage emerges from the action.

2. **Everyone has action preferences**
   You may find that you prefer *pull to* over all the other actions. Characters are written with preferences, too. Sometimes your preferences will match the character and sometimes they will not. You must recognize both your and the character's preferences and be able to play all actions.

3. **Actions tend to resist change**
   Inertia is a fundamental physical law and it holds true in behavior. We tend to keep performing an action until change occurs that prompts a new action. However, most theatrical events condense and intensify action, so changes occur more rapidly than in real life. Therefore, it is necessary that you increase your receptivity to change.

4. **All behavior has duration directly proportional to the energy of the action**
   Actions are not perpetual, they play only until a task is accomplished or another task is taken up. An action only has so much energy and when that energy is exhausted so are the behaviors arising out of that action.

Ki *Points*

- Trust that the action will give rise to behavior. If you have prepared for playing, then your body, voice, imagination, and feelings will align with your intent. You have spent your whole life behaving, so allow your acting tools to do what they were designed to do. If you encounter difficulties in moving, speaking, imagining, or feeling, then it is likely that your energy is blocked—your acting tools are not free and flexible and responsive. See if you can identify the blocks and take steps to overcome them. Your teacher/coach should be able to assist you, or possibly refer you to someone who can, such as a movement or voice specialist.

- You may like to *pull,* others to *push;* some find *hold* difficult to locate in their bodies and elusive to play, while others discover that *release* is not an action they can easily master. The discovery of action preferences is extremely useful. Armed with it, you can effectively double or quadruple your repertory of actions. Knowledge of preferences also leads to understanding why a particular moment, or a character, may be troublesome. Characters are written with preferences. An actor who likes to *push* may find herself playing a character more apt to *pull.* We will discuss this in greater detail in Chapter Eleven—**Playing Character.**

- Although we resist change in real life, the actor must cultivate the ability to change with ease and grace—for that is often demanded by the theatrical event.

- When working with the *Four Actions* using improvised dialogue, you may run out of things to say. Change actions! Don't think of things to say, but concentrate on focusing *ki,* on playing the action and attending to your partner. A new action will compel new behavior, thus new dialogue, until the improvisation has run its course. Once you have grasped the concept of behavior arising from action, you can approach text from an active, rather than a recitative or passive point of view (i.e., line readings—"How do I say this line?"). We will explore this idea in more detail in playing with text in Chapter Ten—**Playing in Plays.**

Blending with the Actions (F, T, E). It is not enough to be able to play an action. You must also be able to play actions with others. Like *Casting Spells,* this exercise physicalizes the interplay of actions, but focuses on refining your ability to blend with the action of another. Leave plenty of room to play this game. Also, it is very important to maintain as constant a force as possible.

1. Pair up and grab your partner's hand (left or right). Keeping your feet planted in place, allow your upper body to be pulled toward your partner.
2. When you feel the impetus of the pull diminish, pull your partner back toward you. Continue pulling each other back and forth in a kind of seesaw motion.
3. Now, let your partner firmly pull you in his/her direction so that your whole body moves to the side and behind your partner. Allow yourself to be pulled forward so that, in effect, you exchange places with your partner.
4. As you pass your partner and the impetus of his/her pull diminishes, begin pulling your partner toward and past you so that, in effect, your partner exchange places with you.
5. Continue exchanging pulls, allowing yourself to move your partner and be moved by your partner. Allow yourselves to travel about the space, letting the pulls take you where they will. Try not to control it, but rather give over to the "dance." (Of course, some measure of control will be necessary so you and your partner maintain safety.) Once you get the hang of it you can:
   - improvise a dialogue
   - exchange memorized solo text
   - do the dialogue from an open scene or from a play

Blending with Push (F, T, E)

1. Place your hands firmly against your partner's hand, palm to palm, and your feet one in front of the other in a modified en garde position. (Your partner's feet should be identically placed as yours, so that if your right foot is in front, your partner's right foot should also be in front.) Push against one another with equal force to find an initial balance.
2. Allow your upper body to be pushed back.

3. When you feel the impetus of your partner's push diminish, push your partner back. Your upper body should move forward and your partner's upper body should now move back. Continue pushing each other in a kind of seesaw motion.

4. Let the motion become circular, so that you and your partner's upper bodies describe a circle.

5. Now, allow your whole body to be pushed by your partner back and to the side in a circular direction. In effect, you will be exchanging places with your partner. Allow yourself to be pushed, but direct the push to your right.

6. When you feel the impetus of your partner's push diminish, push your partner back. S/he should direct your push back and to the side in a circular direction, in effect exchanging places with you.

7. Continue to exchange pushes, moving your partner and allowing yourself to be moved. The result will be a kind of looping, circular dance. Once you get the hang of it you can
   - improvise a dialogue
   - exchange memorized solo text
   - do the dialogue from a ambiguous scene or from a play

■ Pushing is a bit more challenging than pulling because you must allow yourself to move backward while maintaining constant force with your hands and arms.

Action Improv

1. With a partner, choose a simple **What,** such as "deciding where to eat dinner," or "deciding what movie to see."

2. Begin the improv with *push to,* so that you are urging your partner to go along with your choice.
   Ki Point: Maintain your focus on your partner—is the action working? Is your partner changing? Is your partner changing you? Are you allowing yourself to change?

3. After a minute or so, your teacher/coach will call, "Pull to!" Change your action to *pull to.* Pull your partner to the dinner or movie you want.
   Ki Point: Maintain your focus on your partner—is the action working? Is your partner changing? Is your partner changing you? Are you allowing yourself to change?

4. After a minute or so, your teacher/coach will call, "Hold!" This is the moment before a decision is made. Play the action. Physically hold your partner if necessary, or allow yourself to be held.

5. After a few seconds, your teacher/coach will call, "Release." Let go of your partner, and one of you give in and go along with the other to the movie or dinner or what-have-you.

Ki *Points.*   As you watch the improvisation, notice how change is manifest in the body and voice. When switching from *push to* to *pull to,* positions may

TABLE 8.1   Action List

Push		Pull		Hold		Release	
To:	**From:**	**To:**	**From:**	**To:**	**From:**	**To:**	**From:**
nudge	shove	tug	snatch	grasp	block	allow	unchain
urge	tai chi	yank	extract	contain	bar	untie	let go
poke	brush off	snatch	ensnare	freeze	block	unfetter	unblock
prod	flick away	grab	twist	bind	halt	open	admit
punch	ignore	drag	rip	inhibit	interrupt	give in	give up
tickle	prick	stroke	hook	envelope	stifle	ease in	ease up

change. When players "held," they may have stopped moving. Words may also have come out easily and naturally. If the focus of the playing was on the action (and not coming up with clever dialogue), the players may never have to search for words, especially when pushing and pulling. Perhaps when holding, at the moment when a decision is pending, words may have ceased. At the release, movement and speech may have begun again.

All behavior arises out of action. As characters emerge in playing *Tambourine Tag,* scenes emerge from playing actions. This probably has more to do with our own tendencies to make up stories than any story creation intrinsic to action. But, it is this impulse to enact that gives rise to the art of theater, and it is the contention of this book that all of theater is built upon these four fundamental actions.

At last we have arrived at employing the tools and the fundamental actions in service to the theatrical event. So far, we have examined and explored the elements that are employed in creating theater. Now we are ready to put them together.

NOTES

1. Some of the ideas and exercises in this chapter were originally published by the author (in a slightly different form) in *Theatre Topics* (V9, #2). The John Hopkins University Press. Baltimore, MD. 1999.

2. A validation of the four verbs may be found in early childhood development studies. See Cole and Cole, *The Development of Children* (New York: Scientific American Books), Chapter 5 for a basic survey and a good bibliography of additional sources.

3. There are other names that could be used, but as an action, "hold" offers both positive and negative connotations and does not seem derivative of another action, such as "stop." While "stop" indicates a *kind* of hold, the converse does not seem true.

4. Although the action "free" may seem more basic than release, in practice "free" is vague to enact specifically.

1 The Theatrical Illusion

Your preparation is nearly complete (actually it is never complete, but we will proceed as if it is). Your acting tools are freer and more flexible and you now have a vocabulary of actions with which to play. Up to this time, however, we have not focused on your developing abilities in service to the form of theatrical events.

Recall at the beginning of the book it was stated that art symbolizes the nature of change. Each art has a commanding form by which it imitates life processes. This imitation creates a virtual world, an illusion. The illusion theater creates is the appearance of energy between actors. The energy appears in the form of actions. Actions always arise in an attempt to create or forestall change. The composition of actions makes the theatrical event. The theatrical event is always about some aspect of change.

The Willingness to Believe

Acting is believing—but primarily for the audience. Although you must be committed to your playing, your full commitment and belief in your action will not mean much if the audience does not go along with you. As in the *Tug-o-War* game, you must be fully engaged in the action, really pulling away, so the audience "sees", or believes in, the rope. Belief, however, is an elusive term. Belief means having a conviction in something that may or may not be fact. A belief does not make something real that is not real. You can believe that the world is flat, but all your belief will not make it so. Beliefs are prerational. You do not believe something because you have reasoned it out, but because it *feels* right to you. Reason comes after the intuitive sense of rightness. We make up reasons to justify our beliefs. So, belief is the correct term when talking about an actor's work—the actor playing Hamlet is not really dying, but we go along with the game—we believe it (hopefully). The conviction of the effectiveness of an actor's work is subjective. But because belief functions at a prerational level, it tends to get mixed up with the real. We skip ahead to real, even though our beliefs only *may* be real. That's why arguments about the effectiveness of an actor's work will always happen. You can become more discriminating in your judgment and more specific in your analysis, but finally it is all window dressing. In the classroom or studio we can only help each other and arrive at a mutually agreed-upon set of aesthetic values—beliefs in what is or is not effective acting.

The "willing suspension of disbelief" is a phrase that was coined by Samuel Coleridge. The phrase purports to describe what an audience does when it encounters the imaginary world of a play. For example, you go to a show and some cowboy comes out on stage and starts singing. You say to yourself, okay, I realize this is a lot of nonsense, but never mind, let's enjoy the show. Coleridge's construction is in the negative. However, in the experience of this author, people tend to go along with something rather than stop doing something. Most people go to the theater and want to participate, want to have fun and be entertained—*willing to believe*. They say *yes,* they *blend* with the conventions of the theatrical event. Actors begin with the audience's goodwill (mostly, but not always and not everyone, of course). But if the acting is ineffective or the situation/dialogue improbable, then that feeling of goodwill is jeopardized. In order to go along with improbable action, the audience must suspend its disbelief. If the play continues to demand suspension of disbelief, audiences may become *un*willing—and leave!

Effectively creating the illusion of the play of energy requires the commitment of your entire being to the task. Putting those tasks together into some composition is the next step in creating theater. For the last 2,500 years or so, playwrights have been in charge of composition. While there have always been troupes of actors who compose their own theatrical events (Commedia troupes and improv groups, for example), playwrights have taken on the burden of putting actions together and words in the mouths of actors. It must not be concluded, however, that theatrical events are primarily a written art. They are not. Words are only a phase of the action. But most plays are written, and you must be able to discern and enact the composition of actions beneath the words to which that action gives rise (see Chapter Ten— **Playing in Plays**).

Theatrical Illusion of Time

In the opening soliloquy in *Henry V* by William Shakespeare, the Prologue says,

"For 'tis your thoughts that now must deck our Kings,
Carry them here and there: Jumping o're Times;
Turning th' accomplishment of many years
Into an Hourglass . . . "

Theatrical events unfold over time, of course. But time passes differently for the characters in the play than for us in the audience. While the acting we see actually happens in the time it happens, within the imaginary world of the play, time is much more malleable. We jump over hours, days, even years. Sometimes, even though fifteen minutes have passed over the course of an intermission, in the world of the play perhaps only a few seconds may have passed, or no time at all. The playwright manages the time of the play, the audience perceives its flow, but the actor *embodies* it—and therein lies the difference.

The change to time that must be considered has to do with how actors must deal with time. It is not how time passes externally to the audience and the characters in the imaginary world of the play, but rather how time passes internally for the actor playing the part.

Remember from Chapter One, that *everything* that happens in a theatrical event is offered to the audience's perception. Everything means something on stage—or at least is taken to mean something by the audience.

2 A Warm-up

This is a sample of how a warm-up can be constructed. It may be done as a group or individually. Once a warm-up is learned, it can be adapted to the circumstances of the class—either sped up or slowed down. Once you learn the warm-up, it is important that you pay attention to your needs. If a particular body part or aspect of your voice requires additional time, give it that time, if possible. When time is limited, do the physical and vocal work before class. Ideally, the warm-up needs about 15–20 minutes in order to cover all the elements. Practically, however, do what you can in the time you have.

1. Before entering the playing space, make sure you leave at the door any baggage, real or psychological. Bring your mind to bear on the task at hand. Be sure to wear loose fitting clothes, preferably sweatpants and a t-shirt in solid, neutral colors. If possible, do the warm-up in bare feet.
2. Enter the playing space in silence. Come to Actor Ready. Inhale and exhale three times.

Body

3. Yoga
   - Sun Salute
   - Triangle Pose
   - Dancer Pose
4. Isolations/Articulations from head to toe. Be sure to warm up the wrists, fingers, and ankles.
5. Body Wave
6. Dimensional Scale
7. Three Feelings Dance with a memorized text
8. Group Dance
   (If music is available, form a circle and begin dancing. Begin a movement that is in time to the music and is relatively simple. Everyone in the group should dance the step. After eight or sixteen counts, the next person in the circle does his or her own step, which is then imitated by the whole group, and so on, until everyone has had a chance to do a step. This encourages

exploring range of motion, rhythm, Laban Movement Efforts, and can be quite fun.)

Voice

1. Return to Actor Ready. Inhale and exhale three times.
2. Inspired Breathe
3. Sighs of . . .
4. Loose lips, Dropped Jaws, Tripping Tongues
5. Sliding Scales bottom to top two or three times
6. Articulation exercises and tongue twisters
7. Sonnet or memorized text
8. Group sing
   (Sing a song you all know at the end of the vocal warm up. It encourages breathing, sounding, and articulating. It is also fun.)

Imagination

1. Weave—stopping and jumping simultaneously
2. Walkabout—different players might be asked to call out where, when, and what. At each stop, imagine things you see, taste, touch, hear, and smell
3. Casting Spells

Feelings

1. Name and Bow Solo (do the exercise without coaching)
   - Go to Actor Ready
   - Say aloud an inventory of how you feel—sensations and emotions
   - Allow an "ah" so as to connect your voice to your feelings
   - Nursery rhyme
   - Sonnet or other memorized text
2. The Exchange

Action

1. Four Actions
2. Basic Tasks (see Chapter Nine)

PART THREE

Playing

9 The Basic Tasks

"I wanted to change the world. But I have found that the only thing one can be sure of changing is oneself."

—Aldous Huxley

In this chapter we will:

- Identify and explore the basic tasks
- Examine the nature of relationships
- Explore a fundamental improvisation

Acting is *never* done alone. It is *always* done in relation *to* something. Acting is performing an action, determined by theatrical circumstances to accomplish a task. The task is always *managing your relationship* to that something—be it a person, place, or thing. Managing a relationship can mean *changing* or *maintaining* the relationship. You manage relationships through clear and specific actions that you take. In taking specific actions, the nature of the relationship emerges.

You now have the fundamental actions necessary to accomplish any task. Now we shall examine the kinds of tasks you are likely to encounter in a play.

The Basic Tasks

Stanislavski used the word "task" to define what an actor was doing at any particular moment in a play. In other places, "objective" or "intention" has been used. However, Anatoly Smeliansky, associate artistic director of the Moscow Art Theatre (and editor of a new English translation of Stanislavski's work) has stated that "task" is a more accurate translation of the Russian word used by Stanislavski.[1] Task is a useful term because it is simple and open—both important virtues from the point of view of this book.

If there are fundamental actions that are applied to a task, then it follows that there are fundamental or basic tasks you will undertake. Essentially your task is to change or maintain your relationship with something else. There are four basic ways to do this. They are similar to the fundamental actions, but are more general. We alluded to them at the beginning of Chapter Eight. They are:

1. to Attract
2. to Repel
3. to Sustain
4. to Free

Each of these tasks is also simple and open; simple in terms of their *direction* and open in terms of the *means* by which the task may be accomplished. The Fundamental Actions provide the means. You manage relationships by pushing, pulling, holding, and releasing. You may attract, repel, sustain, or free by any of the actions, and by any combination of the actions. Finally, *resistance* is implied in each task. If the task is "to attract," the implication is that the something to be attracted is resisting the attraction. Actions are taken to overcome resistance.

All tasks are forms of the basic four tasks. For example, a common task in a play is "to seduce," an obvious form of "to attract." Another common task is "to intimidate," a form of "to repel." "To encourage" is a form of "to sustain," while "to enlighten" is a form of "to free."

We begin with four basic tasks because, as with the fundamental actions, it provides a foundation upon which playing may be built. As you rehearse your tasks and actions will naturally become more complicated, subtle, and will also change. If you begin with these basic tasks, then right away your energy will be aligned and you may play effectively. But bear in mind that every play will demand clear tasks, and every time you play, your actions will change, determined by theatrical circumstances—what is happening to you, to your scene partner, in the environment, and the imaginary world of the play.

***Basic Tasks* (F, T, E).** This exercise ideally continues right out of the Fundamental Actions exercise as part of the warm up. The goal of the exercise is to put actions in play. It is also a useful prelude to the *Yin/Yang* improvisation.

1. Pair up and choose competing tasks—attract/repel, sustain/free.
2. Improvise accomplishing the task.
3. When your teacher/coach calls out "Stop," name the action (push, pull, hold, release) your fellow player was taking.
4. Begin again, but try to accomplish the task with a different action.
5. When the teacher/coach calls "Switch," change your task to that of your partner's.

As you work together over the course of a semester or the length of the class, you might try a variety of tasks derived from the four basic ones, such as seduce/reject, please/displease, encourage/discourage, or rouse/calm. A longer list of tasks appears in the Appendix.

Ki *Points*

- You need not *be* the thing you want to do. In other words, you need not be excited to excite your partner. See what actions work, and if an action isn't working, change your action!
- Blend. When confronted with your partner's action, use it. If you are being pushed, allow yourself to be pushed. Your opportunity to assert yourself will come. Start with the energy from your partner, honor that, and see what happens.
- Come up with a list of tasks. There are numerous resources for your list in most acting textbooks (including this one), but first think about the kind of tasks you attempt. Just as writers are exhorted to write what they know, actors too must act what they know.

This exercise works on one side of the acting process—**performing actions** required for accomplishing a task. The following exercise is about constructing a series of small (immediate) tasks for yourself that all fall within one overarching (central) task. But you are also required to add two more important elements— **urgency** and **value.** These values are derived from your imagination. By imagining conditions under which the task must be accomplished, you are working on the other important side of the acting process—the **theatrical circumstances** that determine your action.

The Single Task Challenge **(G, F).**   Your focus is on maximum efficiency and minimum effort—applying only the necessary and sufficient energy to accomplish the task. You can quickly and easily see whether or not behavior is necessary and sufficient or rather extraneous and superfluous to accomplishing the task at hand.

1. Set yourself a simple task and try to accomplish it.
   - From an off-stage point, enter the playing space and retrieve an object (a book, notebook, etc.) and exit. This is to be done simply—just come in, get the book, and leave.
   - Do only that which is necessary to fulfill the task.
2. Set a time limit for accomplishing the task.
   - Compressing the event increases the energy of the event. This will add a sense of **urgency** to the task by focusing your energy. There literally will be no time for extraneous behavior. In order to create this time limit or sense of urgency, you will have to—
   - **a.** pre-set a time in which the task may reasonably be accomplished—play around with timing the task. Begin without a limit, then have someone

actually time it and reduce the allotted time to one minute, then 45 seconds, 30, and finally 15 seconds. What happens to your behavior and feelings? What do behavior changes do you see in your fellow players as time is of the essence?

   b. imagine circumstances that engender the desired behavior. An example might be, "I'm late and I left my book in this room." This changes the sense of urgency from externally driven (time) to an internally driven (feeling). You must commit to the imaginary circumstances you have created. But simply stating to yourself, "I'm late," may not be sufficient to generate the necessary playing energy to render the performance of the task compelling and believable.

3. Endow the task with value.

   In addition to limitations of time, endowing the task with value will also heighten the energy with which you attempt to accomplish the task. Continuing with the example, you might imagine that you're late for *class*. You're late for a class you are *failing*. Not only are you late for the class you are failing, but also you've almost left behind the one thing that could help you (namely, the book you need to do your homework).

Your imagination must set the direction of your action and ignite a psychophysical readiness to act. All this is focusing your energy *before* you enter the room. You are *aligning your energy with your intent*.

   You enter the room. Do you know where the room is? Is it your room, or just a room? Do you know where the homework is? Is it in the book? Is the book in the room? All this might go through your mind *if* the situation were real. But you've made all this up. You're pretending. You're acting *as if* the situation is real. The test is, of course, whether we (the audience) believe what you are doing. The audience is ready to believe. But if you *show* us you are looking, instead of really looking for the book, then we will not believe. Behavior that is extraneous to the task is confusing and disrupts belief. When you show us that you're looking, your true task might be "to impress the teacher/coach with my skill," rather than "get the book." This type of extraneous behavior occurs all too often and it has a name—"indicating" (see Text Box—**Indicating**).

Relationships

You are in continual relationship with the world around you. In physics, the relationship between things is usually described mathematically. What the math describes is the *value of energy* inherent in each thing, and the *change* in those values when the things interact. $E = MC^2$ describes the relationship between mass and energy. This description is useful because it is concise and simple. A conceptually convenient way to describe human relationships is

   R = P/D
   Relationship equals **P**ower divided by **D**istance

Indicating

We tend to do most things with a great deal of extraneous behavior, and there is a tendency in performing (since performance is an act designed for perception) to use more energy than necessary to insure perception. This is what is often called "indicating." You are *showing* you are doing the task rather than just doing the task. But of course you are showing what you're doing. So, what is really meant by indicating or overacting in theater?

Everything we perceive in theater is offered to our imaginations for contemplation. All gestures—vocal and physical—are signs by which the audience perceives the theatrical event. Everything means something, or at least, the audience *assumes* that everything presented in a theatrical event means something. So scratching, wiggling, coughing, every tic, and vocalization will be assumed to be part of the show. Some theatrical events are open enough to admit those behaviors without damaging the illusion. Some events do not seem to admit that kind of extraneous behavior. It depends on the event. That is a determination you can only make in working with the artistic creators of the event (the director, designers, etc.). In general, then, it is useful to *minimize* the signs associated with the application of energy to a task. You can always allow more if necessary. A good rule of thumb is to begin in Actor Ready—start with a (relatively) blank slate. Allowing behavioral signs is much easier (in general) than limiting behavioral signs. *The Single Task Challenge* is a useful exercise in eliminating extraneous behaviors associated with a task.

Relationships between human beings and the world cannot be directly measured or quantified, but only *felt*.[2] This holds true whether you are in a relationship with a prop or a person, a set piece or lights, the text, or the audience. By understanding the value of the relationship, you may then more effectively generate the necessary and sufficient energy so that an audience perceives your behavior—vocal, physical, imaginative, felt—as consistent with the relationship evoked by the theatrical event. If the play says you and your partner are lovers, some understanding of a love relationship will be useful for you to play effectively. You will not make that person your lover. You will do the things that lovers do, and the audience will judge the relationship to be loving.

Performance is taking a position relative to an Other (see Chapter One). The position is a manifestation of the power dynamic—degrees of dominance, submission, and equality. All acts are taken to effect change, and power *is the relative ability to effect change*—a little or a lot or none at all. Inherent in any position relative to an Other is *distance*—both actual *physical* distance and (for human beings, anyway) *psychological* distance. For example, you have almost complete power over a pencil—that is, you can almost completely change it. You can do many things and are only limited by the strength of your body and imagination. But if the pencil is out of reach your power is greatly diminished. So, unless you change your position (actually move closer), you no longer have power over the pencil. If you are an older sibling, you certainly know the power in being bigger, stronger, and more experienced. At one time (hopefully no longer), you could limit your younger sibling's ability to make choices, often simply by threatening action. Your sibling could only change the power dynamic by running away or bringing in reinforcements (calling "Mom!" for example). More subtly, your sibling might bargain or *negotiate* with you, agreeing to your demands only if you agree to theirs ("I'll take out the garbage if you drive me to the mall"). If you agree, you give some of your power away to get what you want. Your relative positions have changed and a new relationship is formed. You may attempt to reassert your former relationship (total dominance), but it is very difficult (and often leads to violence). You remain the older sibling (and always will), but the distance between you both has increased by virtue of the bargain made—your sibling/pencil has rolled almost out of reach.

From the audience's point of view characters *assert power* and *manage distance* in order to meet a need (maintain balance). From the actor's point of view, you want to attract, repel, sustain, or free and you do this by pushing, pulling, holding, and releasing. The clearer your task, and the more specific your action, the more well-defined the relationship and the more effective your playing.

Although managing a relationship is the central task of the actor (and of human beings, really), **a relationship is not something you make—it** *emerges* **from the action** (see Text Box—**You Can't Make Me**). The actions you take create the relationship. But the kind of relationship created is a *judgment*—it is outside of the action.

The following exercise plays with power and distance. As you watch, see what kind of relationship emerges simply by altering power and distance. As you play, play with managing power and distance.

You Can't Make Me

An effective task is free of judgments and manipulation. Sometimes, when you examine a text or see a play, you might think a character is really annoying another character. This appears to be the task, but in reality, this is a *judgment* made about the task. You (almost) never set out to irritate someone. You set out to get rid of them (repel), so you push them from you. The person you are trying to get rid of may find your behavior irritating, but that is a judgment (and someone watching may make that judgment, too). Similarly, you almost never set out to manipulate someone. You take an action to satisfy a need. To someone on the outside, it may *appear* manipulative, but this is a judgment about what you are doing, not what you are actually doing.

You cannot *make* anyone consciously do anything. You may limit someone's choice or overcome their resistance, but they still will choose. That is not to say if you give in to a terrible choice you are somehow to *blame* for what may happen to you. If you are unconscious or otherwise unable to make a choice, then you have lost the ability to choose and may be manipulated—treated like a tool. However, if you are conscious, no matter how dire the situation, you cannot be manipulated. You may be overpowered and compelled to make a terrible choice, you may be fooled into making a foolish choice, you may give in, or you may relent. But in the end, you choose your next action. The choice may be stark, and in a great deal of dramatic material, the choices a character may face *are* stark—that is what makes them dramatic.

Status

Keith Johnstone has some wonderful insights into the nature and use of status. Status is the relative position, or standing of, a person to another. Your status (or anyone's status) is determined in two ways.

1. Externally

    Conferred *upon* you by your circle of friends and family, and by the society/culture in which you live, for example. A person with high external status is someone with something valued by society—wealth, knowledge, talent, or celebrity. A low status person might be someone who *appears* to have little or nothing valued by society—no wealth, knowledge, talent, or celebrity. Remember, this has nothing to do with what someone deserves, but only how society, in general, may look upon a person. Many plays have to do with the change in status of an individual, from low to high (Prince Hal in *Henry IV, 1 and 2*) or high to low (*Oedipus Rex*).

2. Internally

    Created by you based on how you feel about yourself in various circumstances. Most of us have a "habitual status." That is, you walk around with a general feeling about your relative value—the king of the world or a speck of dust or (most likely) somewhere in between. There are numerous plays that deal with changes in internal status from low to high (Nora in *A Doll House*) or high to low (*Richard II*).

By playing with status, a relationship with another person or an object will quickly emerge. You can play with status simply by utilizing the actor's tools.

You probably know people who "carry themselves with pride" or "act like they own the place," or "lord it over everyone." You also probably know people who are "shrinking violets" or "creeps" or "wallflowers." This is the clue to playing with status—it manifests itself first in the body. You can create or alter the *perception* of your status simply through alignment. Laban Body level work (see Chapter Four) gives you the vocabulary. By lengthening, widening, shortening, narrowing, bulging, or hollowing you take up more or less space. The more space you take up, the greater your status will seem to be. The less space you take up, the lower your status will seem to be.

Taking Stage/Giving Stage (F, T, E)

1. You and your partner come up with (or receive from the class) a Who, What, Where.
2. Choose either to take up as much or as little room as possible using Body (lengthen, shorten, etc.), and Space (forward, backward, up, down, right/left). What observations can you make about your internal sense of status?
3. After the improvisation, get feedback from the class on their perception of your status and that of your partner.

A second way to play with status is with your voice. As with the body, a voice that takes up space (through volume, range, and tempo) confers high status. A voice that takes up only a little space confers a low status.

Speak Up/Speak Down (F, T, E)

1. You and your partner come up with (or receive from the class) a Who, What, Where.
2. Using your voice take up as much space (volume and range) and time (tempo) or as little space and time as possible.
3. After the improvisation, get feedback from the class on their perception of your status and that of your partner. What observations can you make about your internal sense of status?

Utilizing your imagination is a more indirect means to play with status, but it is very similar to how you might explore and rehearse a play.

King of the World/Scum of the Earth (F, T, E)

1. You and your partner come up with (or receive from the class) a What and Where.
2. Imagine you are the king/queen of the world. Your partner will imagine being the scum of the earth.
3. Play the improv.
4. After the improvisation, get feedback from the class on their perception of your status and that of your partner. What observations can you make about your internal sense of status?

Naturally, status will emerge by the level of energy with which you push, pull, hold, or release.

Status in Action (F, T, E)

1. You and your partner come up with (or receive from the class) a Who, What, Where, and one of the fundamental actions with an energy level of 1 or 10 (1 = lowest, 10 = highest).
2. Play the improv, focusing on playing the action at the designated level.
3. At some point, your teacher/coach (or a classmate) should call "Switch," and you alter your energy level from low to high or high to low.
4. After some practice, play with subtler levels of energy and different combinations of fundamental actions.

Ki *Points.* Do some actions have inherently higher or lower status? Or is the significant factor the level of energy? Certainly a nudge has less energy than a shove, but does that necessarily mean the status is lower? As you play with status, decide for yourself what factors are significant for you and what tool provides you the most effective entry point. How you take up or give up space most effectively is for you to discover. But certainly, managing power and distance is always part of the task at hand.

***Yin/Yang* (G, F, T, E).** This is a highly structured Who, What, Where improvisation—a full actor workout, if you will.[3] The improvisation focuses on the *actual* theatrical circumstances that determine your actions. That is, the *Yin/Yang* improvisation works on your ability to use (transform and exchange) the energy you receive from your partner. As stated earlier, the highest value is placed on the play of energy *between* players. Although this improvisation uses imaginary circumstances to clarify tasks, it is the actual circumstances that most concern us. What occurs in the moment, in the here and now, is of utmost importance.

Examine the Yin/Yang symbol (see Figure 9.1). Within the single circle there are two opposing, but balanced forces. The boundary between the two forces is curved, not straight, implying that one force moves into and toward the other. The small circle within each side represents an element of the other—there is a bit of Yin in Yang, a bit of Yang in Yin. The symbol is active, not static, meaning that Yin can change (transform) into Yang and vice versa.[4]

Yang is the irresistible force, and Yin is the immovable object. Yang attracts, Yin repels. Yang's actions are generally **to** (push, pull, hold, release), Yin's actions are generally **from** (push, pull, hold, release).

For the purposes of playing, the playing space should be set up in such a way that Yin is in a room, Yang is outside the room. There should be a threshold of some kind—a door or entryway—through which Yang must gain entrance into the room.

1. Choose a **relationship**—siblings, partners, lovers, friends, etc. One person is in the room (Yin) and the other person is outside the room (Yang).
2. Choose a **central task**—Yin's task always begins as "to repel." Yang's task always begins as "to attract." However, the task must be related to something Yin has that Yang wants, but under almost no circumstances would Yin allow Yang to accomplish the task. The task can be *to obtain an object,* such as money, keys to a car, a ring. The task can also be *to change the relationship.* For example, Yang wants a love relationship with Yin.

FIGURE 9.1   The Yin/Yang Symbol.

3. Choose an **imaginary past.** Yin/Yang has a history of some kind directly related to the task. If the task is to obtain money, the imaginary past might be that Yang is a continual borrower who doesn't repay. If the task is to change the relationship, the imaginary past might be that Yang broke up with Yin two weeks ago for some reason (and there should be *some* reason).

4. Choose an **imaginary present.** Yin will not want to give the object to Yang not only because of the imaginary past, but also because of current circumstances—the imaginary present. In the money example, Yin may be short of cash for some reason. In the love example, Yin may have met some-one new. In the money example for Yang, the imaginary present might be that Yang needs the money to repay a more serious debtor, or to pay for an opera-tion or to buy Yin a present. In the love scenario, Yang has learned that Yin is the true love of his/her life. Since the imaginary past and present is rarely revealed in the course of the improv, it is most important that *the imaginary circumstances are endowed with value.*

5. Choose an **immediate task.** The immediate task deals with something in/directly related to the central task. For example, if obtaining money is the task, Yin might be paying bills. If the central task is renewing relationship, Yin might be getting ready to go out on a date. Yang's immediate task is to get in the room. Yin must play his/her part by providing resistance and *not* letting Yang in.

Example.   Yin and Yang are college roommates and best friends (*relationship*). They are both taking the same class; however, Yang is failing, whereas Yin is the best in the class. Time and again Yang has come to Yin for help. In fact, Yin has done Yang's homework on several occasions. Yang, meanwhile, has had a tough semester in school and runs out to have fun and drown her troubles instead of doing her work. Yin is sick and tired of being taken advantage of while Yang goes out and has fun, leaving Yin distinctly out of it (*imaginary past*).

At the top of the improv, Yin is late for class, having just finished her excellent homework (*imaginary present*). Yin knows that Yang has not done her homework, but will not give it to her again (*central task*). Yin is getting ready to go to class and cannot be bothered, especially by Yang (*immediate task*).

At the top of the improv, Yang has not done her homework again but now real-izes that her fooling around has been a mask to cover her insecurities and fear of failure (*imaginary present*). Yang has to get the homework and save her school career (*central task*). She knocks on Yin's door to gain permission to enter the room (*immediate task*).

The basics that you and your partner need to know should take about a minute to figure out. The rest is imaginary work for each of you. You must paint yourself into an imaginary psychological corner, so that your impulses to act (recover bal-ance) take over. The imaginary circumstances must be endowed with value in order to affect your acting tools (voice, body, feelings) and maintain the direction of your energy. The desired outcome of the improvisation is the collision of actions, which result in organic psycho-physical behavior. The scene comes to life when you and your partner are:

- Playing off one another, using and adjusting to the energy you give to each other
- Sensitive to the "spells" being cast, allowing yourself to *blend* and be *affected*
- Applying the necessary energy to accomplish the task (getting the money, getting on with your life)—the push/pull/hold/release of the moment

Ki *Points*

- The task is the *modus operandi*—the means by which your ability to play actions is developed.
- Blend—allow the energy emitted to change you, but redirect that energy to create the change you desire.
- Strive for maximum efficiency, minimum effort. Keep behavioral signs to a minimum. Avoid playing a "scene."
- The test of an effective improv is in the audience—did they sense the energy was generated, transformed, and exchanged effectively?
- All improvs are about power or love, or some combination of the two (see Text Box—**The Power of Love**). It is useful to identify what you are playing for—love or power—for it focuses your attention on what you are trying to achieve, what need you are attempting to fulfill.

The Yin/Yang utilizes all of your acting tools—body, voice, imagination, and feeling. It develops specificity of action and clarity of task. It plays with power and distance. It is like a scrimmage or preseason games—very much like the real game, although not quite. It is also a very challenging exercise and a good deal of time ought to be spent on playing it. The importance of this kind of work cannot be overstated. The essence of theater is the play of energy between actors. If the theory about the development of art is correct, then character and words are later developments in the formation of theater. However, most of what the actor does is derive performances from words. So, the next step is to take the Yin/Yang setup and apply it to a simple dialogue, or open scene.

The Power of Love

It is not certain to whom the notion that all plays are about love can be first attributed, but it is a common statement in many acting studios and books on acting. The idea that plays are about power is nearly as common. Consider some plays or movies you have seen and discuss what you think it finally is about—power or love. For example, the play *Glengarry Glen Ross* might be considered almost exclusively about power.

Open Scenes **(G, F, T, E).** This is merely a dialogue between two or more people that awaits imaginary circumstances. Any basic conversation about an innocuous or banal subject (like the weather or time) will do. Write one with your partner, but remember to keep it as simple as possible. You might want to return to the dialogue you created in the *Found Theater* exercise from Chapter One. A sample open scene is provided at the end of the chapter.

1. Stay with your partner from the last Yin/Yang improv. Use exactly the same setup (tasks, shared history, and preparation) as before.
2. Play the scene using only the dialogue you have written.
   Nothing should change in terms of your playing—only now you are speaking words chosen for you.
3. Identify the central task of the scene and jot it down in the margins of the text. Also jot down any actions that you played.
4. Play the scene again, but with awareness of the central task and your fundamental actions.
5. Go through the text and agree upon a moment in the text where a change of task might occur.
6. Select one of the four actions to play for the first unit, one for the second unit.
7. Play the scene with the selected actions, *holding* (to or from) at the change, and *releasing* into the next action.

Units of Action. The change you created (or discovered) is a unit of action—or what is commonly called a beat. A play is made up of many units of action, each with a shape and rhythm of its own, but typically relating to the shape and rhythm of the whole play. A unit is defined by **a series of acts aimed at creating or resisting a single change.** When a change occurs or resistance is successful, a new unit begins. In some plays this change is clear and orderly. In others, the units are ambiguous, and perhaps random—but they are there. A unit is like an at-bat. The batter gets on base or does not. The at-bat is over when the change occurs. Some units, like some at-bats, are more important than others. An at-bat in the third inning with two outs, nobody on with your team leading by nine runs is not such a big deal. An at-bat in the bottom of the ninth, two men on, your team behind by one is rather important. In *Hamlet,* the famous "to be or not to be" is a significant moment to be sure, but it is a much different moment than the moment he kills Polonius. You must recognize and understand the *value of the moment* and the pattern and shape of the units of action.

The choice as to when a unit changes can be an intellectual one initially. You examine and analyze the text and decide when a change occurs. But in rehearsal you may find the unit changes at a different moment. It all depends upon the play of energy between you and your partner. Change does and must occur. But when and how it occurs is a matter of discovery in the moment, based on your analysis and rehearsal. When it comes time to perform you must simply play.

It is important to remember that identifying units of actions and the nature of the task are conceptual conveniences—they are merely means to get at effective playing, but they are not the ends. It is useful to think of units of action as musical phrases. A phrase has a shape, a beginning, middle and end, and an effective player attends to its structure. However, playing the phrase is only one aspect of making music. Playing the unit is only one aspect of making theater.

When you work on a playtext, you may find it useful to identify these units (or beats) and chart the units in terms of the task, the action, and behavior (movement and speech). We will examine this in Chapter Ten.

You have now done everything essential to playing. The open scene may be the culminating experience for your first acting class. You may also play a monologue or a scene from a play. Most acting classes end up with a performance of scenes from plays. Like musicians learning passages from great orchestral works, you may wish to try your hand at passages (scenes) from the great theatrical works. There are good reasons to study and perform scenes from dramatic literature. You are introduced to good drama. You may learn about concepts and philosophies other than your own, you may learn about cultures and historical eras other than your own. Exposure to good drama, like exposure to any good art, can only broaden and deepen your vocabulary of feelings, enrich your acting, develop empathy, and help you become a more effective player.

Sample Open Scene

A: Where have you been?

B: Around. You know.

A: Did you get my message?

B: I think so. Maybe.

A: Maybe. OK. Whatever.

B: Where are you going?

A: Oh, you know. Around.

B: I'll come with.

A: I don't think so.

B: Whaddya mean?

A: Hello! What do you think I mean?

B: I think you're way overreacting to an unreturned phone call.

A: All right, just come on then.

B: Hey. I'll call you first next time.

A: Fine.

B: You're welcome.

A: You can be such a . . .

B: So can you. Let's go.

A: OK.

N O T E S

1. Smeliansky, Anatoly. "Stanislavski Revisited." Panel Presentation. Association for Theatre in Higher Education. San Francisco. 1995.

2. While that feeling may manifest itself in sensations, emotions and thoughts, the relationship can only be perceived by an audience through actions taken by the actors.

3. This is a variation of a Meisner exercise ("Knock on the Door") taught to me by Manual Duque that I have further adapted.

4. There are numerous sources of information regarding the Yin/Yang symbol in books, journals, and the worldwide web.

10 Playing in Plays

". . . Suit the Action to the Word, the Word to the Action, with this special observance: That you o'er-step not the modesty of Nature; for anything so over-done, is from the purpose of Playing, whose end both at the first and now, was and is, to hold as 'twer the Mirror up to Nature; to show Virtue her own Feature, Scorne her owne Image, and the very Age and Body of the Time, his form and pressure. Now, this over-done, or come tardy off, though it make the unskillful laugh, cannot but make the Judicious grieve; The censure of the which One, must in your allowance o're-way a whole Theater of Others . . . "
—*Hamlet*, Act 3, scene 2 by William Shakespeare, from the First Folio, with some modernized spelling for the reader's convenience

In this chapter we will:

- Examine briefly the process of impulse to speech/text
- Propose an operating definition for a playtext
- Examine dramatic structure, theatrical conventions, and "realism"
- Explore an analytic process to determine tasks and actions

Most actors begin with improvisation. But for some actors, sooner or later improvisation just doesn't do it anymore. Some actors, filled with great heart, want great lines to go with it. As you may know from theater history, someone got the bright idea to start writing things down. Thespis is the first playwright to get credit, but doubtless there were many, many before him. However, the transition from improvisation to the written word—the playtext—is not seamless.

From Impulse to Text

You may recall from Chapter One that organic systems act to achieve or maintain balance. The energy applied to the task of achieving or maintaining balance is

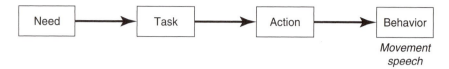

FIGURE 10.1   The Path from Impulse to Text.

always directed outward to enact change. Change is enacted to create or maintain balance. *Im*balance in an organic system creates a **need**—to fight, flee, feed, or pro-create. A conceptually convenient way to chart the process of managing balance is shown in Figure 10.1.

The Play (text)

> A play is a composition of action revealed in resistance to change and is about a pattern of change.

To compose is to put together; the playwright puts together a series of actions. Resistance to change is usually characterized by **conflict.**[1] Conflict arises out of competing actions—push, pull, hold, release—occurring moment to moment. Change may occur quickly, slowly, in a certain rhythm, or in a certain rise and fall of energy. A playwright conceives a pattern of change and composes a series of actions that capture the nature of the change. For example, "coming of age" is a pattern of change. Many plays (and films, novel, songs) are concerned with that particular pattern, and each offers a unique conception of how that change occurs. You, the actor, are the agent of change. You play the actions that collide with the actions of your fellow players. The audience perceives the actions that are revealed in that collision (conflict), and goes on the ride of the play through a pattern of change. At the end, hopefully, the audience recognizes at some level the pattern of change. To a greater or lesser degree, they connect to the truth of the play's conception. It is a tricky business from start to finish—as are all artistic endeavors!

As the agent of change, you need to have a process for not only playing the action, but discerning it as well. We have explored *how* to play. Now we must examine *what* to play. The process of discerning what to play begins with analysis.

Dramatic Structure

All plays, scenes, scenarios, and improvisations have structure. They begin and end, and something happens in the middle. If theater is a game, a script is like a *description* of a game from which we discern the rules of playing. We take external behaviors—gestures and utterances—and through analysis (and intuition) determine the various tasks and the energy necessary to perform the tasks.

By understanding the fundamental pattern of change inherent in the text, and being able to reenact that pattern, you can play effectively. From the description you must figure out the rules of how to play. Analysis helps you determine the rules for playing.

There are always three worlds present in a theatrical experience—the world at large (your life), the world of the theater (the kind of show, the kind of theater), and the world of the play (see Figure 10.2). Each world tells you about itself through signs. In your world, there are a vast amount of signs, fewer (but still many) in the world of the theater, and fewer in the world of the play. The signs you encounter in each world help you to negotiate your way through that world. Some signs, like a stop sign or a red light, you interpret. You understand what it is you are supposed to do when you encounter that sign (stop), because you've been

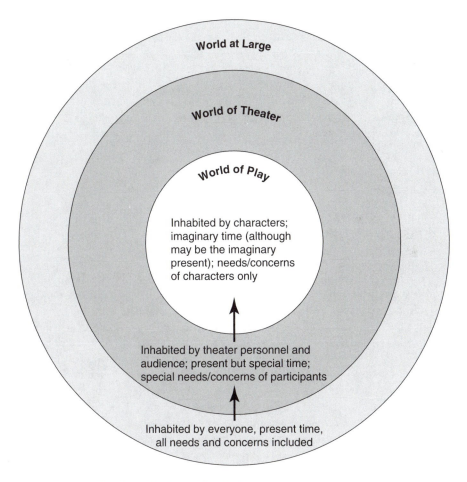

FIGURE 10.2   The Three Worlds at Play in Theater.

taught to "read" it. Some signs you intuit—a slippery road is a "sign" for you to slow down. Plays present you with signs to *interpret* and *intuit* what is going on. A play often utilizes recognizable signs, but changes them in certain ways. The changes reveal the nature of the world of the play. So, for example, in *Hamlet* you understand from almost the beginning that Denmark is in a state of alert and that ghosts appear to be real.

Some plays play games with the signs, taking signs that you would ordinarily recognize and altering their usual function—like a funhouse at an amusement park. A funhouse toys with your perceptions. A mirror in the funhouse distorts your image and you laugh (maybe) because you know what a mirror is supposed to do—and the mirror you encounter in the funhouse isn't doing it. Playwrights have been playing with signs since the beginning. The comedies of Aristophanes (fifth century B.C.E.) toyed with audience expectations and mocked their social structures in plays like *The Birds* and *Lysistrata.* Shakespeare made jokes in his texts about the fact that a boy was playing the female character in plays like *Twelfth Night* and *As You Like It.* The actor/clown Bill Irwin specializes in disrupting the conventions of the theater in theatrical events such as *The Regard of Flight, Largely/New York,* and *Fool Moon.*

This may sound more complicated than it actually is. You are always dealing with signs, negotiating your way through life via these signs. Bert Lahr (the cowardly lion in *The Wizard of Oz*) might have summed it up best when he said, "If it's a comedy, wear a funny hat." The funny hat is a sign that tells you to laugh. The funny hat is a *convention* of comedy—a sign to help the audience interpret what they are seeing and hearing.

Conventions

Recall games you played as a child and you will likely remember that a great deal of time was spent establishing and arguing about the rules. Breaking a rule is "not fair" or "not allowed," ruins the game and someone usually storms off. When rules are broken in sports, there are penalties—free shots, yellow cards, ejections, and even forfeits. In the game of theater, rule violations have a similar effect. At the beginning of a theatrical event, the conventions are established and usually the audience will go with those conventions, even if they cannot fully articulate them. Conventions are conveyed by signs and behaviors. For example, the rising or falling curtain is a convention that signals the beginning or end of an act. Music plays, an actor begins to sing—this establishes a convention that the people in this theatrical event break into song. Most of the time an audience will completely accept these conventions, no matter how strange or random—and some conventions are quite apart from ordinary reality (see Text Box—**Theater for New Audiences**). The audience will go along with the actors as long as the conventions are maintained, even the convention of breaking conventions. The conventions tell an audience how to participate in the theatrical event. If, however, you or any other artist violates any of the rules established, the audience will not be sure how to participate, will grow anxious, distracted, and ultimately bored. Sometimes, of course, there are accidents—set pieces

---

Theater for New Audiences

People new to any game will often be bored because they don't understand the conventions—they literally don't know what they are watching and how to participate. At the movies, we're invited to "sit back, relax, and enjoy the show." This is a convention of movie viewing; however, it is antithetical to participating in a theatrical event. Theater requires a communion between actor and audience—there is a kind of spell that binds them together. The spell is difficult to establish and difficult to maintain—it requires the active engagement of all involved—actors and audience to be sure, but also director, designers, ushers—everyone involved in the conception and production of the theatrical event.

Young people often have no clue as to how they should participate—there are cultural and generational differences that must be taken into account when constructing a theatrical event targeted for a young or student audience. That is why there are classes in art appreciation.

---

falling down, lines dropped, entrances missed—that reveal the tenuous nature of the theater. But these accidents are forgivable—that is, the connection to the audience is not usually lost when accidents happen (and indeed, often these accidents are galvanizing moments for they are actual events rather than imaginary).

Realism

The dominant form of theater in this country and throughout the West is what is known as realism. These are plays, written by playwrights, which primarily deal with human beings in situations that appear to correspond to the current understanding of reality. People do things because of some motivation or need. *Most* of what is seen on Broadway, Off-Broadway, in movies and television falls into this category.

> "Realism . . . describes a number of artistic movements that arose at particular points in our cultural history, where they paralleled other kinds of discourse, political, scientific, and philosophical. Realism is always material—built of words, paint on a canvas or bodies speaking and moving through space—and so is always a *fabrication* of reality."
> (Counsel, 24)

Realism is a style just as any other type of theater—such as restoration comedy, drawing room comedy, or neo-futuristic-dada-drama. Whatever one may call it, what it boils down to is that all forms are just that—forms. These forms can be seen as types of games, with their own rules that a performer must follow. Realism is just another game to be played.

One thing that distinguishes modern realism from other genre is a sense of cause and effect. There is also a sense that what occurs is inevitable. This feeling of an impending future or destiny has been with us since at least the Greeks. In realism, actions appear to be psychologically related, motivated by some underlying need or desire indicated by the manner in which the character is written. Analyzing a play to determine the needs, tasks, and actions, is a very useful skill for you to develop.

Play Analysis[2]

Reading a play is like detective work. The words are only the method by which the author communicates her/his vision of the action. Often, plays are a series of stage directions (see Samuel Beckett, for example). It is necessary to dig into the work and ferret out its structure. All plays are compositions (formal structures). Actions are chosen by the playwright (or scenarist) and ordered in such a way as to reveal something about the nature of change.

There are three primary elements to the play analysis. Each element builds upon the other, aiding you in understanding the game and how it is to be played.

1. What are the imaginary circumstances?

   The imaginary circumstances refer to the "rules" of playing, that is, how the play is acted. There are three areas you must assess: the physical, psychological, and theatrical environment.

   a. The physical environment refers to the information provided by the playwright that sets up the action—the *where* and *when* of the play (what the French call the **milieu**). Where does it take place and how does that place affect the action of the play? A place is not just a location; it is an environment. When does the play take place and what are the social/political/historical salient points that affect the action of the play?

   b. The psychological environment refers to the *who* and the "feeling" of the play; that is, the characters and the mood and tension inherent in the action. For example, *How I Learned to Drive* has a significantly different feeling than *The Importance of Being Earnest*. Who are the main characters and what is the psychological balance at the top of the play? In *How I Learned to Drive* we meet a woman sexually abused when she was young, her uncle, and a chorus of actors who play her family, and other individuals as she tells her story.

   c. The theatrical environment refers to the circumstances special to the play, or the genre—*how* the play will unfold. For example, *Hamlet* is a play in which ghosts appear; it is a revenge play (you may assert). This tells you a great deal about the kind of play in which you're acting. What is the actor-audience relationship? (Do the characters talk to the audience?) What kind of imaginary things happen in the play (things that may or may not occur in "real life")? Identifying and understanding the genre helps you play the game of the play.

2. What is the main action and when does it begin?

The main action is the pattern of change being enacted. The basic pattern of change is initiation, growth, peak, and decline. As described earlier, Erik Erikson identified eight crises each person goes through in life from birth to old age that correspond with the basic pattern. Joseph Campbell examines mythic journeys, such as the "Call to Adventure," "The Road of Trials," and "The Vision Quest" (*The Hero with a Thousand Faces.* Princeton University Press. 1990.). The film world provides a simple way to describe these patterns— "coming of age," "falling in love," "finding your destiny," or "facing death." Each play will have a main action, which specific pattern is revealed over the course of the play. Identify that action with a phrase that seems to encompass the events and major characters of the play. For example, *Oedipus Rex* might be "to discover and destroy the scourge of Thebes." For *How I Learned to Drive* the main action might be, "to come to terms with the past." There is no correct answer, but only answers that harness your playing energy to greater or lesser effect.

There is a moment in every play when the action is fully engaged. It is often near the beginning and occurs at the moment an action taken by the main character meets resistance and the pattern of change the play enacts is revealed or alluded to. Here is a metaphor that may assist you in understanding (and discovering) this moment. Imagine you are blindfolded in an amusement park. Your friends pack you on some sort of ride. You feel the seat of a compartment as you sit, a bar comes across your lap and you feel the compartment begin to move forward. Suddenly, you feel the compartment move upward—and you realize you are on the roller coaster. The moment you feel the direction change and the journey is revealed is when the main action begins. This moment has been variously called the inciting incident, the dramatic or point of attack. At this moment, the audience understands the ride they are in for; not the specific twists and turns, but the general shape.

3. What is the main conflict and what are the significant complications of the play? When does the crises and climax occur?

   - Conflict arises from the various needs/desires of the characters and the obstacles that prevent them from achieving those desires and satisfying those needs. Who's fighting whom and for what?
   - The complications are the obstacles confronted by the characters (either events or people).
   - The crisis occurs when all the conflicts come to a head. This is the moment when the character is forced to make a decision. The climax occurs at the moment of decision. This decision leads inevitably to the denouement, and a new equilibrium is achieved.

A complete analysis would consider more elements—the language, subplots, and theme, for example. However, for the purpose of playing effectively, the above elements will provide a solid basis. But it is also important to recognize that analysis is always ongoing. The more you know and understand, the richer your playing will be. The best players are always going back to the script to ferret out the telling detail or to gain a firmer grasp on the structure.

Scene Analysis

Just as a play may be analyzed, separate scenes in the play ought to be analyzed. Scene analysis is similar to play analysis, but delves into the text with greater depth. In addition to the analysis you perform on an entire play, when you play a scene you must also consider the following.

1. Place the scene in context of the entire play, i.e., when does it take place, what precedes and follows it? What is its importance in the structure of the play? What are the specific circumstances of this scene relative to the play—location, time of day, and any special conditions—that are significant? For example, a play may be set entirely in a kitchen, but there will be some changes and your job is to understand the significance of those changes.
2. Describe the 4 C's—the **main conflict** and **significant complication(s)** of the scene. Identify the moment when the **crisis** and **climax** occur and explain how they move the play forward.

Analyzing Text

Along with analyses of the play and scene, the text itself should be examined. Text arises from *action*—the character speaks to accomplish a task. Literary analysis can tell you a lot about meaning and structure, and this is important. There is a wealth of material concerning this kind of analysis so it will not be reiterated here. Your main concern as an actor concerns primarily *what* is said, and *how* it is said. This must be understood in order for you to play the action clearly and effectively. The speeches and suggestions below provide examples of the concepts useful in text analysis.

1. *What is said* deals with word choice.
   a. Are the words formal or colloquial?
      LOUIS. Why has democracy succeeded in America? Of course by succeeded I mean comparatively, not literally, not in the present, but what makes for the prospect of some sort of radical democracy spreading outward and growing up?
                    from *Angels in America, Part One: Millennium Approaches.*
                    By Tony Kushner

NORCA: Doncha "Norca" me; you takin' her side!! Why you gotta take her side??!! Everywhere I go, someone tryin' ta take the other person's side!! Why can't someone take my damn side for once in a while!!

from *Our Lady of 121ˢᵗ Street*. By Stephen Adly Guirgis

b. Are the words short or multi-syllabic?

LUISA: I take for walk and show to friends mind baby shvester. Make me feel good. Happy. Then gone. And many years no sister but picture from America and letter from Papa and lady who takes care of.

from *A Shayna Maidel*. By Barbara Lebow

LUCKY: . . . in spite of the strides of alimentation and defecation wastes and pines wastes and pines and concurrently simultaneously what is more for reason unknown in spite of the strides of physical culture . . .

from *Waiting for Godot*. By Samuel Beckett

c. Does any of this change and, if so, under what circumstances?

In *A Shayna Maidel,* Luisa's speech changes depending upon whether or not the scene is in the past (in which she speaks fluent Polish), or in the present (in which she speaks broken English).

2. *How the words are said* deals with thought.

a. Is the grammar formal or informal?

BOHR: Throughout history we keep finding ourselves displaced. We keep exiling ourselves to the periphery of things. First we turn ourselves into a mere adjunct of God's unknowable purposes, tiny figures kneeling in the great cathedral of creation. And no sooner have we recovered ourselves in the Renaissance, no sooner has man become, as Protagoras proclaimed him, the measure of all things, than we're pushed aside again by the products of our own reasoning!

from *Copenhagen*. By Michael Frayn

LINCOLN: Who see thuh black card who see thuh black card? You pick thuh red card you pick a loser you pick that red card you pick a loser you pick thuh black card thuh deuce of spades you pick a winner who sees thuh deuce of spaces thuh one whe sees it never fades watch me now as I throw thuh cards.

from *Topdog/Underdog*. By Suzan-Lori Parks

b. Are sentences short or long?

RALPH: This. Er. I fell off a roof. Blacked out. Bosh.

from *Frozen*. By Bryony Lavery

CUSINS: I love the common people. I want to arm them against the lawyers, the doctors, the priests, the literary men, the professors, the artists, and the politicians, who, once in authority, are more disastrous and tyrannical than all the fools, rascals, and impostors.

from *Major Barbara*. By George Bernard Shaw

c. Are the ideas simple or complex?

FICK: I mean if I had these couple—of big buddies—fighters—you—you know—if I had a couple of guys—like—big guys—that—you know,

there's like nothing—I could, like if you walked around with these buddies, I mean you could do, man—you could do anything . . .

from Balm in Gilead. By Lanford Wilson

YVAN. Catherine adores her step-mother, who more or less brought her up,
she wants her name on the invitations, she wants it and her step-mother is
not anticipating, which is understandable, since the mother is dead, not
appearing next to Catherine's father, whereas my step-mother, whom I
detest, it's out of the question her name should appear on the invitation, but
my father won't have his name on it if hers isn't, unless Catherine's step-
mother is left off, which is completely unacceptable . . . "

from Art. By Yasmina Reza

  d. Do they follow a straight path, or do the thoughts meander?

Shakespeare provides excellent examples of both, sometimes in the same
play. In Henry V, the King builds a stirring emotional case for fighting in the
famous St. Crispin's Day speech (Act IV, scene 2), whereas the Hostess, in
recalling the death of Falstaff, goes this way and that in her remembrances.

  e. Does any of this change and, if so, under what circumstances?

Many characters in the plays by Christopher Durang have large changes in
how they speak, depending upon the emotional charge of the moment (and
their particular obsessions). See Beyond Therapy, Betty's Summer Vacation
or Laughing Wild for some fine examples.

You should look at the speech of all the major characters in the play, but of
course you should make a highly detailed analysis of your character's speech. At
advanced levels, greater detail (regarding rhythm, imagery, and literary devices
employed, for example) is useful, but in the early stages of training, considering the
"what" and "how" of your character's speech is a good start.

The Promptscript

The promptscript is a way to organize your playing. If the text is a rendering of the
action, then the promptscript is the blueprint. From the promptscript, you can see
how the play was crafted (built) and develop a plan of how to play it. But since a
playtext is a rendering, with only words to hint at the underlying structure, you must
begin with the words and/or behavior indicated in the text. A good rule of thumb is
to read the scene or play at least three times—the first time as an audience member,
the second time as a director, the third time as an actor.

Obviously, the first time you read any play, its impact upon you will be (more
or less) as if you were watching the play. You'll follow the story and characters and
be left with some sort of impression about the journey of the play. The second time
through, you may begin to visualize and hear how the play might go in greater
detail. Like a director, you will begin to get a grasp of the main conflict, the overall
action and the major tasks the characters are engaged in. The third time you begin to
see the play from the point of view of the character you will play. You may now start

to feel, hear, and see what you might do in the part, but more importantly, you will experience the play from the character's perspective. This is the crucial point. If you begin playing from a single reading you may tend to play the end results—what the audience sees. Playing after a second read you may have some general ideas about your actions and tasks, but you may still be focused on the overall game. The third time through, you will be an **advocate** for your part. You will begin to see how your part functions in the play, what your specific tasks and actions are, and how the character experiences the world of the play.

Of course, it is difficult to read a play too many times. There is an anecdote about Ethel Merman, a great musical theater performer of the twentieth century. She played the character Mama Rose in *Gypsy,* and it was said that before each show, she read the play back to front, so as to prepare her for her first entrance. Merman played Mama Rose more than 3,000 times.[3] That's a lot of reading. But it also provides some insight into the acting process. You must go backwards from the text to the underlying impulses that generate a task, fulfilled by an action, which results in behavior.

Your promptscript should first and foremost be useful to you. There are many ways to create a promptscript and your teacher/coach will undoubtedly have preferences. However, at the very least, the promptscript should contain the following elements.

1. The task at hand. One task per unit of action. Start with one of the basic four. In psychological realism, an effective way to articulate the task is in the form, "I want X to Y," X = one of the four basic tasks, and Y = the person you want to change. The task usually is an attempt to change some Other. "I want to attract Kim," for example. Directing the task beyond yourself also provides a good test for the task. You will perceive if the task is effective or not based on what your partner does.

2. The actions to take. In a unit, there will typically be several different actions applied to accomplish the task. Start with the fundamental four. "I want to attract Kim. How shall I accomplish this?" Pull to, hold to, etc. As you rehearse, you may find more and more specific actions to play—tickle, nudge, squeeze, for example.

3. The move to make. As we will explore in Chapter Twelve, movement on stage is almost always a positive move—a movement to something. Although to an audience it may appear that a character is running away from something, in truth, the character is running to a better place. The questions are 1) where are you going? and 2) how will you get there? Often, the director will offer movements to you, but if your impulse is to move away, move away (to a better place).

If you look closely, each of these things are leading toward speech. The impulse is revealed in the task; the task generates an action, the action results in behavior—movement and speech. You derive your choices by examining the text.

After reading the scene or play a number of times, you will begin to sense the task and action implied in the text. Try one. Let's say the character says simply, "Hi!" Is it a push, pull, hold, or release? What task seems to be at hand—to attract, repel, sustain, or free? What move might you make—to what and how? Two units of a scene in promptscript style might look like this:

	TASK	ACTION	MOVE	TEXT
First unit				
	Attract	Pull to	step in	KENNY Hi.
				WOMAN Hi?
		Hold to	stay	KENNY Hi.
				WOMAN Hi?
		Push to	step in	KENNY How are you?
				WOMAN How am I?
		Nudge	offer hand	KENNY How are you?
				WOMAN How am I?/What are you, some sort of nice guy?
New unit	Repel	Push from	move away	KENNY Am I a nice guy?
				WOMAN Are you a nice guy?
		Brush off	stay still	KENNY Am I a nice guy?
				WOMAN Are you hard of hearing too?
		Hold from	step in	KENNY Am I a nice guy?
				WOMAN Are you?
		Release from	walk out	KENNY Not to a jerk like you!

FIGURE 10.3   Promptscript—*The Session:* "Kenny."

You can generate choices for tasks and actions fairly simply, and alter them as simply if they prove ineffective. However, the best approach might be to understand the role you are playing first. As you work on a scene, whether it is an open scene or a scene from a play, you will find that in order to effectively play you not only need to understand the game you are playing, but the part you play and your place in the field of play. The next two chapters consider each of these in turn—character and staging.

NOTES

1. Conflict is only one means by which theater is created. Conflict is a subcategory of inertia, or resistance to change.

2. This form of analysis goes back to Gustav Freytag, a nineteenth century German critic. James Thomas's book, *Script Analysis for Actors, Directors, and Designers* (Butterworth-Heinemann. Newton, MA, 1992) offers a clear and thorough exploration of this form of dramatic analysis. Of course, there are many approaches to analyzing a text. Any form of analysis is useful if it opens up your imagination and ignites your energy for playing.

3. James Hoskins, a teacher and professional actor/dancer who worked with Merman in the 1960s, related this story to me.

11 Playing Character

> *"In drama, characterization depends on function; what a character is follows from what he has to do in the play. Dramatic function in its turn depends on the structure of the play; the character has certain things to do because the play has such and such a shape."*
>
> —Northrup Frye, *Anatomy of Criticism*

In this chapter we will:

- Examine the concept of character
- Apply our knowledge of acting to the realization of character
- Propose an analytic tool for character

"Bovary, c'est moi," the famous writer Gustav Flaubert said about his fictional character Madame Bovary. That's fine for him. But if you play Madame Bovary, she ain't you and you ain't she. You are you. You are not Hamlet, or Rosalind, or Sandra Dee. You stay you. You do not *become* Hamlet, Rosalind, or Sandra Dee. A character is simply marks on a page that indicate behaviors (movement and speech). You give life—*yours*—to those markings. Let the audience think that you are Hamlet, Rosalind, Sandra Dee. That's what they are supposed to think! You may feel different when playing Hamlet—why wouldn't you? Hamlet is a prince in Denmark and (arguably) a little crazy who goes around killing people and accusing his mother of incest. If these behaviors are not ordinarily part of your daily life, then it should be no surprise that when playing Hamlet you feel differently. But, do not confuse *feeling* different with *being* different.[1]

The actor performs a function within a structure and the particular function performed is perceived as character. Your *role* is *what* you do in the play. Playing *character* is *how* it is done. For example, in baseball, the third baseman is a role. One of his functions is to guard the left field baseline to midway between third and second base. *How* he plays third base is his character. The center in basketball is a role, but Shaquille O'Neal plays it much differently than Yao Ming. Their playing style characterizes them.

Physical and vocal choices of the actor are essentially **pathways** of energy through the body/voice, and **patterns** of energy manifest in action. This is made evident by the selection of actions performed. All genres and forms require specific and appropriate choices regarding the pathways and patterns of energy. Designations such as leading, supporting, or bit roles are descriptions of the actor's job (or function—see Text Box—**Play *Your* Part**).

Creating a character is one of the more controversial aspects of acting. The various American schools—Strasberg, Meisner, Hagen, and Adler to name a few—have significantly different takes on the matter. Richard Schechner compares the character-building work of the Stanislavskian actor to the trance state of a Balinese dancer,[2] what Stanislavski himself called "living the part."[3] In *A Practical Handbook for the Actor,* one of the chapters is entitled, "The Myth of Character" denying the existence of character altogether.[4] David Mamet (the godfather of *A Practical Handbook for the Actor*) states that actors are not to create characters, but to speak the author's lines clearly. He seems to mean that the actors he casts are already intrinsically "right" for the part and therefore need not alter themselves in any way.

Every actor worth her salt says she can play any part, and of course this is true. The real question is can she play the part *more effectively* than someone else? Text is a manifestation of energy, as has been discussed previously in this book. This energy has a pattern, a rhythm—a quality that is unique unto it.[5] Human beings also have an intrinsic energy—the way energy flows in and out and through the self has a pattern, a rhythm—an intensity. Although this pattern may be, and often is, altered by changing circumstances, there is a general predictability, or predilection, to this energy. When an actor is "right" for a part (and there is no final answer to this, it depends on time, culture, well . . . everything), what might be more accurately said is that the actor's intrinsic energy is more or less *aligned* with the intrinsic energy in the text. Playwrights and actors have recognized this since the beginning, thus the prevalence of types in nearly all cultures.

Jungian psychologists have identified certain archetypes in human beings (Stevens 1982). But Aristophanes used types in his comedies, and one can presume that these types were recognizable long before he got around to playing with them.

Play *Your* Part

If a third baseman encroaches on the shortstop's territory, errors may occur—the play is botched. Similarly, if you are playing a chorus role and steal focus when the leads kiss, you have violated your function, stepped out of your role and consequently botched that moment of the play. Understanding and effectively playing your role, your function, is critical to the success of any performance.

The *Commedia dell'Arte* codified comic types (which arose out of Greek and Roman types). So, while actors may complain of type casting, it is natural and in some ways makes sense. Of course, in art there are no "rules," and visionaries and/or delinquents soon break any rules constructed. Interesting effects may be achieved by "casting against type," revealing new truths in a work, for example, casting Romeo and Juliet as an older couple. It may be compelling, it may be terrific theater, but it cannot be denied that the intrinsic energies of the actors do not align with the intrinsic energy of the text. This intrinsic energy—which is essentially **a pattern of acts**—*is* **character.** Your job is to understand that pattern and to effectively perform the actions that are perceived as character.

Character Studies   Utilizing many of the exercises you've done so far, you can begin to explore the pathways of energy through your actor tools that will result in the creation of "character." First, however, you must clarify your own preferences—how you use your body, voice, imagination, and your action preference. There are a number of ways you can do this. Laban suggests examining your preferences through how you move, and this is a particularly effective approach since physical behavior is the most easily observed. The model in Table 11.1 is adapted from LMS.

Practice the following exercises again—first examining your preferences, then experiment by altering one or more preference.

Character Studies (F, T)

1. Body Wave
   - Choose to remain in one of the five positions. Play "Casting Spells" or "Zip-Zap-Zop" or "Freeze Tag Improv." Observe and note any changes in yourself and classmates.
   - Walk and speak in one of the positions, interacting with classmates or scene partner. Try each position, exaggerating the position at first, and then modifying it to a more subtle and "realistic" manifestation. What position feels "right?" What position of your partner's seems more believable?
2. Dimensional Scale
   - Shape level—choose one shape choice: lengthen, shorten, widen, narrow, bulge, or hollow. Begin by simply walking with the shape. Next, play with the choice in various exercises and improvisations, as above. Then, create combinations of two—lengthen/widen, narrow/shorten, for example. First just walk, and then experiment in exercises and improvisations.
   - Directional level—choose a direction in which to place your energy.
     a. Imagine that your energy is projected from your center vertically (up or down), horizontally (left/right), and sagittally (forward/back). Take a walk and note what happens to you and your classmates as you focus your energy in different directions.

TABLE 11.1   Preference Chart

	Voice	**Body**	**Imagination**	**Feeling**	**Action**
Take in	What kind of breath do you take as you assimilate energy?	Where in the body do you allow energy to enter?	What senses are stimulated? What is the tendency toward the perverse, profane, obscene or other associations?	How does energy received make you feel? E.g., defensive, offensive? Giddy? What is your "go to" feeling?	Push-Pull-Hold-Release? To/From?
Transform	Where does the energy resonate—chest, head? What sounds tend to arise? What articulations?	How and where does the energy move through you? E.g., does it wriggle, flow, jump?	Where does the energy take you? E.g., What do you see, hear, taste, smell, etc?	How do your feelings change as the energy moves through you?	Push-Pull-Hold-Release? To/From?
Send out	How does the sound come out? Through which resonators? Articulators?	Where in the body does the energy arise? Core? Periphery? When you send it out, do you always use your arms? Hips? Head?	Is your energy monstrous, angelic, sexy, gentle, playful? How would you *characterize* the sights, sounds, smells, tastes you experience?	How do you feel as you send energy out? Anxious? Daring? Angry? Sad? Happy?	Push-Pull-Hold-Release? To/From?

b. Imagine placing your energy in different planes, shifting the center of the plane from your one-point to the extremes of the dimension. As you experiment with the placement of your energy, add text and/or behavior and afterwards reflect upon what was effective.

- The Table (horizontal) plane—imagine you are standing on the table, that you are under the table, or that you are in the center of the table.
- The Door (vertical) plane—imagine you are behind the door, that you are in front of the door, that you are in the middle of the door.
- The Wheel (sagittal) place—imagine you are on the left side of the wheel, that you are on the right side of the wheel.[6]

3. Efforts

   Efforts are manifestations of your relationship to space, weight, time, and flow. As discussed in Chapter Four, you have personal preferences along a continuum in each effort. A character will have preferences as well. To gain facility in altering your preferences, play with the efforts in various exercises and improv as described above. *Casting Spells* is particularly useful in exploring the Efforts.

   - Weight: Cast spells as if you were sending cotton balls or balloons—maintaining a sense of **lightness.** Cast spells as if you were sending bowling balls or a ton of dirt—maintaining a sense of **strength.**
   - Time: Cast spells as if you had all the time in the world—**sustain** the spell as long as you can. Cast spells as if you had no time at all—cast as **quickly** as possible.
   - Space: Cast spells with laser beam accuracy—send them **directly** out and to someone. Cast spells in a broad swath—send them **indirectly** to two or more people.
   - Flow: Cast spells with ceaseless motion—**freeing** the flow of energy. Cast spells as if your body is locked tight—**binding** the flow of energy.

   The Efforts can be explored endlessly. As with any discipline, a full and thorough study of the work is necessary to master the concepts and skills. This is merely an introduction into some of the aspects of Laban's work.

4. Fundamental actions

   Just as you have action preferences (as explored earlier) characters will have action preferences. Of all the above-mentioned explorations of character, action preferences are the most succinct and simplest to enact. Choose each in turn and apply the action using some text. You will discover the action that seems to align with the text most effectively.

5. Put it all together

   For example, push in a light, direct way, bulging and leading with your hips, initiating movement from your core.

Inner Dynamics (**T**).   One of the central challenges of contemporary characters is embodying internal conflict. Many characters in modern and contemporary plays want one thing, but hide their desire. The inner dynamic is the source of energy for many characters. The conflict between what is desired and what is allowable creates an inner dynamic upon which you may draw to enliven your portrayal. The "body level" work of Laban Movement provides a clear mechanism for creating this inner dynamic.

1. Choose one body level orientation—lengthen, shorten, widen, narrow, bulge, or hollow—and take a walk.
2. Choose the opposite orientation of what you just chose and take a walk.
3. Go back to your first choice, then mask or cover that choice with its opposite. For example, if you choose shorten, cover that with a feeling of length-

ening, but don't lose the feeling of shortening altogether. Take a walk. Speak a text. Interact with a partner. If you feel overly tense, then shake it off and begin again.

Ki *Points.* If you have embodied the choices effectively, you probably felt a pull or tug within your core. Try to maintain flow and ease throughout the rest of your body—don't tighten and tense up. It takes a great deal of energy to maintain this inner dynamic and that energy is a good source for your acting.

In the play, *Angels in America,* the character Joe is struggling with his Mormon faith and his secret homosexuality. In the scenes with his wife, Harper, his true nature might manifest itself in a hollowing—a movement away from her. He might cover this hollowing with a lengthening—keeping up a brave front. The energy generated by these counter moves will be the sign an audience could interpret as Joe's secret desire. However, without such an inner dynamic, the energy will not be consonant with the intrinsic nature of the character and the audience will not believe the playing.

The energy it takes to mask the true intent of the character in fact reveals it. Of course, people mask their true feelings in life all the time and usually we know that they are masking something. In psychological realism, we usually want to create a sense in the audience that a burst of energy comes from somewhere. Otherwise, they will stop watching the play and say, "Where did *that* come from?" Inner dynamics generate the energy necessary to arrive at outbursts of feeling by doing rather than showing.

Character

Nobody, no matter how "right" for a part, aligns perfectly with a character (see Text Box—**What's Your Line?**). For one thing, it is impossible to know perfectly what the intrinsic nature of the character is. One can only discern in a general way and then create the greater specificity necessary for an effective evocation of the character. Therefore, analysis is a practical and necessary aspect of the actor's work.

What's Your Line?

In earlier times, actors took on what were called "lines of business"—leading man, leading lady, ingénue, comic, etc. Old movie musicals are filled with these types. They are descendants of the melodramas of the nineteenth century, which in turn are descended from earlier work all the way down to even before plays were written down. Contemporary theater still employs types or lines of business, but they tend to be more specific and less general than the old ones.

The fundamental question you must ask is "What is the change from me to the character?"

1. Nature of the energy. You must discern the general nature of the intrinsic energy of the character. There are two ways to get at this (besides reading the text, of course).
   a. What is the foundation of the character? That is, from what type is the character derived? Look to commedia, or myths and archetypes for clues.
   b. How did others play it? If the play is not an original, find out what choices other actors made.[7] If the play is original, ask the author.
2. Analysis of the Energy. The actor must make choices regarding the pathways and patterns of energy, including physical, vocal, imaginative, emotional pathways, action patterns (that is, preferences to push, pull, hold, or release), and how energy is generated, exchanged (assimilated, emitted), and transformed.

Type Casting Part I (F)

1. As a group, watch a specific set of programs, including the commercials, on television for a week. Keep a detailed log of the various types you see.
2. As a group, create a list of the types you saw. Break the characters down any way the group decides—tough mom, goofy dad, obnoxious brat, cute boy/girl, geek, etc.—it doesn't matter.
3. Make your own list of your fellow actors and match them to the various roles in the programs/commercials and identify each actor as one of the designated types the group came up with.
4. Cast yourself in the programs/commercials and identify your type.
5. Exchange your lists with your classmates and see how they've cast you.
   ■ Discuss the similarities and differences between what you and your fellow actors thought about each other. Note any consensus or dissension. What does this tell you about what you project and what you "sell?"

A type is simply a very basic character—that is, recognizable patterns and pathways of energy. Over time, these patterns have been given different names, depending upon the historical/social/political milieu. But these character patterns are evident in many (if not all) cultures and times. Artists employ these patterns all the time, recreating and reimagining them for their own uses. Types function as signs for an audience, creating expectation, anticipation and suspense regarding what will happen. There are numerous sources for you to research regarding a character type (*Commedia dell'Arte*, Kabuki and Noh theater, contemporary movies, to name a few), but a convenient way to map types, and therefore to help you locate yours, is using our mandala with four points: Hero, Villain, Lover, and Clown (see Figure 11.1).[8]

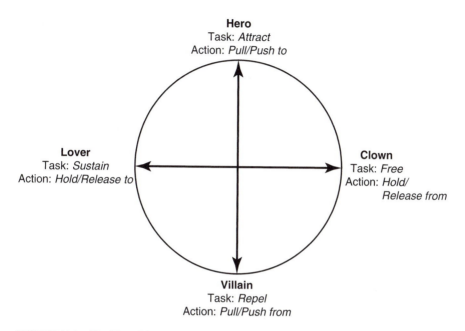

FIGURE 11.1   The Type Mandala.

The Hero represents constructive, creative energy. The Villain represents destructive, chaotic energy. The Lover represents connective energy and the Clown represents disruptive energy. As you may guess, these types correspond to the four basic tasks. The Hero's task is to attract—bring forth an answer, unite the troops, build a city, save the day. The Hero's fundamental actions (how the Hero accomplishes the task) are to *pull/push **to***. The Villain's task is to repel—to drive apart an alliance, to break the peace, to destroy the world! His/her fundamental actions are to *push/pull **from***. The Lover's task is to sustain—to keep love and hope alive, to heal wounds, to maintain the peace, and urge others to "let go." His/her fundamental actions are to *hold/release **to***. The Clown's task is to free and keep at bay—dispel tensions, burst bubbles, escape the rules; his/her fundamental actions are to *release/hold **from***. Most types can be boiled down to one of these four essences and certainly down to some combination or other of two, three or even all four (although a combination of all four would be more like a full human being rather than a limited type).

Type Casting Part II (F)

1. Return to your list and see if you can boil down the types the group created to one of the four or some combination of two or more.

2. Now return to your perception of yourself and your peer's perception of you. Which of the four or combination seems to fit you? Discuss each of your types as a group and note what conclusions you reach.

The following is one way to discover the pathways and patterns of energy inherent in a character. There are as many ways to examine character as there are characters. Analysis is an entry point—a way in to the pathways and patterns.

Character Analysis

As in all analyses, the place to start is the text, so any ideas you have about the character should be supported by evidence you find in the text. On the other hand, sometimes you have to use your imagination and just make things up!

1. What is the character's type?
   a. Define type—hero, villain, lover, clown, father, mother, etc. and find a historical/literary/mythological/theatrical antecedent. For example, a mythic hero is Hercules, a historical villain is Caligula, a literary lover is Anna Karenina, and a theatrical clown is Touchstone.
   b. Specify characteristics
      i. What is said by the character and how
      ii. What is said about character by others
      iii. What is said about the character by the playwright
2. What is the character's function?
   a. What does the character actually do?
   b. What is the *essential* task and action?
3. What approach will you take in creating the character? What are the major challenges and the major opportunities?
   a. Vocal choices (See Chapter Five)
   b. Physical choices (See Chapter Four and this chapter)
   c. Action Preferences

We began this chapter with a strong statement that you are not the character and cannot become the character. But, in another sense, you *are* the character. When you are playing a part, the character is you. You are playing the actions, performing the behaviors, and giving life to the words—no one else is. There is no character without you. Characters are finite—and you are not. There is a description of what Hamlet does and says, but no matter how wonderful that description may be, it is finally only some words on a page. You, by your very existence, are more than Hamlet ever will be. There is no Hamlet until it is played, and when the curtain comes down, he ceases to exist. But after you go on, you go on. You are real, Hamlet is imaginary. This is a useful thing to keep in mind when playing such a notoriously difficult and challenging part such as Hamlet or Rosalind, or even Sandra Dee.

N O T E S

1. There is some recent evidence that the hemispheres in the brain are somewhat independent. Some discoveries are also being made in examining patients with so-called multiple personalities, which indicate significant neuro-chemical changes in each "personality." On the other hand, there is no documentation of shape-shifting accompanying shifts in personality!

2. Richard Schechner. *Performance Theory.* (New York: Routledge, 1988), 75.

3. Constantin Stanislavski. *An Actor Prepares.* Elizabeth Hapgood, Tr. (New York: Theatre Arts Books, 1936), 15.

4. Bruder, Cohn, et al. *A Practical Handbook for the Actor.* (New York: Vintage Books, 1986), 74.

5. There is serious argument about whether the emotions in a work of art (in this case a playtext) are consonant with the emotions of the artist. This energy *may* or *may not* reveal something about the artist—but that is not relevant.

6. Note that each plane has a secondary plane affinity, that is, there is a tendency to cycle through planes—horizontal falls into the vertical, the vertical falls into the sagittal, the sagittal falls into the horizontal. A single plane is inherently unstable and thus placing your energy in one you will feel a pull to the secondary plane. The energy required to maintain balance in an unstable position is great and becomes a terrific source of acting energy. Characters also tend to be inherently unstable, and try to maintain a precarious balance. For example, Oedipus' desire for power might manifest itself in placing his energy beneath him—so he's standing on the table of his energy. From this position Oedipus "falls."

7. Some actors feel that knowing about or seeing the work of another actor in the same part will somehow negatively affect the performance. However, especially at the beginning of your study, it is probably a good idea to see and use whatever you find compelling. Artists build upon the work of other artists.

8. This mandala is suggested by Northrup Frye in his *Anatomy of Criticism* as well as by the work of Claude Levi-Strauss, Joseph Campbell, and many others.

12 Playing the Field

"A stage setting has no independent life of its own. Its emphasis is directed toward the performance. In the absence of the actor it does not exist."

—Robert Edmond Jones, *The Dramatic Imagination*

In this chapter we will:

- Examine the fundamentals of the playing space
- Propose guidelines for moving on stage
- Discuss the proscenium stage and how to play in it
- Explore playing with light, sound, and costume

"Cheat front! Find your light! Hit your mark! Hands out of your pockets! Don't fidget! Louder! Faster! Funnier!" Perhaps you've heard these words yelled from the back of the auditorium. You may wonder what happened to the caring, nurturing theater teacher you loved in class. You may be confused. I'm doing all the acting things I've learned in class (you tell yourself)—attending to my partner, playing strong actions guided by clear tasks and shaped by the imaginary circumstances. What gives?

The fact is, no matter how wonderfully you are working, if it isn't "getting across the footlights" it won't play. By this point, if you have attended to the process and are doing all the things you need to do (or most anyway), stage technique will take care of itself. However, there are some useful things to know when playing on stage. Now that we are reaching the point where you will likely be working on a scene for possible presentation in front of people, it seems an appropriate time to turn our attention to how to play on stage. But, as we have done throughout the book, we are going to dig a bit deeper than is typical. The more rich and thorough your understanding of stage technique and its necessity in playing, the more effective your playing will be.

Stage Technique

Like all games, theater is played on a field. The field delineates actual and imaginary boundaries and does much to determine how the game is played. Essentially, the field of play shapes relationships and behavior of all participants: actor and audience, support staff (backstage crew, house management) and actor, staff and audience. The effectiveness of any performance is largely determined by the clarity of these relationships and the quality of the behavior of each participant. Like all elements of theater, the field supports certain tasks, and asserts specific energy—push, pull, hold, and release—that engenders change.

Architecture is the art of shaping human interactions in space.[1] Effective architecture typically enhances the activity for which the space was designed—form follows function.[2] There are always three functions occurring simultaneously in performance—1) living functions, 2) social functions, and 3) imaginary functions. The living functions refer to bodily activities. A performance space *usually* includes enough air for everyone to breathe, a place to sit, restrooms, drinking fountains—those things required for the safety and comfort of the audience and the workers (actors, crew, staff, etc.). The social functions refer to those specific activities the space is designed to support. A traditional proscenium theater usually includes an auditorium, a stage, dressing rooms, and space for scenery, among other things. The imaginary function refers to the inner or psychological aspects that the space is designed to support. An effective theater space supports the play of imagination of both the actors and the audience. This is the most crucial aspect of the space and the area of which you need to be most aware.

Four Questions for the Space

1. What are the primary relationships supported by the space?
2. What are the primary functions (tasks and actions) supported by the space?
3. What are the opportunities created by the space?
4. What are the obstacles created by the space?

1. The primary spatial relationships to be considered are actor-audience, actor-actor, actor-crew, and actor-object. How does where you are on stage relative to someone else tell us something about the relationship? How does where someone is on stage relative to an object tell us something about the play, character, etc?

2. Some spaces feel free, others constricted. Some spaces have a wide expanse; others have a great deal of depth. What can you do in the space? What behaviors feel inhibited? What conventions of staging (proscenium, thrust, arena, or environmental) must you follow (see Text Box—**Hit Your Mark**)? How does the space support your basic tasks and actions? What can you do in the space to support your tasks and actions?

Hit Your Mark

Finding your light and hitting your mark are expressions of energy enhancing spatial opportunities. The skilled actor has learned how to find the light and hit the mark and has a knack for finding the audience or camera. Find your light by glancing up into the lighting instrument and finding the "ring" of light in the center of the lamp. Hitting your mark simply means going exactly to the place where the light is focused—be it on stage or on camera. The mark is usually just a bit of tape on the floor and your job is to stop at the tape without looking down at your feet.

---

3. Like a hitter's alley in a baseball field, each space has areas that add to playing energy. Where are the hot spots? What architecture (levels, walls, etc.) can you exploit to enhance your playing?

4. Every space presents impediments, hindrances to playing energy. What kind of access to quick changes, access to stage areas, access to audience exists? Awareness of areas to avoid (if possible) is just as important as knowing where the sweet spot is.

The Impulse to Move

In Chapter Four we discussed developing a vocabulary of movement from which the actor may draw in creating a performance. Working on the body nurtures the impulse to move as well as developing a fluency in movement. All movement must be imbued with energy in order to be effective. In real life we rarely move with clear purpose. In fact, we move a lot less in real life than on stage. In heated discussions, most people don't cross meaningfully to the window and look longingly across the fields toward Moscow, for example. This would be unnatural. But in the theater, of course, it makes complete sense. You must nurture the impulse to move and allow it expression.

The basis of all movement, like all behavior, is to create or maintain balance. Recall from the Feelings Pyramid (Chapter Seven), at the base is our urges and drives—the origin of the impulse to move. The two fundamental urges are approach and withdraw, but the net effect of either move is to get to a better place. Therefore, all movement is toward *positive change*. If balance is achieved or already exists, there is no further urge or impulse to move—you stay where you are. Any movement on stage has the same two options—go or stay—move toward positive change or maintain your ground.

In the dominant form of theater it is necessary for movement to appear as if it arises out of character need—or, a *motivation* (see Text Box—**What's My Motivation?**). The two key questions you must ask of any movement you make are: Why this? Why now? The key to moving in the field of play is awareness. You must be responsible for every act, every movement, and every utterance you make. Without awareness of the demands of the field, your playing will be less focused and effective. Imagine playing baseball without understanding the difference between a fair and foul ball or knowing the rules of running in the baselines. The game falls apart without adherence to the rules. The same is true of playing in theater.

> The challenges of moving on stage are to allow the impulse to move to occur, and direct that impulse in such a way so it reveals the action of the play.

Seven Guidelines for Playing the Field

The effective actor is the master of the space, not its victim. There are a number of useful guidelines for playing the field. But, as always, guidelines are most useful when the limitations they propose free your playing.

1. Know where the focus is. Your energy must support the moment. If it's your moment, take stage. If it is someone else's moment, give focus by adjusting your body and energy toward the focus. If you know where the focus is you will never upstage yourself or others. (Upstaging means to take focus inappropriately, either through your position on stage or by your behavior.)
2. Know your function.
   - If you are the focus, keep in the open—don't hide behind scenery or other actors.
   - If you are part of a group, make a group (triangles and other odd sided shapes are useful configurations).
   - If you are part of a group, create levels.
   - If you are working with a partner, delay contact—keep away from them as much as possible, until you *must* move toward them.

"What's My Motivation?"

There is the legend of an actor who, when asked to make a specific movement, stops rehearsal and asks the director, "But what's my motivation?" The director then angrily replies, "Your paycheck!" or "So the audience can see you!" The actor's question is a good one—it's just misdirected. It is the actor's job to fill movement with meaning, purpose, and energy. You must ask yourself, "How do I get there from here?" If you are not sure, then simply make the move and see if the motivation for it reveals itself. If you are still unsure, then you might say, "I'm having trouble filling this move; can you help me find a stronger action to get me where I need to go?" Most directors will do their best to help you. But if they do not, simply choose a strong action and play it fully. In this way, the director has something to respond to and will almost certainly tell you whether or not your choice is effective.

- Adjust and change. Theater is about change. Audiences like change and variety.

3. Move smart. When is it the perfect time to make a move—crossing the stage, sitting, standing, etc.? What impact do you wish to make in that moment? Is it organic or is it calculated? Some moves are stronger than others. Movement towards something or someone tends to be stronger than movement away (this includes moving toward or away from the audience). If you understand the value of a moment, you will move smart. Sometimes the move is *not* to move. Lee Strasberg used to say, "Just don't do something—stand there!"

4. Share. Can you share yourself with the audience as well as your scene partner? How you give yourself to your partner or the audience changes with each theater configuration (proscenium, thrust, arena, alley, etc.).

5. Gesture smart. The world of the play will guide you in the size, scope, and meaning of your gestures. Gestures are signs and the signs you make must be part of the world of the play, whether that world is fantastical or ordinary. Unnecessary gestures are substitutes for playing action. For example, pointing is a substitute for doing. If you're really focusing your energy into push-pull-hold-release, you won't need to point (maybe once or twice a show). The same goes for craning the neck, only more so. Craning is a substitute for focused energy and also makes the audience uncomfortable—when you strain, they strain. Relax completely and let your energy flow through you.

6. Choose wisely. Leave yourself alone (concentrate on what you're doing). Less is more. Cut 90 percent. The craft of acting is in the selection of actions, gestures, and utterances. Can you make do with one move instead of two—or better, no move at all?

7. Make an entrance, make an exit. Movement into or out of a space *always* changes the energy of a scene. How do you come into the space—alone, to another, from somewhere? What impact do you wish to have or not wish to have? How do you leave a space? What impact do you wish to have or not wish to have?

Everything that happens on stage is offered to the audience for contemplation and entertainment. From the smallest scratch to the largest leap of joy, every utterance and expression will mean something.

Playing the Proscenium Field

Stage techniques are tried and true methods of dealing with typical staging problems, primarily on the proscenium stage.[3] The proscenium stage is being used less and less by many theater organizations, but is still the primary field of play on Broadway and many theaters throughout the country.[4] The proscenium stage became the de facto playing configuration due to a number of historical, political, and practical factors. It is important to have a basic understanding of these factors because if you understand the values behind the configuration of the proscenium stage, you will be able to play more effectively.

In Europe up until about the seventeenth century, scenic art was limited to an occasional backdrop or simple scenic element that indicated different locales. The Greeks employed three-sided panels called **periaktoi,** on which scenes were painted and rotated to indicate a change of locale. In the Elizabethan theater, elements such as banners or wooden thrones would signal location to the audience. Primarily, however, characters would announce their location ("Verona, for a while I take leave, /To see my friends in Padua . . ." *The Taming of the Shrew* I-ii). The structure of a theater was **formal,** that is, the form followed the function—the presentation of performances. Actors, and to some degree costumes, were the means by which the performance was delivered. But when theaters moved indoors, the possibilities for scenery greatly increased. In fifteenth century Italy, painters discovered the principles of perspective. This basically involved creating a vanishing point in a painting, towards which the lines and shapes were drawn, creating the illusion of three dimensions in a two-dimensional plane. In the Italian court, artists got the clever idea of adapting perspective techniques for the theater, so that it would appear as if the actors were playing in a "real" place. Side panels, backdrops, and a frame (the proscenium arch) were all added to the playing area to facilitate and maintain the perspective. To further the illusion, the stage floor itself was angled (*raked*) so that it rose toward the back of the playing area—or up stage. The actors would play at the front of the playing area (down stage). Scenic elements were built along the perspective line so as to increase the illusion. From the audience's point of view (actually, from the point of view from the best seat in the house—the king's), houses or trees would appear realistic, even though their actual size could be quite small.[5] Actors had to avoid moving upstage, or they, too, would destroy the illusion. This forced all playing down and in front of the audience. In order for audiences to get the best perspective, they were crowded together and moved away from the playing area. This in turn, led to all the unnatural behaviors demanded by the proscenium—cheating front, turning toward your upstage shoulder, pivoting, counter crossing, stage whispering, and on and on. This was an exciting novelty for the audience (remember, at the time three-dimensional representation was quite new—not unlike computer animated graphics in films today—and quite astounding). But this change was not very good for actors. The movement of theater indoors was of huge significance and profoundly changed the nature of playing. It was the beginning of the dislocation of actors from center stage, who were replaced as the central artist in the theater by playwrights, designers, and ultimately, the director.

The important thing to understand is the displacement of the actor caused by the proscenium stage. Performances went from being heard to being seen. Actors, who once worked on the imaginary forces of the audience using only their voices and bodies, now were part of the scenery. Where once there was an intimate connection between performer and audience, now a gulf had literally opened up between them. Once on the road to representation, audiences demanded greater and greater verisimilitude. This has led to such extremes as chandeliers and helicopters dropping from the flies or famous actors making an entrance as they strangle a wolf.[6] In order for the illusion of three dimensions to be sustained, the actor actually has to limit his own dimensionality, so he becomes just part of the scenery. One may argue the merits of this change, but the dominant stage configuration is the proscenium, like it or not. So, the skilled player must be able to traverse the field of play with a solid understanding of the rules of movement the space requires and his relative place in it.

The illustration of the proscenium stage areas (see Figure 12.1) provides a map of where you *can* go. And it is from these areas that most blocking notation is derived. Blocking notation is simply a shorthand way of describing a particular basic movement from one place to another on a proscenium stage.

Blocking Notation

X = cross
D = downstage
C = center
U = upstage
R = right
L = left
XDC = cross down center

(Any abbreviation will do for furniture or characters—chair might be "ch.";
Petruchio might be "P." The only "rule" is to be able to write it quickly and in a form that will actually mean something to you!)

Planes

In addition to the basic areas, the proscenium playing area can also be seen as a series of horizontal planes from down to upstage. The width of these planes is often determined by the scenic demands, but typically a plane is about three to four feet wide. Thus, a stage with a depth of 30 feet could be divided into 7–10 planes. In addition, there is often side masking (called legs or wings) that divides the stage into fewer and larger units. In musical theater, for example, playing in front of scene curtain (often on the forestage or apron) is called "playing in one." This allows for a scene to happen while scenery is being changed behind the curtain. With advances in stage technology, this device is less common than it once was. However, the language is still employed and the skilled player needs to be aware of it.

It is important to understand what plane you are in relative to your fellow actor in order to keep open and not upstage yourself or your partner. Playing in the same plane avoids upstaging problems, but it does force your body front to keep your playing out to the audience (see Figure 12.2).

Crosses

Movement in the playing field usually entails traveling in a direct line from one place to another—or a cross. Crosses are usually along a diagonal (although not always). Since everything that happens on stage means something, a cross usually

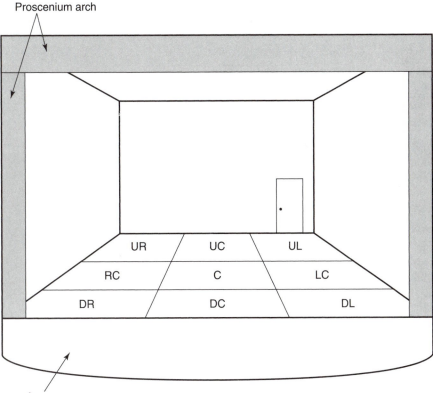

FIGURE 12.1   **Areas of the Proscenium Stage.**

means quite a lot. We don't cross often in real life but, as stated above, on stage it is not only useful, but also necessary.

There are three major kinds of crosses every actor should know (see Figures 12.3 and 12.4): The direct cross, the counter cross and the curved cross. Each has a different function and is, of course, variable in time and distance. Each subtle nuance you employ in a cross will reveal the action of the play slightly differently.

- The direct cross is obviously a movement directly from one place to another. The movement implies, but is not limited to mean, a direct intent—for example, confronting (if the move is to someone) or avoiding (away from someone).
- The curved cross is a movement that describes an arc of varying curvature from one point to another. This movement implies, but is not limited to mean, an indirect intent—for example, worming in (if the movement is toward someone) or dodging (if the movement is away from someone).
- The counter cross is a parallel movement, performed in opposition to a cross by another actor, usually your scene partner. The movement is primarily a

FIGURE 12.2 Playing in Planes.

simple way to stay in the clear and balance the stage. The counter may be as small as a pivot that gets you out of the way of the actor making the cross, or it can be several steps and a pivot. This is something almost purely of the stage and therefore highly artificial. But it is a very useful technique and the skilled player should use it almost automatically. Although the movement is primarily functional, the skilled player will fill it with intention, for example, "keeping up" or "staying even" or "getting out of the way."

Body Positions

Almost everyone knows what a profile is—a flat side view of a face or body. Profile is a common body position on stage, and one you want to employ judiciously. Body positions signal to the audience a *level of involvement*. Each position and each shift from one position to another connotes a change in relationship, with the audience and your scene partner (see Figure 12.3).

- Full front. Facing the audience directly. This is a very open and direct position. If the play allows for direct address to the audience, you will often use full front. If you are not playing to and with the audience, but to an imaginary

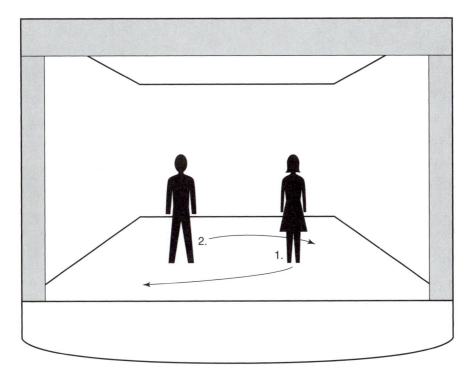

FIGURE 12.3   The Counter Cross.

person or thing (an environment or some imagined scenic element such as a wall or mirror or window), this is a very vulnerable and revealing position. It is very difficult to hide in this position and because of the direct relationship it asserts with the audience, it must be used with care and awareness.

- One-quarter right/left. Facing toward the audience, but at a 45 degree angle, either to the left or right. This is an oft-used position because it allows for two actors to share the space, keep open, and appear as if they are relating to one another. It is artificial (because usually we face people directly), but it also allows you to avoid direct contact with both the audience and your acting partner. This is actually quite freeing. You are then able to allow the free play of feelings to be manifest in your body (and face) without having to mask them from your scene partner or reveal them fully to the audience. It lets the audience in without asking them to participate or confront you.

- Profile. One-half of the body, either left or right. Profile away from your scene partner allows you to completely hide your intent/feelings from your partner, while giving the audience at least a glimpse of what's going on. Profile facing your partner is a direct confrontation—you are literally face-to-face. This is a very strong (and favored) position for the actors, but it actually hides half the playing from the audience. You want to employ the profile with great awareness

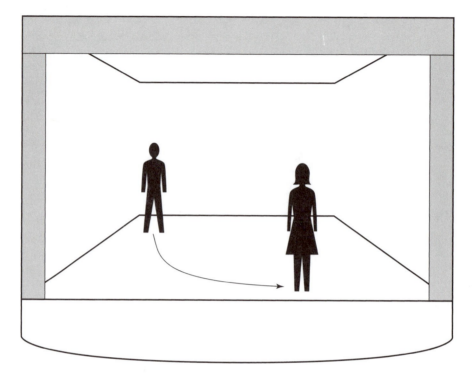

FIGURE 12.4   The Curved Cross.

of your intent—either to confront or hide. A good guide for using profile is to use it at the last minute and get out of it as quickly as you can.

■ Three-quarters right/left. The body is facing mostly upstage, away from the audience. This is used primarily to hide you in plain sight. The signal to the audience is usually read as "this person is not important right now." In the classic detective-type plays, a character who is about to reveal some secret will often steal up to some corner of the stage, three-quarter position, only to turn strongly to the one-quarter or full front to make the big revelation. It also is a useful position to mask any technical business, such as retrieving a property (such as a notebook, pencil, or phone) or adjusting a costume. As a hiding position, it is a useful one to take when you are not the main focus of the scene and you want to draw as little attention to yourself as possible.

■ Full back. The back is fully given to the audience. There is an old "rule" never to turn your back on stage. As with all rules, this one is meant to be broken, but it is useful to examine why this "rule" came about. As with full front, full back is a direct relationship to the audience—one of **denial.** The signal sent to the audience is that you are actively cutting yourself off from the audience or scene. It is a very strong position and draws focus. Used judiciously, it can be very effective, especially when you shift into or out of the full back position. However, it is also a vulnerable position. You can't see what's going on, yet you can feel the eyes on you. It takes confidence as well as full involvement of your body when playing in this position. Your primary means of expression—the face and voice—are negated by this position. You must allow your action to be revealed in your posture and in the very muscles and bones of your back. This is not easy to do without forcing, so it is wise to get in and out of this position as quickly as possible, and when you are in it, to increase the energy of your playing. When you do turn, it can be a powerful and revealing movement.

The following exercises allow you to play around with all the information above.

Should I Stay or Should I Go? (T, E)

1. With a partner, come up with a *What* that requires a decision to stay or go. For example, deciding whether or not to approach someone you are attracted to.
2. Begin with choosing to go. As you begin to walk away, your partner simply says, "Are you sure?"
3. Stop. Your partner says, "Are you sure?"
4. Consider and go. Continue three or four goings and stayings, then switch. Other examples might be deciding whether or not to go to somewhere (class, a concert, movie), or to get something (food, jewelry, electronics), or to avoid someone (an ex-, a creditor, an enemy). You may improvise any dialogue, but come up with a key phrase, such as "Are you sure?" to cue you to move or stop.

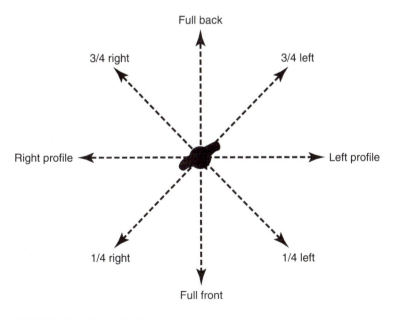

FIGURE 12.5 **Body Positions.**

Hocus Focus (**F, T, E**). Refer back to the *Like You/Loathe* game (page 78). Play it again, but this time your teacher/coach will call upon you or one of your fellow players to take focus. When it is your turn, turn it on. When your turn is over, give over.

Weave II (**F, T, E**). Play *The Weave* (page 34), but this time on a proscenium stage (or in a similar orientation in your classroom).

1. The entire class should play simultaneously.
2. Your teacher/coach will call "Go!" and everyone will a) move into small groups of three or four; b) within each group choose high, medium, or low levels; c) find the audience.
3. The teacher/coach then calls out a player's name and a stage area. The player called moves to the designated spot on stage while the ensemble shifts their orientations to give focus to the player.
4. The player then speaks a prepared text, sings a line or two of a song, does a dance, improvises, or otherwise has "a moment" in the spotlight.

Enter! (**F, T, E**)

1. Choose an entrance line from a play, or make one up (a sample of entrance lines are in the Appendix).
2. Using what material you have on hand, create a threshold of some sort (a doorframe, a curtain, two chairs, or even the door to the classroom, if necessary, will do).
3. Choose a "Who," "Where," "What," as well as *where you are coming from* (including the imaginary place, event, and/or condition).
4. Enter the playing space and speak the text.

Take stage and announce your presence! An entrance has to make space for itself and your fellow players must accommodate and adjust to the new conditions.

This exercise ought to be played quickly, so there should always be someone "on deck" for the next entrance.

Variation. In groups of three or four, come up with Who, Where, and What. Two or three of the group are to be in the playing space, while one of you makes the entrance. Adjust to the entrance physically as well as imaginatively. Shift your position in the space and orientation to the audience to accommodate the new player.

Exeunt! (**F, T, E**)

1. Choose an exit line from a play, or make one up (a sample of exit lines are in the appendix).
2. Identify a boundary that is "off stage."
3. Choose a "Who," "Where," "What," as well as *where you are going to* (including the imaginary place, event, and/or condition).

4. Begin *in* the playing space, speak the text, and leave the playing space.

Often, you will find it necessary to use the text to get near the exit and leave the space at the last possible moment. An exit marks a significant change—leaving a void that must be filled by the other players.

Variation.   As in *Enter!,* in groups of three or four, populate the space, choosing Who, What, and Where. One actor exits (using some text), while the remaining players adjust their positions in space and orientations to the audience.

Any changes that occur when you enter or leave a space are derived from both the imaginary and actual theatrical conditions. You must actually adjust to the reduction or enlargement of space created by exits and entrances. You must also adjust to the change in imaginary circumstances—guided by your relationship to the "character" that has come in or has left the space.

***Composition Improvs* (G, F, E).**   Although primarily a directing exercise, this is very useful for learning how every gesture on stage creates meaning.

1. Draw a composition (either perspective or overhead view) of three people in some kind of basic spatial relationship using levels, body positions, and even facial expressions. Be specific. Include one move for each person using stage terminology.
2. Using blocking terminology, place actors in the desired positions/postures on stage.
3. Allow the class to identify the following:
   a. the primary focus. This is typically the apex of the triangle, but not always. Different levels, different orientations will affect where the primary focus is.
   b. the secondary foci. Usually, there is one other person or couple to whom the eye will travel.
   c. the primary and secondary couples (if there are any). Audiences tend to group things together—what relationships do you see in the composition?
      Basically, this is an analysis of the flow of energy in space. Audiences tend to see how they read—left to right in most Western countries, right to left in some Middle Eastern countries, up and down in some Asian countries. The eye will go to where it habitually goes to begin reading. So, for example, a person upstage right (audience left) will draw the eye first. The eye then will travel along the imaginary lines established by the primary and secondary foci and relationships.
4. Let the class make up a story—a Who, What, and Where based on the composition. Clarify relationships by making any adjustments necessary (experiment with shifts in body orientation, redirecting the head and eyes, altering levels, etc.)
5. Once the imaginary circumstances are established, allow the actors to improvise the scene.

This exercise immediately and clearly reveals the power of subtle alterations in spatial relationships, and the importance of understanding your place in the space.

Costumes, Lights, and Sound

In addition to the field of play, there are at least three other technical elements that shape your actions, tasks, and relationships. How you and others dress, how you and the space are illuminated, and the aural environment all have a major impact on your playing. You must ask the same questions about each of these elements as you do for the space.

1. What are the primary relationships supported by the costumes/lights/sound?
2. What are the primary functions (tasks and actions) supported by costumes/lights/sound?
3. What are the opportunities created by the costumes/lights/sound?
4. What are the obstacles created by the costumes/lights/sound?

Costume

Dressing for success is a major collaboration between the designer, director, and the actor. On your very person the three worlds of the theater intersect. First, it is really *you* in costume—how it fits (or doesn't fit), how the colors work with or against your coloring, the behavior the clothes release or inhibit—in the world at large. Clothes assert specific energy upon the wearer—do they push, pull, hold, and/or release? Do they attract, repel, sustain, or free? In what way and under what circumstances? Within the world of the theater the costumes are major signs telling the audience about the nature of the play they are seeing. Also, as they are designed for the stage, they are made differently than everyday clothes—sometimes sturdier and sometimes more expediently. A costume must last as long as possible (depending on the run, whether it will be stored later or rented out, for example). But it is made for the audience's pleasure, not the actor's. If the audience will only see the outside of a coat, there is no need to labor unnecessarily on the lining inside. Finally, the costume is part of the world of the play and signals aspects of character, time, and place. You must understand all aspects of how costumes function in order to effectively play in costume.

Costume Parade (**T**).   Watch people go by and characterize them by their clothes. How do you dress—for what role? What messages does your clothing send?

1. Assemble any outfit before class and assess the message. Play a few lines of a speech and see how the costume affects your behavior.
2. Parade around the space and let the class deconstruct you. Play the speech again. How was your behavior altered?

3. Alter the costume in some way (un/tuck shirt, take off shoes, etc.) and discuss how the message is altered, how behavior is altered.
4. On subsequent classes, come dressed as other "selves" or other people you know. After deconstruction, make alterations. Try different speeches, including period speeches that seem opposed to the costume.

Light

The effect lighting has on your playing is more difficult for you to assess because only someone outside the playing area can really see how the lights are functioning. You can see (to a lesser degree than the audience) how light affects your playing partners, but the best you can do for yourself is to know 1) when you are in the light, 2) what part of your body is being illuminated, and (to some extent) 3) the *kind* of light you are in.

Light is energy. The light you encounter in playing gives you something as surely as your scene partner. It casts a spell on both you and the audience. Allow yourself to be changed by the light and let it fuel your playing.

You absolutely must know if you are illuminated or not, and whether you should be illuminated. An actor who cannot be seen when necessary or is seen when not necessary is most distracting to an audience. Like a ballplayer being out of position, it looks like you don't know what you're doing. Following is an exercise designed to help you adjust to changing lighting conditions.

You also must adjust your playing to the **frame** created by the light. If only your face is illuminated in a tight spot, then your face must carry the burden of the moment. If the light illuminates half of your body, play within the space delineated. Although the light may inhibit your playing, it also presents an opportunity. There are few greater thrills for actor or audience when the opportunity arises to turn into a light meant only for you at a critical moment in the play.

Finally, you must also adjust to any special lighting effects, such as color or projections. How you play in an amber light will be different than how you play in a blood red light. Your body is also a potential screen upon which images may be projected, whether it may be the simple shadows cast by a gobo (a filter that creates shadow effects in a variety of shapes) or an actual film. Video projections, computer animation, and holograms are all available to the lighting designer. Your job is to facilitate the functioning of these effects.

Finding the Light (T). Using a simple lighting instrument (or even a strong flashlight), focus the light on the face or upper body of one of the actors in a basic Who, What, Where improvisation. The light operator should move the light from actor to actor and then away from both of them.

1. When the light is on you, take focus.
2. When the light is on your partner, give focus.

3. When the light moves, find it and try to stay in it, all the while maintaining the improv.

Sound

The aural environment—underscoring, sound effects (telephones, door buzzers), and the naturally occurring sounds of the world—all have a major impact on your playing. Sound is energy. You must allow your playing to be changed by the sound. But the change must be dictated by the world from which the sound arises. The world at large brings in many sounds, most of them unwelcome and distracting. Airplanes overhead, sirens screaming, rain beating on the roof, cell phones ringing in the audience, CB radio chat broadcast over the house speakers—all these and more may occur during a performance. What can you do? It depends upon the nature of the intrusion on the world of the play. Sometimes the sounds may be ignored, as long as you can still be heard. Sometimes you must wait until the sound abates, but maintain your alignment with the world of the play. Sometimes the sound destroys the illusion of the play so thoroughly there is nothing for it but to acknowledge the intrusion, smile with the audience and get on with it. If you understand the nature of the play and the relationship with the audience, you will feel what adjustment you must make. Panic, fear, and indecision will hinder your effectiveness. Experience is the best teacher, but if you trust yourself and the audience you will know what to do.

Sounds within the world of the theater demand a more subtle adjustment. Although you hear the underscoring in a scene, the character does not. Yet, you must allow yourself to be altered and play with the underscoring (whether it is musical or a special imaginary sound effect). Often you will be required to time your behavior to the length of the sound. Like any limitation, initially this may be challenging, but in the end, if you have adjusted well (and the sound is effective), your playing will be enhanced. The key is to blend with the sound—is it pushing, pulling, holding, or releasing you?

The character hears sounds that occur within the world of the play and you must adjust to those sounds based on how energy travels through the pathways of the character. Like all other relationships, the character will have a relationship with sound based on the value of the moment. A knock at the door, a telephone ringing, a clock striking—these sounds will impact upon the character based on the situation and the nature of the character. If you have done your analytical work and understand the action asserted upon you by the sound, you will play effectively.

Sound Effects (**T**).   Compile a collection of sound effects including various forms of music. Construct a basic Who, What, Where improvisation. The sound operator should turn the sound on and off and change volume.

1. When a sound effect occurs, *blend* with it and let the scene change.
2. Begin the scene with one underscoring of music. When the music changes, allow the scene to change as well.

There are many challenges in dealing with the technical elements of playing. But even the most skilled actors supported by the finest designers and cutting edge technology will make mistakes or find themselves in the dark, costume falling apart and the phone that is supposed to be ringing totally silent. These things happen. The skilled player handles these things in the same way as any improvisation—by blending. The skilled player adjusts to changing circumstances with grace and aplomb. This will win the goodwill of the audience and the approbation of your peers.

NOTES

1. Of course, every structure has a relationship with its environment, but only human beings are able to perceive that relationship—the tree does not notice the house, but we notice whether or not the house and tree are in a harmonious relationship. See Langer, *Feeling and Form,* for an excellent discussion of the art.

2. This famous statement is not a **rule** but an **observation.** Form does indeed follow from function, but the nature of human interactions is such that it is impossible to determine exactly what form best suits a function. That is what makes architecture an art and not a science.

3. The word proscenium is derived from the Greek **pro,** meaning before or in front of, and *skene,* meaning house. In ancient Greek amphitheaters, audience sat on steeply raked (inclined) tiered seats three-quarters around the **orchestra** (or "dancing place"). At the back of the orchestra was a house-like structure from which actors would make entrances and exits, called the **skene.**

4. Richard Schechner has some interesting things to say about the proscenium stage in *Performance Theory* (161–164), as does Marvin Carlson in *Theatre Semiotics* (41–55).

5. Elements downstage would be approximately "real" size, while objects further upstage would be smaller and smaller in order to maintain the illusion created by the perspective.

6. *Phantom of the Opera, Miss Saigon,* and the famous nineteenth-century actor Edwin Forrest.

13 You the Player, You the Artist

"In human life, art may arise from almost any activity, and once it does so, it is launched on a long road of exploration, invention, freedom to the limits of extravagance, interference to the point of frustration, finally discipline, controlling constant change and growth."

—Susanne Langer

In this chapter we will:

- Examine the rehearsal process from inception to production
- Propose an effective working relationship between actor and teacher, actor and director
- Examine the actor's relationship to the theater

As we stated in the Preface, you cannot learn acting from a book. You have to do it to learn it. You cannot fully learn to act in class—you have to play in a show. You'll have to prepare an audition—either a monologue or a "side" from the script (see Text Box—**Audition Basics**). With all you have learned, some coaching and a little luck, you may get a part. Then a new kind of fun begins! There are few things more exciting than getting a call ("You got the part!") or seeing your name next to a role on a cast list ("I got the part!"). After the anxiety and intensity of the audition process, the thrill of being selected for a role can release a great deal of energy. Whoops of joy are not uncommon (as are tears of frustration and sadness if you do *not* get a part). But, once cast, the reality of putting a show on in two, three, four, or five weeks sinks in. How will you learn all those lines? How will you put all you know into practice?

The Rehearsal Process

Soon after being cast in a show you will be given a script, and told where and when to meet the other participants in the endeavor. Hopefully, there will be a clear

Audition Basics

There are many books on auditioning, and most classes will touch upon preparing an audition. We will not reiterate that here except to provide some of the audition "lingo" and to name a few resources to aid you in preparation. In essence, however, playing an audition is the same as all acting—performing actions determined by theatrical conditions to accomplish a task. There are two types of text-based auditions—monologues and cuttings from the play itself (or "sides").

The monologue—this is a short solo piece, usually one to three minutes, usually taken from a play. In consultation with a teacher/coach, you select a piece appropriate to the play (and part) for which you are auditioning. Most actors have a number of comic and serious monologues from several genres at the ready (Shakespearean, contemporary, modern, classic, Restoration—the list can go on and on). If you sing and audition for musicals, you will also need a selection of songs (from 16 bars to entire verse and chorus) from a variety of musical forms and composers.

"Sides"—this refers to scene(s) from the play with the part for which you are auditioning. You may be asked to prepare (break down into units, choose tasks and actions) the "side" and will read with another actor or a stage manager or an audition reader. Sometimes you will have to do a "cold reading" (that is, with little or no preparation), but more often you will have a day or at least a few hours to look over the text.

Once you have performed an initial audition, you may receive a "**callback**"—an invitation to do some further auditioning. Callbacks have various forms, often determined by the nature of the play and the level of production. You may be asked to improvise. You may read with several actors so the director may see how you play and look with your potential partners. You may have several callbacks. Then you wait.

Here is a very short list of audition resources:

Audition! Michael Shurtleff. Bantam; reissue edition (January 2, 1980)

www.theatrebooks.com/actors_acting/auditioning.html is a good site for a list of books.

Backstage.com is the website of the trade journal. It often has articles on auditioning, as well as casting calls for professional (Equity and nonequity) productions.

The search for audition tips and audition monologues is endless. Your fellow players and your teacher/coach are ultimately the best resource because you can perform for them. Seek advice, use what you can, discard what you can't use, and find the fun. Sigourney Weaver said that for her, auditioning is her chance to play the part. With this attitude she is in charge of her performance. You cannot really know what the director or casting person wants. To play to what "they" want places all the power outside of your self. Place the power with you—be prepared, hit your marks, play your actions, find the fun. These are things *you* can do, and doing them, you walk out of the audition successfully, whether or not you get the part.

---

rehearsal schedule, a contact sheet of all the artistic and technical personnel, a competent stage manager to keep things running smoothly, and a skilled and nurturing director who will facilitate your playing.

The first thing you ought to do, naturally, is read the script. Earlier we discussed that it typically takes at least three full readings to begin to come at the script from the perspective of the role you are to play (whether or not this involves creating a "realistic" character or not). Often it is useful to have some place to record your impressions, thoughts, and reflections on the script—a journal or notepad (actual or electronic). This is a good place to write down the tasks you perceive you must play and the actions you might take to accomplish those tasks, the demands of the role on your actor's tools, and what special preparation you'll need to do to effectively play. It is also useful to mark important structural moments in the play, as you perceive them—units of actions, complications, obstacles, crises, climax, etc. Of course, the director will undoubtedly have done the same, and may have different thoughts on these matters—but no matter. If you have time, the more you know your script, the better. When you come to rehearsal for the first time, you're concentration will not have to be on reading words, or making choices, but more properly on learning about your fellow actors and the play of energy between you all.

In general, homework is where you make and reflect upon choices. Rehearsal is where you play. You cannot both play and reflect at the same time. That is not to say that choices will not be made in rehearsal. They will be, of course! But in rehearsal, choices are discovered in the playing. In baseball, the pitcher will select his pitches based on his understanding of the batters he will face. In the course of the game, however, he may discover that those choices are not working and he must therefore adjust his pitching. Actors come to rehearsal and performance with tasks and actions chosen and worked out. But in playing, new things occur between you and your fellow actors, audiences will be different, costumes, lights, sets all will be slightly changed from one night to the next. Your playing must adapt and adjust to those changes, if it is to be effective.

Read-throughs

Read-throughs, or table work as it is sometimes called, are often the first rehearsal activities you will encounter. The read-through is just that—you read through the play. Each director approaches readings and table work differently but, typically, the first time you read the play (with the stage manager or director reading pertinent stage directions) you will read it from beginning to end without interruption. Thereafter, you may read scene by scene or even unit by unit and stop to discuss aspects of the structure, delve into meaning, clarify unusual language, and examine the salient social/political/historical elements of the play that may be unfamiliar. Depending on the play (and time set aside for rehearsing) this can take a day or two or even a week or more. If you are prepared, the first read-through of a play is the time to immediately begin playing.

Although every director will ask for different things, the following are some *Ki* practices you may always employ in these first rehearsals.

1. Follow the *Ki* guidelines—Keep One-point, Extend *Ki,* Maintain Ground, Allow *Ki* to flow.
2. Find Actor Ready Seated—usually you will sit during the first reading and table work, but you may still play in Actor Ready. Find the optimal balanced

position you may comfortably maintain. Usually this means feet flat on the ground, about shoulder width apart, spine lengthening, and widening, free your neck, let your head rise and come forward.

3. Maintain Contact—when speaking try to give as much of the dialogue to your acting partner as possible. Get a sentence or two in your head and lift your gaze from the script to your partner. Use a pencil or your finger to help you keep track of where you are. When listening, try to give your eyes to your partner. The script isn't going anywhere, so you needn't read along. If you have done your preparation, then you will already have a good idea of when it is your turn to speak.

   This can sometimes take more time than is available, so the director may prefer that you concentrate on simply reading the words. But you will still have opportunities to make contact, and ought to take all opportunities you can.

4. Trust the process. There is a tendency in all actors to "get to the good part" whether it is a line, a scene, or performing before an audience. When you place your attention on the future it is obviously not where it ought to be—in the moment! The good part is *now*.

5. Observe and Note. As you progress through readings and table work, you may find it useful to make notes in your script (in pencil, of course) and/or in a handy journal. A hash mark (/) might indicate a change in action, a line across the page a change in task. You might write out the subtext for a line to help clarify your action, you might ask a question about the value of a moment. In your journal, you might jot down notes from the director, dramaturg, or designers about their conceptions and ideas about the play as well as your own. You can build a list of properties you'll need, information you need to find out, or resources to deepen your exploration of the role. There are always two parts of the process—doing and reflecting upon the doing. Both are required for effective playing.

A great deal of rehearsing involves discovery. As an infant discovers her abilities to move and sound, or a child discovers the wonders of a new toy, the actor needs to meet discovery with the same sense of wonder and joy as the infant or child. Rehearsal is playing, and your playing ought to be imbued with joy, wonder, and delight.

Homework

As mentioned above, homework is making choices. You reflect upon the discoveries you have made in rehearsal and prepare for the next rehearsal by choosing. This is not to be taken as instruction to play an attitude or indicate feeling. The choices you make are about the actions you *might* take. For example, in rehearsal, you may discover that *pushing* is just not helping the scene move forward. So, upon reflection, you might consciously choose to play *pull* or *hold* when next rehearsing the scene. You choose your action and see how it plays. Often, these adjustments are made in rehearsal ("Try that again, but this time *pull* instead of *push,"* a director might say). But often as not, only you will feel that a moment is not playing effectively—either because that moment is not of immediate concern to the director or that you simply didn't have time to fully explore it. Homework is essential for the play to progress effectively. You cannot wait to do everything in rehearsal.

Learning your lines is only one part of your homework. It is essential that you learn your lines, of course. But the end of any utterance in a play is to accomplish a task. **Speech is a mode of action.** Sometimes memorization by rote can lead to empty line readings, devoid of action. Upon reading a script you may almost hear the lines being said. A line that so specifically ignites your imagination is probably an indication of a good line. However, hearing how the line sounds can lead to imitating the sound you hear in your head rather than playing an action. Your speech act will not be directed at creating or maintaining balance of the character, but of *you.* The act is directed at you, so your energy will not be outer-directed or in the world of the play.

Rehearsing

Rehearsing is about discovery—of what your fellow actors are giving you, of what actions play effectively, and what tasks you must accomplish. But rehearsal is also about moving toward performance, which means mastering the material (both language and behavior), clarifying tasks, and specifying actions.

Mastery of material means having utter command of the words you say and the moves you make. You ought to know your lines so well you can speak them under almost any circumstances—standing on your head, knitting a sweater or dancing a jig! Only then, with such mastery, may you employ the words with complete freedom to accomplish the task at hand. The other material aspect of your playing involves behavior—movement, activities, blocking, and bits of business you have discovered are necessary to the play. You ought to perform all your behavior with grace and ease. When you can perform your moves uttering any text—a nursery rhyme, the Gettysburg address, or the phone book—then you have achieved mastery of movement (see Text Box—**Never Let Them See You Sweat**).

Mastery has meaning *only* if the scene is fully lived.

Peter Brook has said that he completely prepares almost every aspect of a play before he begins rehearsal, but then is prepared to throw it all out at the first rehearsal. You must have the same fearlessness. The true test of mastery is not in repeating exactly a performance each time, but rather in allowing the performance to go where it will and trusting that all the work you have done will support your free, simple, and graceful playing.

Never Let Them See You Sweat

The hallmark of effective playing, be it in theater or sport or game, is a sense of *effortlessness*. Strain, stress, "hard work" are indications of energy not effectively applied.

"Economy is the last thing you add."
Joel Friedman, professional actor and teacher

Specificity of action means finding the exact variety of push-pull-hold-release you are playing. We developed a short list at the end of Chapter Eight, but you must find the action specific to the play, moment, and role. *Push from* probably is not specific enough, for example. What kind of *push from*—a shove, nudge, punch, tweak? Rehearsal is about discovering and refining your actions. Once your action is specified, then it will finally be **determined by the theatrical conditions to accomplish a task.** That is, how it finally and exactly plays in performance is unknown until you perform, and depends upon the theatrical conditions—what energy you receive from your fellow actors, how your playing is shaped by the design elements, and the impact of the audience's attention on your playing. Your actions will **never** be static, but will inevitably and necessarily vary slightly (or sometimes even considerably) each time you perform. As you study, you may find it useful to develop your action vocabulary. There are many resources from which to derive your list, most importantly from your own work in the classroom and rehearsal. In the Appendix you will find a longer list of specific, outer-directed physical actions to play.

The specific action is the one that can accomplish the task.

Clarity of task means knowing exactly what you are attempting to accomplish. Attracting, Repelling, Maintaining, or Freeing are not clear enough. They will do for a start, but you must discover clearer tasks that will focus your energy for playing so that it aligns with the intent of the theatrical event. A list of peformable tasks appears in the Appendix, but a clear task will always be directed at creating a perceivable change (whether the task is aimed at another person or an object). Unlike actions that necessarily vary rehearsal to rehearsal, performance to performance, the task does *not* change. You still will discover the task in rehearsal (and upon reflection), but once discovered and considered to be appropriate to the playing of the play, the task is set. How you accomplish your task must and will change. The task is predetermined. However, you may (and probably will) find over the course of the run of the play (be it one, two or fifty-two weeks), that the task you have chosen may require greater clarity. You might discover in playing that a slightly different task is more effective in focusing your energy for playing. Unless the task is radically different than the one you rehearsed (and chose with the director and your fellow actors), try it and see.

The Task at Hand

1. Using an open scene or a scene from a play you are rehearsing, select a unit of action and play the unit without any clear task in mind. Simply take in, transform, and send out.
2. Play the unit again, this time choosing a basic task—attract, repel, maintain, or free. Note any differences. Solicit feedback from your fellow players and coach.
3. Play the unit again, this time clarifying the task further. As discussed in Chapter 10, the form of the task will typically be "I want X to Y." How did it play? Was it more or less effective and believable?

Ki *Point*

A basic task always involves changing or maintaining a relationship; however, tasks are rarely so straightforward and general. Often, the theatrical circumstances demand the task be clarified by certain conditions—**temporal** and **behavioral.**

4. Play the unit once again, and clarify the task even further by adding conditionals to the task. These conditionals refine the task so that they are accomplished in a certain way. For example, "I want Dad to give me the car keys *immediately.*" This is a **temporal** condition, the test of which lays in your determination of what is meant by *immediately.* Another type of conditional is **behavioral**—or the manner in which you perform the task. "I want Dad to give me the car keys *gently.*" These kinds of conditionals are judgments. Only you can judge if your task was accomplished effectively (if the keys were given *gently* or not).

> A clear task aligns your energy.

Run-throughs

When rehearsals reach a certain point, typically in the third or fourth week, you will begin to play through entire scenes or acts or the whole play without stopping. This is a run-through, and it makes demands on the players that require clarification. There is a great deal of difference between the initial run-through of a play and the final run-through, or dress rehearsal. There is a tendency to think that once run-throughs have begun, the work is over—but really it has only, finally, just begun.

Once tasks are chosen, actions specified, and material mastered, real play may begin. No longer are you working on moments or units—now you are stringing those moments together into some sort of coherent whole. At this point, you must enlarge your view of the game, as it were. While you must attend to the task at hand, live fully in the moment, and blend with the energy of your fellow players, you must now widen your attention to include the ebb and flow of energy as the play moves from beginning to end. This is often referred to by the elusive phrase *tempo/rhythm*. It is during run-throughs that actors will sometimes hear the classic "Louder, faster, funnier." What the director is saying, however inadequately, is that attention must be paid to enacting the play and that the play has a drive of its own. Sometimes the pace is steady, sometimes slow, and sometimes rapid—it depends upon the nature of the moment. If you have done your work, the tempo/rhythm will take care of itself. But your director's job is to deliver the play to the audience and you are only *part* of the play. What may feel like a crucially important moment to you (and to the character), may be less consequential to the play moving forward. On the other hand, you may be involved in a crucial moment in the play that is not at all a big deal for your character. Know *when* in the game you are, and *what* your part is at that moment. At last, however, you will arrive at the penultimate and most complicated time—technical rehearsals.

Tech

Technical run-throughs typically include adjusting lighting, working on moving scenery, integrating music/sound, and costume. The week before a play opens is exciting, but it requires maximum focus and patience from the actor. The initial technical rehearsal is often done without actors. The set, lighting, and sound design-ers concentrate on finishing touches to the scenery, creating mood through lighting, and setting volume levels (among a myriad of tasks). The director discusses options with the designers and the stage manager orchestrates all the comings and goings of scenery, the placement of "cues" for lighting changes, sound and other special effects. The next day the actors are called for "10 out of 12." This means rehearsing 10 hours out of 12—with an hour for lunch or two hours for dinner, depending upon the starting point. Often, the actors will rehearse "cue to cue"—or from one design element change to the next. Often, this will mean that the actors must begin a line or two of dialogue before the actual cue and proceed through the running of the cue. This can take a long time. However, it is also an opportunity to work with the design elements to enhance your playing. Attending to the actual theatrical circumstances offered by technical and design elements can facilitate your playing. You will get a sense of the timing of a light or scene change or a sound cue and use it to your advantage. For instance, say a spotlight is to hit you at a specific moment. As the cue is rehearsed, you may play around with when you give your eyes to the light. Since the focus of the rehearsal is on the technical elements, you can work on your techni-cal elements—timing, position, pace, to name a few. While this kind of rehearsal can be tedious for the inexperience player, the seasoned player uses it to hone and perfect choices.

Opening Night

Well, you did it. You made it to the first performance. This is an exciting time—maybe too exciting. Nerves are at the breaking point and everyone is on "red alert." The inex-perienced player will use the adrenalin rush of opening night as a way to make amends for lack of preparation and serious rehearsal. Often, inspiration, in the form of enormous energy, will lift a less than well-prepared performance to higher levels. But this is a false high and may only serve for opening night. The seasoned player understands to simply play the part as rehearsed—no more or less. Opening night is *not* the time to "jazz it up" or really act. Opening night is the time to give over to the audience, serve the audience and enact the play simply and clearly—just as you presumably have rehearsed it. And when it is done, offer yourself in gratitude to the audience for their kind attention (see **Curtain Call** on page 181 for more about the bow).

There is an old myth that second nights are a letdown. This may be true for the inexperienced player who relies on the inspiration of opening night. But the seasoned player delivers a cleaner, more economical performance each time they perform. John Basil, Artistic Director of the American Globe Theatre in New York City, once offered this advice for second nights: Dedicate your performance to someone who cannot be at the show—a loved one far away, a relative or friend who is ill, someone who has died, or to a cause about which you feel strongly. Your performance becomes an offering to that which is more important than you and the show itself. This may release tremendous joy as well as humility, and your playing that night will be a gift—as it always is.[1]

Playing Well with Others

In your study and practice of playing you will encounter several significant relationships that will have a tremendous impact on your development. Who you are as a player and artist is greatly influenced by your teacher/coach and the director. Let us examine these relationships in depth.

The Student–Teacher Relationship

If you have performed in a show or completed an acting course, you may decide you'd like to continue to learn. There are many classes and teachers out there. It is important to consider not just what you'd like to study, but with whom. The relationship to your teacher is a critical part of your development as a player (see Text Box—**What's Your Style?**).

Studying is the surest way to achieving artistry. Certainly there are those who have made a career for themselves without much study (or even talent sometimes), but they are the exception, not the rule. Every actor should enroll in an acting class. Continual practice on the discipline, craft, and art is imperative for growth. Pavarotti, the great operatic tenor, took voice class throughout his career. If it's good enough for him, it's good enough for everyone, frankly. If you feel you have nothing left to learn you are a dead artist.

There are many classes you can take and you should take as many as you can afford from as many different teachers as possible (see Text Box—**A Student's Bill of Rights**). Not all classes will suit you, but nevertheless you can learn something from each class, if you have the proper working attitude. The proper attitude begins

What's Your Style?

You learn in several different ways, and you will be taught in several different ways. The above-mentioned relationships are derived from the interplay of learning and teaching styles. Often, the teacher asserts a relationship and you must agree. Resistance to a teaching style can result in frustration and little learning. On the other hand, simply accepting a teaching style may result in feelings of powerlessness—not the best feeling for effective learning. Like any mature relationship, the student-teacher relationship ought to be negotiated. How do you best learn? How does your teacher best teach? How can you both adjust and collaborate?

Learning Styles—auditory, visual, kinesthetic/tactile

See www.chaminade.org/inspire/learnstl.htm for a good summation of learning styles.

Teaching Styles—Formal authority, personal model, facilitator, delegator

See http://tlt.its.psu.edu/suggestions/research/teaching_styles.shtml for a good summation of teaching styles.

A Student's Bill of Rights

You have the right:

1. to audit a class (but you do have to be flexible)
2. to a thorough and clear explanation about the basic approach, the nature of an exercise, and the expectations of the instructor
3. to a dignified and respectful attitude from both instructor and classmates
4. to say no to any demand by the instructor (with reason)
5. to a refund
6. to change scene partners
7. to disagree with the instructor
8. to study with anybody (who'll have you, via audition/interview)

with a clear understanding of the relationship between the teacher and the student. The following three relationships between student and teacher seem to offer the most positive experience while achieving the most positive results. They vary only slightly, primarily to do with the relationship to the work rather than the relationship of the teacher to the student.

Collaborators.   Exactly like it sounds, collaborators work together to make theater. Everyone has a job to do, but anyone can do any job. There is little or no hierarchy. When expertise in some area is called for, the individual who has the aptitude or interest takes the lead. The teacher offers challenges to be met and tasks to take on. Classes are workshops in which you work on developing skills and using the actor's tools. Each exercise has a set of rules or blueprints that must be followed. The facilitator's job is to keep actors on task and following the blueprints. Often these classes are outgrowths of existing theatrical companies. A group of people comes together to work on the craft and individuals take turns leading the class. This can be a wonderful and freeing way to work, and may lead to developing a group style that is strong, original, and compelling. But there are two cautions. First, a class without a strong leader can become aimless and unfocused. Second, some groups can become cultish and exert a pressure to conform to the "way" of the group.

Player to Player.   Acting is a game to players, and a fun game, too. Improvisation troupes and classes often utilize this approach. It isn't work; it's play. Spontaneity is the primary value in these classes. Depending on the teacher, this class will probably be the one you never miss. The problem can sometimes be that you never want to leave the classroom. Also, such classes can degenerate into a sort of daycare for actors—everything is ok, nothing is wrong, discipline is a bad word. But with the right group of players, you will learn a lot.

Artist to Artist.   Making art is a collaborative and process-oriented activity. The intensity level is high, the demands on your creativity and discipline are high, but the rewards are great. On the other hand, this can be a license for Svengali-like teachers to wreak havoc on your nervous system.

The Actor–Director Relationship

The director's function is to ensure the play is delivered to the audience. The director's tools are, among others, composition and movement (see Text Box—**The Director's Tools**). But the director's primary task is communicating. The director channels, literally directs, the action based on a conception of the theatrical event. This conception may be exclusively the director's, but it often arises out of collaboration with the other artists—playwright, designers, and actors.

Every director directs differently, of course. Often directors are in a position of authority and also have a special bond with actors. The issues of power and distance that characterize any relationship are the same, but in some ways heightened

The Director's Tools

- Composition: the structure of the visual and aural elements of the event
- Movement: the changes that occur moment-to-moment and the pattern of change that occurs over the course of the event
- Communication: expressive means (verbal, nonverbal, visual, aural, etc.) by which the composition and movement is discovered and aligned in collaboration with the other artists

or more obvious because of the intensity of the rehearsal process. Every director will wield power and manage distance differently. As in any relationship, adjustments and negotiations will inevitably occur. This relationship is not always discussed, but it is surely present and shapes behavior. Naturally, relationships thrive when there is mutual respect and trust for each other and the process. Optimally, a director will facilitate the creativity of all the artists involved in production, and similarly, you ought to offer the director the same. It is important that boundaries are honored, but are also negotiable. It is important to take the work seriously, but not yourself or others too seriously. Finally, if all goes well, you will find joy in creating for an audience. But no matter what the exact nature of the relationship is between actor and director, your job as actor remains the same—to transform description into action.

Skills a Director Wants.   Once you are in a play and rehearsing, there are four basic things most every director wants. Your job as actor is to **provide** these skills.

1. *Motivate movement*—toward, away from, remain. The movement is related to the action. See Chapter Twelve—**Playing the Field,** for more on moving on stage.
2. *Understand stage technique.* Know where you are, how to get to where you're asked to go, and how to adjust yourself to the specific demands of the space.
3. *Know where the focus is.* As the ball of energy that is the scene moves about the space, know what your relationship is to the "ball" and how best to support its journey.
4. *Provide choices.* If you are asked to perform some task, be sure to have at least three ways to accomplish it, thus giving the director something to choose.

Director to Actor Communication.   The director will communicate with you through composition (your relative position to another—see Chapter Twelve) and through movement (Chapter Four). The director will also give "notes" during and after rehearsal. Your job is to take those notes and turn them into something you can do.

Many directors are savvy to the language of action and of actors and the best will have the "mot juste" that will give you energy and get you back in the game. Often the note will be posed as a question rather than a directive, allowing you to work out the answer for yourself and discover the most effective action for the moment you are working on.

Often a director will communicate to an actor in images or other nonactive terms. Your job then is to *translate* that image into action. For example, the director may say, "I need that walk across stage to be incredibly slow, as if you're walking in honey." One approach might be to imagine walking through honey. But you can also translate the direction into one of the fundamental actions. Walking through honey implies a great resistance to motion, so that it could be translated as a *pull from.* The advantage of using an action is that it gives you a specific, repeatable thing to do.

Imagining walking through honey, though possibly useful (and perhaps preferable for some) will be more ambiguous and variable than the action *to pull from.* Another director may say, "You need to be angrier here." Anger is a by-product of an action, so you must discern from the by-product the underlying action. Raise the level of energy and clarify the specificity of your action, endow the moment with value using an "as if" to facilitate your connection to the material and perhaps anger will result.

Finally, a director may simply say, "Louder" or "Faster" or "Smile." These behaviors are also results, of course, but of such a general nature that you may find it challenging to discover the underlying action quickly. At such an instance, sometimes the best policy is to simply speak more loudly, move more quickly, and smile. In doing so, you then have a chance to discover the action and the task. Allow the behavior to suggest an action to you—is it a push, pull, hold, or release? If you cannot quite figure it out, after rehearsal review that moment a number of times until you've arrived at *some* choice—then try it out next time.

Throughout this book we have attempted to describe the acting process as clearly as possible and to propose some means for effective training. We have examined physical processes (the body and voice) and mental processes (the imagination and feelings). The goal has been to be as concrete as possible in describing these processes, to clarify the fundamental aspects of acting, and position you, the artist, in a more central and powerful place from where you may discover and realize your talent. As much as possible we have avoided the ineffable and elusive aspects of the art of acting, but let us acknowledge these aspects now. The spirit of playing, really *why* we play, is the topic to which we finally turn (see Figure 13.1 on page 185).

Curtain Call—The Spirit of Play

The effective player is one who has developed the body, voice, imagination, and feelings, and allows the free and organic expression of these tools in applying energy to a task. This is how to play. But *why* do we play? Perhaps we play to practice for real life. Perhaps we play to learn more about our condition and ourselves. Perhaps for the sheer joy of playing—for the pleasure we derive from the investment of our selves in something, not useful or practical, but just because we can.

Initial encounters in theater can be immensely rewarding. Many of us love to act and be in plays. You may have started quite early, took classes at school or in weekend or after school programs, and even participated in community theater. But at the college and university level training can get serious; and when things get serious it can stop being fun. When the mystery and magic of theater is examined and "secrets" are revealed, inevitably there is a sense of loss. But like any love, once through the initial dizzying romance, the relationship then may get much deeper, more interesting, and even more mysterious.

But *joy* is central to the artist's learning and creating. Without joy and the joy that creativity brings, the work becomes work. That is not to say that creation is not attended with agony, pain, misery, disgust, anxiety, and fear. Sometimes, it is. But when the creation comes to fruition, there can be tremendous joy. Finding and maintaining the joy in creativity is central to the spirit of playing. But how do you do that? The spirit of playing includes those things that are intangible, but nevertheless make the difference between a good player and a great one.

On most audition forms there is a blank space at the bottom of the page for intangibles—those things about an actor that don't fall neatly into categories of vocal range, character type and such, but are nevertheless important. In spite of flaws in technique, execution, characterization, and action, an actor may move us, charm us, and even change us. Although an entire book may be devoted to considering these intangibles, let us briefly examine three important aspects of the spirit of playing: Presence, Service, and Openness. If these things are part of the learning or creative environment, then the joy and the fun of playing will be there, too.

Presence

What is it that makes one actor more interesting than another? Beyond skill, beyond imagination, there is some indefinable something that some actors have in meager supply while others have it in spades. Presence. But what is it and can anyone get it?

Presence is "a quality . . . that enables a performer to achieve a close relationship with his audience." (903)² Definitions vary, but presence seems to be comprised of three major elements—confidence, charisma, and conviction. Many of the same words are used to describe presence, confidence, and charisma, but upon closer inspection there are certain important differences that lead to the conclusion that presence is a *product* of confidence and charisma *plus* conviction (you do the math). Essentially, confidence deals with energy within you and charisma deals with energy between you and the audience. Together, they *multiply* the level of your energy. Conviction *adds* direction and shape for your energy.

Confidence is defined as faith, trust, or an awareness of one's powers. (234) Charisma is a little more elusive, but can be described as a "magnetic appeal." (186) Conviction is "the act of compelling the admission of truth." (246) Like all definitions, these are informative, but do little to help you achieve results. However, if you look closer, you can see that these three elements are exactly the same elements required for effective acting. The awareness of one's power is simply clarity of task. You know what needs to be done. Magnetic appeal is simply asserting a strong action to accomplish a task. Conviction is knowing you can do what needs to be done. The actor with presence is grounded, activated, and focused. These are things everyone can do.

But presence also means *being present*. Maintaining your ground, action, and focus in the here and now is a vital aspect of presence. If you linger in the past or fret about the future, you will not be present here and now, and will not have presence. If, on the other hand, you are confident, have command and know what you want, you will be fully present (see Text Box—**The Power of Presence**).

Presence is something everyone can have. It does not detract from a performance or daily life to have a stage or even a world of people with presence. At least on stage, it definitely helps!

Service.   By serving you will be served. Nearly every acting lesson is about focusing your attention off yourself and on the other. Serve your partner, serve the playwright, serve the director, serve the set, lighting, and costume designers, serve the audience—and you will be served. We are creatures driven by selfish motives—that seems to be the way we are designed. But, we are gifted with awareness and able to make choices that place us second or third or later after people and ideas we think are important. We give up our own selfish needs, perhaps only momentarily, and give over to the needs of others. Giving over to something greater than you is the second concrete aspect of the spirit of playing. *Trust* your partner, yourself, and the

The Power of Presence

Presence can be positive and negative as well as quite powerful. Hitler had a great deal of presence. He was extremely confident, had tremendous charisma and total conviction. But his magnetic appeal seems to have been more of a repellent nature, inspiring awe and fear. He demanded complete devotion of his followers, even to death. Mahatma Gandhi also had amazing presence. His conviction was supreme, his confidence total, and his charisma palpable. His appeal seems to have been more of an attractive nature, inspiring fidelity and courage. Gandhi asked people to join him, rather than coercing them into joining him. He was willing to sacrifice his own life for the sake of others. This is admittedly a subjective view. Ask yourself who you believe to have presence and analyze their behavior in the above manner. Then examine yourself. When have you had presence?

Confidence
a clear task

X

Charisma
a specific action

+

Conviction
knowledge of capability to accomplish the task

=

Presence
a glow of energy resulting from the interplay of the actor and
audience's energy (being there)

---

game to be played, and that trust will be returned. *Invest* in your partner, yourself and the game, and your investment will be doubly returned.

Openness.　The third aspect of great acting to be examined is openness. Openness simply refers to *allowing change.* Play is how we learn to manage change. We take small aspects of life experience and make them into games. These games help us to deal with actual changes in our environment and to maintain balance. When we witness great acting, what we are witnessing is the highly effective management of change. The possibility of change creates compelling theater. The mastery of change as personified by the excellent actor is thrilling, compelling, transfixing, and transforming. Mastery of change is finally a matter of openness. You must be open to change, allow change to occur, and have the courage to know that you may manage it.

- *Presence* in the here and now, applying energy to a task with the knowledge that you can accomplish the task
- *Service* to your fellow players, to your fellow artists, and to the audience
- *Openness* to change, to your fellow players, to your fellow artists, and to the audience

That's the game. It is simple, but it takes a lifetime to learn to play well.

At the end of the game, it is good to take a moment to acknowledge the players' efforts. The moment, however, is not for the player's glory, but to give the audience a chance to express itself.

Take a Bow.   The true meaning of the bow (in the west) is an offering of the head. It says to the person to whom you bow that your life is in their keeping. In theatre, bowing is a simple way to express your service to the audience. An effective bow is conspicuous by its openness, by the head fully offered to the crowd, and by a look that says, "How fun this was to do for you, and thank you so much for coming." It is embracing, welcoming, with energy freely exchanging between performer and audience. No matter how serious the play, at its end it is the audience's turn to act. You have returned to the world of the theater, your function as an actor has ceased, and so you offer yourself to the audience. Leave it in their hands.

Take a Bow (G, F, T, E)

1. Enter the playing area as if you belong—no apologies, no excuse, no more nor no less than your whole self, your best self, smiling at the pleasure of playing.
2. Hit your mark—center stage or the designated spot—and allow the audience to look at you, and allow yourself to return that look.
3. Bow deeply from the waist, offering your head, as if to say "All for you."
4. Come back up, smile on your face and step lightly and quickly to make way for the next actor or the continuance of the curtain call.

Postscript

Susanne Langer speculated that the dawn of the human mind began with dreams. She thought that perhaps, long ago, an image from a dream arose during a waking moment. Imagine such a moment. You are on your way to find food, or a place to spend the night. You have no language, just urges to which you respond. Along your way, suddenly, you see something that is not there. It seems familiar, yet this thing you see has no presence, no existence. What was it? Where did it come from? You might attempt to see it again, to recall the image in your mind's eye—to imagine. This is the beginning of the human mind—the imagination. Out of the imagination, we created the world.

In the Hindu religion, the god Narayana is said to have dreamt the world into existence. That is what the artist does—dreams, imagines worlds into being. The actor's magnificent transformation is that the actor not only creates a world to see or

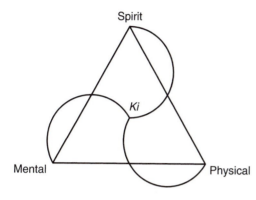
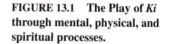

FIGURE 13.1 **The Play of** *Ki* **through mental, physical, and spiritual processes.**

hear, but to live fully in. You, as artist, as dreamer, as part of the next generation of doers—you have an *obligation* to have courage, to keep faith, to hold on to hope. It may appear at times that this is impossible. But *fear not.* At the end, after all the complications, the crises, the climaxes and denouements—it *will* have been worth it, it *will* be of value.

If you have the *courage* to stick to your vision, and *faith* in the value of your vision, you will have reason to *hope* that your vision realized may change something or someone for the better. And it has. You've done it. Look back and see what you have done. Look around you and see whom you have changed. Look into the future and see what you may be. Courage, faith, hope—an artist's trinity.

Change occurs over time, sometimes a long time. But *fear not.* Find the *courage* to encounter change. Keep *faith* in the necessity of change. And hold the *hope* that change can be, will be good. That is what the artist can do, must do.

Now, go out and play.

NOTES

1. After a show opens, it is traditional that friends, family, and well-wishers will await your triumphant appearance before them, face washed clean of makeup, dressed in your actor-best. . . . This is probably not the time to criticize. After a show, it not a time to discuss seriously whether or not the show was good, great, or awful, or say "You looked like you were having fun up there!" Pleasant (or not) as these discussions may be, they really are beside the point. After a show, what we celebrate is the simple fact that you did it. You got through it, the show went up before an audience and was played. In a world where so much is tenuous, the fact that a show was performed is a wonderful reason to celebrate. And so you should. There will be (and probably should be) time to reflect upon the performance—what was effective or ineffective in your employment of your acting tools and your application of the acting process.

2. Webster's New Collegiate Dictionary. Springfield, MA: G. & C. Merriam Co., 1979.

APPENDIX

Action List (Push, Pull, Hold, Release—*from and to*)

A

add to	allow	arrest	attack
admit	alert to	avoid	attend to
affix	arrange	attach	

B

back up	blind	bolt	brush up/off
ban	blot	bomb	bump
bang	box up	bore into	burn
bat	brake	bounce	bury
bathe	boil	bruise	buzz

C

call on	chew out	coach	cover over/up
care for	choke	coil up	crack
carry to	chop	confuse	crash
carve up	clap	connect to	cross up
charge	clean	continue	crush
chase	clear up	correct	curl
check	clip	command	comb
cheer up	close up		

D

dam up	divide	dust	drop on
dare	double up	dress up/down	drown
deliver to	drag	drill	drum on
disarm	drain	drip on	dry up

E

elevate	erase	explode	extend
empty	exorcise	expand	extricate
end			

F

fasten to	fire up	flood	force
fence in	fit in	fold up	frame up
file down	fix (in place)	fool	fry
fill up	float		

G

gather in	grab	grip	guard from
glue to	grate	grease	guide to

H

hammer	harm	heat	hug
handle	head butt	help	hunt down
hang	heap on	hook	hurry up

I

inject	interest in	invite in	itch

J

jail	jog	joke	juggle
jam	join	jostle	jump on

K

kick	kiss	knock	knot
kill	knit		

L

launch	lick	load up	lock up
level	lighten		

M

manhandle	mate	mess up	moor
manage	measure	milk	move
mark	melt	mine	mug
marry	mend	mix up	murder
match to			

N

nail to	nest in	nick

O

offer up	open up	oust

P

pack in	peck	please	prick
paddle	peel	plug	program
paint	permit	point to	protect from
park	pick at	poke	pull
part	pinch	polish	pump
pass	place	pour on	punch
paste	plane	present	puncture
pat	plant	preserve from	punish
pause	play	press	push

Q

quash

R

rain on	reign over	release	repair
raise up	reject	remind	replace
reduce	relax	remove	reply
refuse			

R

rescue from	rock	rub on/off/ over/in	rule over
rinse	roll		rush out

S

sack up	search	soak	stir up
save from	separate from	soothe	stitch
saw	serve up	sound out	stop
scare	settle down	spare from	strap to
scatter	share with	spark up	stretch
scold	shave	spray	strip off
scorch	shelter	squash	stroke
scrape	shock	squeeze	stuff in
scratch	slap	stain	suck out/in
scream	slow down	stamp	suit up
screw	smash	start up	support
scribble	smoke	stay on	surround
scrub	snatch	steer away	suspend from
seal in/up	sniff out	step on	

T

tap	thaw	tire out	trick
taste	tickle	touch	trip up
tease	tie up/down	tow	tug
tempt	time	trace	turn
test	tip over	transport	twist

U

undress	unite	unlock	use
unfasten			

V

vanquish	violate	vacuum

W

walk on/over	wave	whirl	wrap
warm-up	weigh	wipe	wreck
wash	whip	work over	wrestle
water			

X

x-ray

Y

yank

Z

zip

Task List (Attract, Repel, Sustain, Free)

(I Want X to . . . or I Want to . . .)

apologize	employ	irritate
accept	enable	injure
advise	encourage	judge
agree	entertain	nag
approve	excite	prevent
amuse	examine	prepare
annoy	escape	provide
balance	frighten	quarantine
beg	haunt	question
bless	harass	quell
challenge	heal	rob
confess	influence	surprise
compete	ignore	shock
damage	impress	support
deceive	improve	tame
destroy	include	terrify
develop	instruct	trap
delight	interfere	warn
educate	interrupt	welcome
embarrass	introduce	

Sample Entrance Lines

"Here I am! Hello? Where is everyone? Ok, you can all come out now. I know you're in here. Guys, come on. Well, what the—"

"Alone at last. I can't wait to get out of these."

"God! Those people make me sick! If they stay here one more minute I'm going to scream."

"Oh yea? Who the hell are you? Oh. So sorry, I was just . . . talking to a friend. Do you know where the bathroom is?"

"Wow! This is some place, not the kind of joint I usually hang out in. I mean, the stuffed animals alone."

"Ladies and Gentlemen, if you would all move to the next room we can get started. Just place any firearms in the basket there—and any knives or brass knuckles, too."

"Is this heaven? Am I dreaming? Am I hallucinating? Ok—happy? Can we go?"

"Freeze! Hands on your head! Ah! I didn't say Simon says!"

"Oh my god, if s/he isn't the most beautiful, magnificent . . . what did you say his/her name was?"

"Yes! Yes! Yes! Yes! I win, I win, I win. Nyah-nyah-nyah. Oof. I think I pulled something."

(Trips in.) "Don't mind me. I'm fine. Just go on about your business. Pay no attention. Can someone call a doctor?"

Sample Exit Lines

"That's it! I'm leaving. Now. Ok out there, unlock the door. Thank you."

"I can't believe you! Goodbye forever. Call me?"

"I really have to go. Don't ask me to stay, I just can't. As much as I'd love to."

"Let's see, keys, wallet, aspirin. Well, I'm off!"

"Don't forget to water the plants and feed the cats. And no friends over. I mean it!"

"I never meant to hurt you. But it's over and you have to accept that. I'm sorry. For everything."

"I'll be right back. Stay right there. Don't move!"

"Will somebody get that? Anyone? Oh, for crying out loud. Coming!"

"That's everything, I guess. Well, it's been quite a time. I'm going to miss this place."

"Ah. Excuse me, I've got to . . . Which way is the . . . ? Down the hall, to the right, yes? No, don't get up, I'll find it."

"As I say farewell, ladies and gentlemen, let me leave you with one final thought—(*sotto voce*) I'm sorry, what? What? I told you, it's the little red one. . . . " (*ad lib as exiting*)

"Is that the phone? It's probably my mother. I have to get it. Sorry. No, stay! I won't be long."

"I've never been so insulted in my life! I don't have to stand here and take this. And as for you, why don't you drop dead."

"Adieu, adieu. Parting is such sweet sorrow. I've always wanted to say that. Pretty lame, huh?"

SELECTED BIBLIOGRAPHY

Acting

Barton, Robert. *Style for the Actor.* Mountain View, CA: Mayfield Publishing, 1993.

Benedetti, Robert. *The Actor at Work.* 9th ed. Boston: Pearson Allyn & Bacon, 2005.

Bruder, Cohn, et al. *A Practical Handbook for the Actor.* Vintage. New York. 1986.

Chaiken, Joseph. *The Presence of the Actor.* New York: Atheneum, 1972.

Chekhov, Michael. *To the Actor.* New York: Harper & Row, 1953.

Cohen, Robert. *Acting One.* Mountain View, CA: Mayfield Publishing, 1984.

———. *Acting Power.* Mountain View: Mayfield, 1978.

Cole, Toby and Helen Krich Chinoy, ed. *Actors on Acting.* New York: Crown Publishers. 1970.

Daw, Kurt. *Acting: Thought into Action.* Portsmouth, New Hampshire: Heinemann, 1997.

Felner, Mira. *Free to Act.* 2nd ed. Boston: Pearson Allyn & Bacon, 2004.

Huston, Hollis. *The Actor's Instrument—Body, Theory, Stage.* Ann Arbor: University of Michigan Press, 1992.

Konijn, Elly. *Acting Emotions.* Amsterdam. Amsterdam University Press, 2000.

Spolin, Viola. *Improvisation for the Theatre.* 3rd ed. Evanston, IL: Northwestern University Press, 1999.

Stanislavski, C. *An Actor Prepares.* Trans. Elizabeth Reynolds Hapgood. New York: Theatre Arts Books, 1948.

———. *Building a Character.* Trans. Elizabeth Reynolds Hapgood. New York: Theatre Arts Books, 1949.

———. *Creating a Role.* Trans. Elizabeth Reynolds Hapgood. New York: Theatre Arts Books, 1961.

———. *My Life in Art.* Trans. J.J. Robbins. New York: Little, Brown & Co., 1924. New York: Theatre Art Books, 1948.

Movement

Bartinieff, Irmgard and Lewis, Dori. *Body Movement: Coping with the Environment.* New York: Gordon & Breach Science Publishers, 1980.

Barker, Sarah. *The Alexander Technique.* New York: Bantam Books, 1991.

Dennis, Anne. *The Articulate Body: the Physical Training of the Actor.* New York: Drama Books, 1995.

Feldenkrais, Moche. *Awareness through Movement.* New York: HarperCollins, 1972.

Potter, Nicole, ed. *Movement for Actors.* New York: Allworth Press, 2002.

Rubin, Lucille, ed. *Movement for the Actor.* New York: Drama Book Specialists, 1980.

Von Laban, Rudolph. *The Language of Movement.* London: Macdonald & Evans, 1976.

Voice

Berry, Cecile. *The Actor and the Text.* London: Virgin, 1993.

Linklater, Kristin. *Freeing the Natural Voice.* New York: Drama Book Specialists, 1976.

———.*Freeing Shakespeare's Voice.* New York: Theatre Communications Group, 1992.

Rodenberg, Patsy. *The Actor Speaks: Voice and the Performer.* London: Methuen Drama, 1997.

Hampton and Acker, ed. *The Vocal Vision.* New York: Applause Books, 1997.

Theory and Analysis

Barba, Eugenio and Nicola Savarese. *A Dictionary of Theatre Anthropology.* Trans. Richard Fowler. London: Routlege, 1991.

Boal, Augusto. *Theatre of the Oppressed.* Trans. Charles A. and Maria-Odilia Leal McBride. New York: Theatre Communications Group, 1979.

Brook, Peter. *The Empty Space.* New York: Antheneum, 1980.

———. *The Open Door.* New York: Theatre Communications Group, 1995.

Carlson, Marvin. *Theatre Semiotics: Signs of Life.* Bloomington, IN: Indiana University Press, 1990.

Counsell, Colin. *Signs of Performance.* London: Routledge, 1996.

Crohn Schmitt, Natalie. *Actors and Onlookers: Theater and Twentieth-Century Scientific View of Nature.* Evanston, IL: Northwestern University Press, 1990.

Frye, Northrup. *Anatomy of Criticism.*

Grotowski, Jerzy. *Towards a Poor Theatre.* New York: Simon and Schuster, 1968.

Hodge, Francis. *Play Directing.* 5th ed. Boston: Pearson Allyn & Bacon, 2000.

Krasner, David, ed. *Method Acting Reconsidered: Theory, Practice, Future.* New York: St. Martin's Press, 2000.

Langer, Susanne K. *Feeling and Form.* New York: Scribner & Sons, 1953.

———. *Mind: An Essay on Human Feeling.* Johns Hopkins University Press. Baltimore. 1992.

———. *Problems of Art.* New York: Scribner & Sons, 1957.

Schechner, Richard. *Performance Theory.* London: Routledge, 1988.

Thomas, James. *Script Analysis for Actors, Directors, and Designers.* Newton, MA: Butterworth-Heinemann, 1992.

Turner, Victor. *The Anthropology of Performance.* New York: PAJ Publications, 1987.

Background

Campbell, Joseph. *The Hero with a Thousand Faces.* Princeton University Press. Princeton, NJ. 1990.

DuBrul, E. Lloyd. *The Evolution of the Speech Apparatus.* Charles C. Thomas. Springfield, MA. 1958.

Gardner, Howard. *Art, Mind, and Brain: a cognitive approach to creativity.* New York: Basic Books, 1982.

———. *Multiple Intelligences: the theory in practice.* New York: Basic Books, 1993.

Homma, Gaku. *Aikido for Life.* Berkeley, CA: North Atlantic Books, 1990.

Lenneberg, Eric H. *Biological Foundations of Language.* New York: Wiley & Sons, 1967.

May, Rollo. *The Courage to Create.* New York: Norton, 1975.

Trask, R.L. *Language: The Basics.* London: Routledge, 1995.

Wang, William S-Y, ed. *The Emergence of Language: Development and Evolution: Readings from Scientific American Magazine.* New York: W.H. Freeman and Company, 1991.

Zatrsiorsky, Vladimir M. *Kinematics of Human Motion.* Champaign, IL: Human Kinetics, 1998.

INDEX